SAFFET EMRE TONGUÇ

BOSPHORUS

THE ULTIMATE GUIDE

ISTANBUL
METROPOLITAN
MUNICIPALITY

KÜLTÜR A.Ş.

SAFFET EMRE TONGUÇ

BOSPHORUS

THE ULTIMATE GUIDE

Saffet Emre TONGUÇ
www.saffetemretonguc.com
@saffetemretonguc

ISTANBUL METROPOLITAN MUNICIPALITY

KÜLTÜR A.Ş.

Bosphorus The Ultimate Guide, 2020

Project Director
Cengiz Özkarabekir

Publishing Director
Ahmet Bozkurt

Production
D Sinema Destek Sistemleri Ltd. Şti.,2020
info@d-sinema.com

Administrative Coordination
Gökhan Özçevik

Editor
Ahmet Bozkurt

Book's Editor
Duygun Soysal

Proofreading
Nihan Kalle

Visual Arts Cosultant
Utku Lomlu

Photo Editor
Serkan Eldeleklioğlu

Cover Design
LOM Creative, Alper Zeki

Cover Photo
Halit Bilen

Page Design
ademsenel.com

Map Editing
Birkan Demir

Archive Editing
Evren Ertem

Printing and Binding
Seçil Ofset
100. Yıl Mahallesi, Massit Matbaacılar Sitesi,
4.Cad. No: 77, Bağcılar-İstanbul

ISBN: 978-605-7864-79-6
53rd Edition: İstanbul, July 2020

Publisher Certificate Number: 15321
Printers Certificate Number: 44903

ISTANBUL CULTURE AND ART PRODUCTS TRADE CO.
Maltepe Mah. Topkapı Kültür Parkı Osmanlı Evleri
34010 Topkapı/Zeytinburnu/İSTANBUL/TURKEY
Phone: +90 212 467 07 00 Fax: +90 212 467 07 99

PREFACE

Ekrem İmamoğlu
İstanbul Metropolitan Municipality Mayor

Dear Friends,

I must confess, after reading the enjoyable *Istanbul The Ultimate Guide* - which was awarded "Best Tourism Publication" - I had to meet dear Saffet Emre Tonguç regarding future publications in the name of the Istanbul Metropolitan Municipality.

Mr. Tonguç's career caught my attention in recent years; he is an internationally recognized historian, television producer, professional tour guide and an avid lover of Istanbul.

We are delighted to update, enlarge, and republish Mr. Tonguç's books on Istanbul with the most recent photos and in several languages. *Bosphorus The Ultimate Guide* introduces us to the stories of hundreds of waterfront mansions along the Bosphorus while giving us a fresh perspective on historical sanctuaries such as the mosques, churches, and synagogues along the Strait. The book also describes in stunning detail the palaces (the Çırağan, the Dolmabahçe, and others), museums, castles, fountains, bathhouses, and even summer residences of foreign consuls. Hundreds of glossy photographs beautifully display important visual, contextual information. As such, we could say it may well be the most comprehensive and contemporary work on one of the most recognizable bodies of water in the world - the Bosphorus.

So, when you read *Bosphorus The Ultimate Guide*, you will take a journey with Saffet Emre Tonguç while gaining a deeper understanding of the subject matter. I enjoyed reading Mr. Tonguç's books as much as I enjoyed his Istanbul tours. The book in your hands will help you discover the Bosphorus from Cankurtaran to Rumelifeneri, from Kadıköy and Moda to Arnavutköy and Bebek - pretty much the entire strait - while you sail upon the lapis lazuli waters enjoying the sight of the redbuds. Furthermore, it will enhance your knowledge from both historical and modern-day perspectives while gently whispering to you and you alone the secrets of the Bosphorus.

May you enjoy your reading experience...

THE BOSPHORUS *European Shore*

THE BOSPHORUS *Asian Shore*

How to Use This Book?

In researching this book I started off from **Cankurturan** and the **Sea Walls** on the European side of the **Historic Peninsula** and continued along the **Bosphorus** until, with **Rumeli Feneri**, I had visited **21** different areas. Then I started from the southernmost point of the Anatolian side of the Bosphorus in **Kadıköy** and **Moda** and headed along the northern shore until I reached **Anadolu Feneri**, visiting another **13** areas. You can identify the different areas according to the numbers on the map and tick off the boxes next to the numbers as you progress up and down the Bosphorus.

BLACK SEA
Rumeli Feneri 21
Garipçe 21
Poyrazköy and Anadolu Feneri 34
3rd Bridge
Rumeli Kavağı 21
Sarıyer 21
Büyükdere 20
34 Anadolu Kavağı
SARIYER
BEYKOZ
Kireçburnu 19
33 Beykoz
Tarabya 19
Kalender 19
Yeniköy 18
İstinye 18
33 Paşabahçe
Sakıp Sabancı Müzesi (Sakıp Sabancı Museum) 17
32 Çubuklu
Emirgan 16
31 Kanlıca
2nd Bridge
Rumeli Hisarı 15 (European Castle)
30 Anadolu Hisarı (Asian Castle)
BEŞİKTAŞ
Bebek 14
29 Küçüksu
29 Kandilli
Arnavutköy 13
ŞİŞLİ
Kuruçeşme 13
28 Vaniköy
28 Kuleli
BEYOĞLU
Yıldız Park 10
Ortaköy 12
28 Çengelköy
11 Çırağan Palace
1st Bridge
Beşiktaş 09
08 Dolmabahçe Palace
27 Beylerbeyi
GOLDEN HORN
Kabataş 07
Tophane 07
26 Kuzguncuk
25 Çamlıca
Karaköy 06
05 Galata Bridge
25 Üsküdar
04 New Mosque
24 The Maiden's Tower
03 Sirkeci
02 Gülhane Park
01 Cankurtaran
ÜSKÜDAR
ÜMRANİYE
Eurasia Tunnel
23 Haydarpaşa and Selimiye
MARMARA SEA
22 Kadıköy
22 Moda
KADIKÖY

Bosphorus The Ultimate Guide

After months of preparation, my Bosphorus book finally hit the shelves. On the heels of **'Istanbul The Ultimate Guide'**, which received the **'The Best Tourism Publication of 2010'** award, this book represents one of the most comprehensive studies of the Bosphorus. This book got the same award in 2012.

The primary reason why Istanbul has been such an important city for thousands of years is its incomparable geographical location straddling the shores of Europe and Asia. Meandering through the middle is the Bosphorus, which makes its stately way past nostalgic neighborhoods, ancient houses of worship, historic monuments, and magnificent yalıs. Like the Istanbul it is a part of, the Bosphorus is perpetually changing. From the hotels to the restaurants, from the houses of worship to the palaces, and from the museums to the yalıs, the area's make-up has gradually altered over the centuries. For this reason, I saw a need for a new and updated guidebook to highlight the changes and incorporate the latest information and photographs.

While preparing this book, I had a tough time dealing with the yalıs. Most older books about the Bosphorus lack photographs of their interiors and I had to wait six months just to take pictures of one of them. Thanks to the help of friends and acquaintances I finally managed to come up with pictures of more than twenty yalıs or were given the opportunity to photograph them especially for this book. I would like to increase this figure for every edition and would be very grateful for any assistance. I would also appreciate it if you could let me know of anything I have missed out or got wrong.

I hope you have fun reading this book.

Saffet Emre Tonguç

www.saffetemretonguc.com
tonguc2000@gmail.com
@saffetemretonguc

Saffet Emre Tonguç

Saffet Emre Tonguç was born in 1966 and graduated from **Şişli Terakki High School**. He went on to graduate from **Bosphorus University's Tourism and Hotel Management, Political Science** and **International Relations and Ottoman Social History Departments**. Having written a master thesis entitled **'Jews and Ottoman Social Structure'**, he conducted his post-graduate studies on business administration at the **Vienna University of Economics and Business** (Wirtschaftsuniversität Wien). He has been a professional tour guide since 1987, guiding celebrities such as **Oprah Winfrey, Martha Stewart, Robert Redford, Michael Douglas, Catherine Zeta-Jones, Candice Bergen, Matthew McConaughey, Billy Crystal, Kevin Spacey, Penn Badgley, Prince Edward of England, Carlo Azeglio Ciampi, Madeleine Albright, Colin Powell, Eric Schmidt, Calvin Klein, Michael Kors and Eli Tahari** around Turkey. He has travelled to different 134 countries, either for business or pleasure.

BOOKS	AWARDS
Türkiye' de Görülmesi Gereken 101 Yer **101 Must-See-Places in Turkey** **Avrupa'da Görülecek 41 Yer** **Avrupa'da Görülecek 101 Yer** **İstanbul Hakkında Her Şey** **Istanbul the Ultimate Guide** **Boğaz Hakkında Her Şey** **Bosphorus the Ultimate Guide** **A' dan Z' ye İstanbul** **İstanbul Camileri** **İstanbul' da Bilmeniz Gereken 105 Eser** **Saffet Emre Tonguç ile Kapalı Çarşı Turu** **En İyi 50 Butik Otel** **İstanbul ve Gece** **Ayrıcalıklı Rotalar** **Kanatlarımda İstanbul** **Istanbul A Bird's Eye View** www.saffetemretonguc.com tonguc2000@gmail.com *@saffetemretonguc* *@saffetemretonguc* *@saffetemre*	"Professional Outstanding Service Award" by the Rotary Club in 2005, 2010 and 2014 "Travel Author of the Year" in 2006 "Travel Author" award in 2007 (White Crystal Competition) "Turkey's Best Professional Guide" by SKAL Club in 2007, 2012 and 2014 "Best Book of the Year" award by TUREB in 2008 (101 Must See Places in Turkey) "Best Tourism Publication" award in 2010 (İstanbul Hakkında Her Şey) "Best Tourism Publication" award in 2012 (Boğaz Hakkında Her Şey) "Best TV Show" award in 2015 (Priceless Istanbul) "Tourism Incentive Publication" award in 2017 (Privileged Routes) "Best Professional Guide of the Year" and the "Professional High Service Award" in 2017 "Best TV Show" award in 2018 (Privileged Routes) "Best Travel Author" award in 2019 "Professional Outstanding Service Award" in 2020

From Nakkaştepe, you can see all three bridges.

A few thank yous

Numerous people have contributed to the preparation of this book. Duygun Soysal was seven years old when I met her in 1989. Now she reads my books and feeds her intellectual knowledge between the lines. I also extend particular thanks to Zahide Bilsay, Ayferi Ertek, Şirin Bebe Schade, Demet Sabancı Çetindoğan, Arzu Sabancı, Altan Tuzluoğlu, Aslı Özlen, Rana Korgül, Murat Öneş, İbrahim C. Yılgaz, Ebru Mengenecioğlu, Canan Bolak, Ece Kurdoğlu, Gülden Tüfekçi, Fatih Murat Eyioğlu, Ali Aral and Sibel Baykam, as well as to the Tek-Esin Foundation.

The photographers who added color to my book

Most of the photographs in this book were taken by Aydın Sertbaş (@aydinsert) and Halit Bilen (@bildrone), but I also included shots taken by Sinan Doğan, Koray Erkaya, Engin Aydeniz, Rebecca Erol, Serhan Güngör, Gülgün Asutay, Servet Dilber, Ufuk Sarışen, Fatih Pınar, Erman Tezgör, Barış Hasan Bedir and Aydın Kudu. A full list of credits appears on page 338.

Museum Pass

With Museum Pass Turkey, you can visit more than three hundred museums and archeological sites that belong to Republic of Turkey Ministry of Culture and Tourism and enjoy your trip through time. The pass is valid for fifteen days starting from your first museum and archeological site entrance. For more information you can visit: www.muze.gov.tr/MuseumPass

Exploring Istanbul

The city has an excellent public transport system incorporating buses, trains, metrobuses, trams, funiculars, ferries, seabuses, and even cable cars. I suggest that you invest in an İstanbulkart, an electronic purse that can be used on every form of local transport except the private dolmuşes (minibuses). You can buy them at main metro terminals, ferry terminals and transport interchanges, and can refill them at machines dotted about the city. For More information please visit: www.istanbulkart.istanbul

Don't let your photos gather dust

My door is open to anyone who has taken some captivating photos. Don't keep them locked in your archives or computers. If you think your photos, old postcards, miniatures or lithographs are appropriate for this book or my other works, please don't hesitate to share them with me.
I would be very grateful.

Saffet Emre Tonguç
tonguc2000@gmail.com

The ancestors of Bosphorus The Ultimate Guide

In 2010, **Saffet Emre Tonguç** published "**Istanbul Hakkında Her Şey**" and its English version, **"Istanbul The Ultimate Guide",** two of the most comprehensive, up-to-date and lavishly illustrated guides to the city published until then. Each book contained 660 pages, 3,000 photos, maps, lithographs and old postcards. With more than three editions to date, both Istanbul Hakkında Her Şey and Istanbul The Ultimate Guide have garnered praise from such publications as **The New York Times** and **The International Herald Tribune**.

One of his latest books, **Istanbul A Bird's Eye View**, published in 2020, offers you to discover unique angles and captures of the city.

Bridging Two Continents

The Bosphorus and

If there is one single thing that explains Istanbul's awe-inspiring beauty it surely has to be the Bosphorus, the wonderful stretch of water that sweeps down from the Black Sea to the Sea of Marmara, passing through the town center and dividing Asia from Europe as it goes. It's the moods of the Bosphorus that define the city day by day as the color of the sky is re-

its Bridges

flected in its water and then bounced back up to the sky again. Much of the greenery and many of the wonderful old houses that used to line its banks may have vanished beyond recall, but recent years have seen promenades created along long stretches of the waterside, attracting all sorts of fun-loving Istanbul residents.

Stretching almost 30 kilometers from Sarayburnu in the heart of Old Istanbul right up to **Anadolu Feneri** at the mouth of the Black Sea, the Bosphorus is the magnificent stretch of water that separates the European and Asian shores of the city. Even now, when many of the wonderful wooden yalıs (seaside mansions) that used to line the shores have been lost, the beauty of the Bosphorus is still absolutely magnetic, and few things can be more enjoyable than taking a cruise along it, looking out for historic palaces and ancient castles, watching for **birds** and the occasional pod of dolphins, and floating beneath the twin modern bridges without which Istanbul's traffic would grind to a complete halt. At the far end of the strait at Anadolu Kavağı (see p.334) you can stop for a fish lunch and climb up to the remains of a castle offering a view down to the **Black Sea**. Then it will be time to hop back on to the ferry for the return journey via **Kanlıca**, well-known to Istanbul residents for its thick and tasty yoghurt (see p.310).

Zeus, Hero and Io the cow

How the Bosphorus got its name

According to Ancient Greek mythology, the name Bosphorus, meaning "**cow's passage**", is derived from that of the priestess **Io**, the favorite of **Zeus**, the king of the gods. Fearing the wrath of his jealous wife, Zeus had Io turned into a cow, but **Hera** was wise to him and sent a gadfly to hound poor Io who was driven to roam the earth in an attempt to rid herself of it. Eventually she arrived at the Bosphorus, which has commemorated her passing ever since. The story had a happy ending, for when she finally arrived in Egypt Zeus had the decency to return her to human form. In Turkish the Bosphorus is called much less imaginatively "**Boğaz**", or "**throat**".

Strategic importance

The Bosphorus has always held great strategic significance as the link between the Mediterranean and Black seas via the Sea of Marmara, which is one reason why Constantine the Great chose to locate the new capital of the Roman Empire (Byzantium) beside it. The result has been several conflicts, especially the **Crimean War** of 1853-1856 and the **Russo-Turkish War** of 1877-1878, and the struggle over **Gallipoli** in 1915 during the First World War. Under the terms of the 1936 **Montreux Convention** the Bosphorus has been declared an international shipping lane, although Turkey retains the right to bar access to warships and ships of non-Black Sea nations. The strait is one of the world's busiest shipping routes. Every year approximately **40,000 ships** pass through it. Ten thousand of them are tankers carrying oil and other explosive materials.

In 2003 growing fears over the danger of collisions, especially between oil tankers, on this super-busy waterway led to the erection of a series of white **radar towers** along both sides of the Bosphorus, sometimes sited right beside important historic monuments.

The Bosphorus then and now

At the start of the 21st century the shores of the Bosphorus are built-up for much of their length. To understand what they looked like one hundred years ago you have to imagine the coast roads stripped away and, in their place, a succession of discrete villages, mansions and palaces separated by woodland that would have been accessible only by boat. Today the villages may have been subsumed by urban sprawl but some of them are still extremely beautiful.

King Darius

Bridging the Bosphorus

In 512 BC the Persians, under the leadership of **Darius,** built a bridge of 325 boats from Anadolu Hisarı to Rumeli Hisarı, enabling an **army of 700,000 men** to cross from Asia to Europe; Darius is said to have watched them doing so from a spot above Rumeli Hisarı which was called "**Darius' Throne**". More than a thousand years later the Byzantine **Emperor Heraclius** I created a similar bridge of boats and rode a horse across it.

The first modern bridge was the Bosphorus Bridge (**July 15 Martyrs' Bridge**) built in 1973. The second Bosphorus Bridge (**Fatih Sultan Mehmed Bridge**) was built 5 km to the north of the first bridge in 1988. But since the traffic problem was still not resolved, a third bridge (**Yavuz Sultan Selim Bridge**) was opened for service in 2016 with its two piers in **Garipçe** and **Poyrazköy**. Designed as the widest (1875 meters) and longest (1.408 meters) bridge in the World with a rail system.

Küçük Said Paşa Yalı

Yalıs, old and new

In Turkish, the word "yalı" refers to a waterside house. The Bosphorus yalıs are graceful wooden mansions that sit right beside the water with landing-stages for boats to tie up at them. The first yalıs were built in the early 18th-century, during the so-called **Tulip Era**, but most date back to the 19th and early 20th centuries. Unfortunately, as population pressure raised the value of land along the Bosphorus, many were either demolished or caught fire in sometimes suspicious circumstances. Those that still remain are aptly described by the locals as "**the pearls of the Bosphorus**".

Cruising the Bosphorus: Eminönü to Bebek

Long Bosphorus ferry cruises depart from Eminönü. Soon after starting off you will get a magnificent view of **Sarayburnu** (Palace Point), with the **Topkapı Palace, Hagia Sophia** and **Sultanahmet Mosque** throwing up a wonderful silhouette on the skyline. Then, on the left, you will see the future port of Istanbul, Galataport (see p.66) rising as a city project. A little further along you will spot **Kız Kulesi** (Maiden's Tower, see p.211), just off Üsküdar on the Asian shore. The elaborate 19th-century **Dolmabahçe Palace** (see p.74) then looms up on the European side, followed shortly afterwards by the pretty early 20th-century **Beşiktaş landing stage** (see p.87). A little further along you will see the **Four Seasons at the Bosphorus Hotel** and the luxurious **Çırağan Palace Hotel** (see p.100), with its wonderful swimming pool right on the water's edge. On the opposite shore is the late 18th-century **Pink Yalı**, more correctly called the Fethi Ahmed Paşa Yalı (see p.236). As you approach the **1st Bridge** look out for **Ortaköy** (see p.104) on the European shore, which is one of Istanbul's liveliest nightlife hotspots. Facing it, and almost immediately beneath the bridge, is **Beylerbeyi Palace** (see p.242), which resembles a cut-down version of the Dolmabahçe. Then, still on the Asian side, you will spot the twin towers of the **Kuleli Military School** (see p.263). Back on the European side of the strait the boat sails past the lovely **Arnavutköy** (see p.114), which retains many of its wonderful wooden houses. A little further along, you pass the beautiful Art Nouveau building in **Bebek** that houses the **Egyptian Consulate** (see p.120).

Cruising the Bosphorus: Kandilli to Anadolu Kavağı

Over on the Asian shore you should keep your eyes peeled for the long white **Kıbrıslı Mustafa Emin Paşa Yalı** (see p.288), **Küçüksu Mansion** (see p.291) and the late 17th-century **Köprülü Amcazade Hüseyin Paşa Yalı** (see p.302), the oldest surviving wooden mansion on the Bosphorus. Then shortly before the **2nd Bridge** the unmissable castle of **Rumeli Hisarı** (see p.132) looms up on the European shore. Facing it are the less dramatic remains of **Anadolu Hisarı** (see p.297), its older and smaller brother.

The ferry continues past **Kanlıca** (see p.310) and then, on the Asian shore, you'll see, high on a hill, the **Khedive's**

Villa (see p.320), a wonderful Art Nouveau summerhouse built for the last khedive (Ottoman governor) of Egypt in c.1900. On the European side the boat skirts **Emirgan** (see p.138) and the pretty harbor at **İstinye** (see p.151) before coming to **Yeniköy** (see p.153), a particularly upscale suburb where you'll see the 19th-century **Sait Halim Paşa Yalı** and many others.

Further still, you pass **Tarabya** (see p.172) and **Sarıyer** (see p.185) before arriving at **Rumeli Kavağı** (see p.188), which offers a fine selection of fish restaurants. Otherwise you can continue to **Anadolu Kavağı** on the Asian side (see p.335) and the end of the run.

The red building on top of the hill at Kandilli once housed Casanova. Beneath it is the Fuat Bayramoğlu Yalı with the Clifton Yalı to its left.

Jason and the Argonauts

In Greek mythology Jason was the son of the king of Thessaly who had been overthrown by his brother. Jason's uncle had told his nephew that he could only become king himself after bringing back the **Golden Fleece** from Colchis (probably modern Georgia). To do this Jason gathered together a group of heroes, including **Hercules and Theseus**, and set off in a ship called the **Argo**, after which his followers became known as the Argonauts. Together they traveled up the Bosphorus and through the **Symplegades** (see p.335) to reach **Colchis** and retrieve the fleece with all sorts of hair-raising adventures along the way.

Jason holding the Golden Fleece

The Bosphorus in numbers

- Length: 32km
- Maximum width: 3600m (Black Sea entrance)
- Minimum width: 698m (Anadolu Hisarı-Rumeli Hisarı)
- Maximum depth: 110m (Bebek-Kandilli)
- Minimum depth: 30m

The 1st Bridge in numbers

- Built: 1973
- Length (Between its towers): 1074m
- Height to road: 65m
- Height to top of support struts: 165m
- Traffic lanes: 6

The 2nd Bridge in numbers

- Built: 1988
- Length (Between its towers): 1090m
- Height to road: 64m
- Height to top of support struts: 102m
- Traffic lanes: 8

The 3rd Bridge in Numbers

- Built: 2016
- Length (Between its towers): 1875m
- Elevation from Sea Level: 72m
- Length of Towers: 322m
- Traffic Lanes: 10 (8 highways, 2 rail systems)

A Walk Between Continents

When the 1st Bridge first opened, it was possible to ascend the elevators inside the towers and walk across it. Later this was forbidden in an attempt to deter potential suicides, although the determined could still stop their car and try to take their own lives. There are incredible views from both the Bosphorus bridges. Moreover, they are the only places in the world where it's possible to walk from one continent to another. If the bridges were caged like the **Eiffel Tower**, this would prevent people from jumping off them while not robbing millions of others of a simple pleasure or depriving the treasury of a potential source of revenue. For now, thrill-seekers can only walk or run across the 1st Bridge as participants in the annual **Eurasia Marathon** that takes place every October.

Dolphin delight

Dubbed the "street children of the Bosphorus" in a newspaper article, the pods of dolphins that can sometimes be seen swimming in the strait are an encouraging sign that it is becoming less polluted. **Bottlenose dolphins, common dolphins,** and **harbor porpoises** have all returned to the water recently, delighting fishermen and ferry passengers alike with their antics.

Cormorant

The birds of the Bosphorus

No sooner does any ferry set sail than a stream of **black-headed gulls** will gather around it, screeching a hopeful plea for a piece of one of the simits (sesame-seed rolls) many locals buy just to toss to them. They are the most conspicuous of the Bosphorus' multitudinous birds, but you will also see many **cormorants** swimming in the water or sunning themselves with their wings spread open on the buoys, and flocks of tiny **Mediterranean shearwaters** skimming low across the water.

These are the resident birds, but the Bosphorus also lies on an important migratory route and one of the great sights of the city is that of the **storks** arriving back from their winter sojourn in Africa in March and then leaving again in even greater numbers in the third week of August.

2nd Bridge on a winter day.

How the Judas tree got its name

If you visit Istanbul in the spring you will hardly be able to miss the beautiful pink-flowering Judas trees (*Cercis siliquastrum*). Legend holds that **Judas Iscariot**, the disciple who betrayed Jesus Christ, hanged himself from one of these trees, hence its popular name. In reality it is probably a corruption of the French "**Arbre de Judée**", meaning **Tree of Judea** in recognition of one of the places that it grows.

Savarona

Now you see it, now you don't. Moored at Kuruçeşme, the *Savarona* was the largest and most luxurious private yacht in the world. It was built in 1931 for **Emily Roebling**, granddaughter of the man responsible for New York's Brooklyn Bridge, but in 1938 it was bought by the **Turkish government** and used for several cabinet meetings. It was while on-board the *Savarona* in 1938 that **Atatürk** succumbed to critical illness; he was taken from the yacht to the Dolmabahçe Palace where he died. In 1979 the yacht was badly damaged by fire.

Completely restored, the Savarona can be hired for special occasions, and past guests have included **Prince Rainier of Monaco, Prince Charles and Princess Diana** of **Britain**, and **King Juan Carlos** of **Spain**, as well as **Tom Cruise** and **Nicole Kidman**, and **Sharon Stone**.

There are projects underway to use the ship to host foreign statesmen and then use it as a museum. The ship was expropriated in 2014 under the initiative of the Ministry of Culture and Tourism. Now it serves as the presidential yacht.

Stairs of the Savarona

Savarona suite

Deck of the Savarona

Fireworks on 29 October
(Republic Day/Cumhuriyet Bayramı)

Moonlight flits

On summer evenings few things could be more pleasant than taking a **late-night cruise** along the Bosphorus, and plenty of companies compete to offer ready-made or do-it-yourself boat trips. But just think how much more romantic it must have been in the past when wealthy yalı owners would organize caique trips with musical entertainment of the more classically sedate kind that kept going right through until dawn. On moonlit summer nights boats would be rowed in silence from bay to bay, pausing in front of favored yalıs so that the musicians could serenade the owners. **Sultan Abdülaziz** seems to have been the greatest fan of these excursions, but by the end of the 19th century, during the time of Sultan Abdülhamid II they had faded into history.

An intriguing and sometimes dangerous feature of the Bosphorus is that a strong surface current flows from the Black Sea towards the Sea of Marmara while beneath it another current flows in the opposite direction.

How many yalıs are there?

A total of 366 Bosphorus yalıs are registered as first-, second- and third-grade historical monuments. The total rises to 600 if you include those yalıs of no historical value. While Beşiktaş is home to 37 yalıs, there are 136 in Sarıyer, 84 in Üsküdar, and 109 in Beykoz. There are six first-class yalıs in Beşiktaş, 41 in Sarıyer, 24 in Üsküdar, and 18 in Beykoz. Of the 208 second-class yalıs, there are 30 in Beşiktaş, 74 in Sarıyer, 40 in Üsküdar, and 64 in Beykoz. An additional 69 yalıs are registered as third-class structures. While restoration work on first-class yalıs must be done without tearing down the structure, second- and third-class yalıs can be demolished as long as their facades are precisely reconstructed.

THE BOSPHORUS

European Shore

01

Beyond the Stable Gate

Cankurtaran and the Sea Walls

The back streets of Cankurtaran, tucked in between the Topkapı Palace walls and Kumkapı, stand on the site of the remains of the old Byzantine Great Palace whose remains crop up unexpectedly here and there. It is also home to the frequently overlooked Dede Efendi House Museum.

This photo was taken in the late 19th century by the Levantine Pascal Sébah and his partner, Polycarpe Joaillier, who ran the Sébah Joaillier Photography Company. The former Courthouse (Darülfünun), which burned down in 1933, can be seen between the Sultanahmet Mosque and Hagia Sophia, behind Cankurturan.

"Life-saver" might seem rather a strange name for a neighborhood, but Cankurtaran is thought to have acquired it because it was at one time home to a **lifeboat station**. Alternatively, it may have been given the name in memory of a soldier called Ni'me'l-Ceyş'ten Seyyid Hasan Ağa who was nicknamed "**the Life-Saver**" because of his valor in battle against the Byzantines.

Hidrellez festivities in days gone

In the 16th century the Ottoman admiral known to the west as **Barbarossa** (see p.86) had barracks built here to house his sailors when they returned from a voyage. The original buildings were lost to an 18th-century fire; a hotel now stands on the site.

Resident of Cankurtaran

Today this is a district that is rapidly surrendering to tourism. Although hotels are increasingly encroaching on the area, it still has the feel of a traditional Istanbul mahalle (neighborhood) and retains many old **wooden houses** – often in a sorry state of disrepair – and small shops catering for the locals. Still pockets of glaring poverty continue to rub awkwardly against such speedy gentrification.

Akbıyık St (Akbıyık Caddesi)

The heart of Cankurtaran, "**White Moustache Street**" is a funny place, part Turkish take on Bangkok's famous Khao San Road backpacker enclave, part fast-gentrifying hotel-land. Bars, restaurants, cafes, souvenir shops, grocery shops, book exchanges, they're all here, and in summer life on the street can be raucous – although the municipality occasionally quietens things down again by closing all the bars. They soon re-open and life returns to normal. Near the junction with Mimar Mehmet Ağa Caddesi a stretch of the Byzantine **Magnaura Palace**, which formed part of the Great Palace, has been rather crudely restored. It is known to be the largest of the four large palaces built in the region by the Byzantine **Emperor Constantin I**, founder of Eastern Rome, when he settled in Istanbul. The building, which served as the senate and a university in different eras, was acquired by **Istanbul Metropolitan Municipality** in 2017.

Akbıyık Street

İshak Paşa Hamam

İshak Paşa Mosque

Often overlooked despite its position at one end of Akbıyık Caddesi this small mosque dating back to 1482 is one of the oldest in the city as it was built for **İshak Paşa**, Grand Vizier to **Mehmed II** and **Bayezıd II**. Across the road the remains of its large **hamam** crumble away unloved; some parts are incorporated into the garden of a hotel.

Dede Efendi House Museum

This lovely old wooden mansion was once home to **Dede Efendi** (1778-1846) who was one of Turkey's finest composers of classical music. After his death it was used for a while as the local police station before falling into disrepair. Restored in the 1980s, it now houses a small **museum of musical instruments**, but is mostly worth visiting to get a sense of what some of the other houses crumbling away nearby might have looked like in their heyday. Watch for signs advertising occasional **concerts**. Right beside the museum stands an elaborate **fountain** dating back to 1734 and paid for by the mother of the Grand Vizier **Hekimoğlu Ali Paşa**.

dedeefendievi, Tel. 0212 516 43 14, www.turkev.org.tr

One of the rooms in the museum

Who was Dede Efendi?

Born in Istanbul and resident for a while in Eyüp, Dede Efendi studied the **ney** (a form of flute) and wrote hundreds of songs and pieces of music for the **Mevlevi dervishes**. His works were popular with Sultan **Selim III** for whom he often performed. In 1846, while on pilgrimage to Saudi Arabia, he died of cholera. He is buried in Mecca. Some of his songs remain popular even today.

Statue of Admiral Turgut Reis in front of the sea walls

Pearl Pavilion

The Propontine Sea Walls

If you stroll down from Küçük Ayasofya to Kennedy Caddesi and the seashore, you will be able to inspect the remains of the Byzantine sea walls that ran all the way from **Mermer Kule** (the Marble Tower) in the west to **Ayvansaray** in the north. Despite the heavy traffic on Kennedy Caddesi, the coast road, it's a pleasant half-hour **walk** from Ahırkapı or Çatladıkapı to Sarayburnu. As you walk along you will be able to inspect the mish-mash of masonry and look out for two particular landmarks. The first is the support wall that is all that remains of the marble **İncili Köşk (Pearl Pavilion)**, built into the perimeter of Topkapı Palace in 1578. According to the story, at the very end of his life **Sultan Murad III** (r. 1574-95) was listening to music while gazing out to sea from this pavilion when the passing navy fired their guns in his honor, causing such vibrations that part of the ceiling fell down on him. The Pearl Pavilion was also the last known resting place of a famous **organ** sent as a gift to Sultan Mehmed III by **Queen Elizabeth I of England**. Just past the pavilion patterns in the brickwork of the wall and the shapes of arches and windows are all that remain of the 12th-century **Church of Savior Philanthropos** (Jesus the Charitable) which was popular with medieval Russian pilgrims who reported a miracle-working statue there. Greek pilgrims visited an **ayazma** (sacred spring) here until well into the 19th century.

Traces of Church of Savior Philanthropos

Ahırkapı

Cankurtaran lurks behind the remains of the old **Byzantine sea walls**, which, here, have a railway line running immediately behind them. Occasionally there are breaks in the wall where the railway line is forced to run across the old gateways. Ahırkapı (Stable Gate) was one such gateway that offered access to the **imperial mews** in Ottoman times.

Historic Peninsula and Kadıköy

02

Park and Porte

Gülhane Park and Sarayburnu

One of the gems of Old Istanbul is Gülhane Park (House of Roses Park), once the lower part of the Topkapı Palace gardens and now, after considerable renovation, a popular place for local families to pass their spare time beneath a canopy of tall trees amid well-kept flowerbeds. There are several minor monuments within the park, including the ancient Goths Column, as well as a few simple teahouses. The park is at its best in April during the tulip festival and in high summer when concerts and other family-oriented events are held here.

Gülhane Park

Aşık Veysel

At 163,000 square meters, Gülhane Park is roughly equal the size of St James's Park in London. Dotted about its fringes are several minor historic monuments, including the slight remains of what looks like a church but may have been the 6th-century **orphanage of St Paul** which ended up housing the University of Constantinople in the 13th century. There are also several important monuments and buildings attached to the surrounding walls and lining the tram tracks as they head downhill to Eminönü.

The Goths Column

Inside the park on top of the hillside overlooking Sarayburnu (Seraglio Point) stands a 15-meter-tall granite column with a Corinthian column perched on top which the Byzantine historian Nicephorus Gregoras tells us once carried a **statue of Byzas**, the founder of Byzantium. A barely discernible **Latin inscription** on its base reads, "To Fortune, who returns by reason of the victory over the Goths", which leaves it unclear whether it was erected during the reign of **Claudius II Gothicus** (r. 268-270) or that of **Constantine the Great** (r. 324-337), both of whom won battles against the Goths.

Museum of the History of Islamic Science and Technology

Housed in the rebuilt stables that ring the inside of the park walls, this new museum may be of rather specialist interest but is nonetheless very atmospheric, with sections devoted to time, navigation and medicine as well as zoology and architecture. Many of the exhibits are either copies of items held in foreign museums or models based on written accounts, but there are also some fine original musical instruments on display. It's almost worth paying the entrance fee just to see the lovely drawings on the ceiling by the Istanbul artist **Nusret Çolpan** whose delightful miniatures also adorn the tram stops.

Near the museum can be seen a fine **rose garden** as well as a small garden displaying the flora of the Turkish Republic of Northern Cyprus.

Tel: 0212 528 80 65, www.ibttm.gov.tr

Miniature painted by Nusret Çolpan

The birds of Gülhane

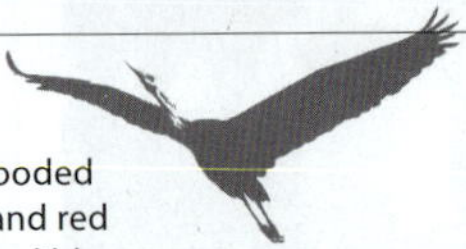

In spring the park is full of birdsong. Look out for hooded crows, turtle and collared doves, and bright green and red parakeets. In winter and spring a large **heronry** is audible and visible amid the naked branches of the trees.

Seraglio Point (Sarayburnu)

If you walk right across the park from the Soğukçeşme (Cold Fountain) Gate on the tramway side you will exit facing Seraglio Point which offers great views across the Sea of Marmara. Here stands what was the first **statue of Atatürk** (or any other Turk, for that matter) to be erected in the country in 1926. Designed by the Austrian sculptor Heinrinch Krippel, it shows Atatürk gazing across to Kadıköy and Haydarpaşa. It was from this spot that Atatürk set sail for Samsun in 1919 at the start of the **Turkish War of Independence**.

A short walk along the road towards Sirkeci takes you past the dainty **Sepetçiler Kasrı (Basket-makers' Pavilion)**, a boathouse with rooms above it whence the sultans would embark on cruises across the Bosphorus or up the Golden Horn. The existing version was built in 1643 for **Sultan İbrahim I** , although there seems to have been a building on the site since the 5th century. Derelict for much of the 20th century, it was restored in 1980 and again in 1990, and is best appreciated from the water as you sail towards Kadıköy.

Topkapı Palace looking down on the Basket-makers' Pavilion.

Zeynep Sultan Mosque

Most people enter Gülhane Park either downhill from the Archeological Museum or via the Soğukçeşme Gate entrance at the bottom of Soğukçeşme Sokak. Across the tramlines from this entrance stands the baroque-style Zeynep Sultan Mosque, built in 1760 for Sultan Ahmed III's daughter Zeynep by **Mehmed Tahir Ağa**, who was also responsible for the Laleli Mosque. The mosque could easily be mistaken for a Byzantine church, not just because of its dome, which undulates around the arches of the windows beneath it, but also because of its alternating layers of brick and stone, a style of masonry that seems to have continued straight through from Byzantine times into the 18th century. Behind the mosque a small building of similar construction was once an Ottoman **primary school** and is now the office of the Osmanlı Araştırmaları Vakfı (Ottoman Researches Foundation). Immediately in front of the mosque is a prominent **sebil**, now housing a refreshment kiosk, which turns out not to belong to the mosque at all but was moved here from Sirkeci when the roads were widened. It dates back to 1778 and used to be attached to the tomb of **Sultan Abdülhamid I**.

The Gülhane Decree

Gülhane Park provided the location for an important event in later Ottoman history. In 1839, during the **Tanzimat (Reform)** era, it was here that **Sultan Abdülmecid I** proclaimed the Gülhane Decree, which kickstarted only partially successful efforts to strengthen the empire by modernizing its institutions. By the 19th century the once vibrant Ottoman Empire was stagnating, nicknamed "**the Sick Man of Europe**" by the Western powers. Starting with the Gülhane Edict (also called the Tanzimat Fermanı) in 1839, the reforming sultans **Mahmud II** and **Abdülmecid I**, and the grand viziers **Ali Paşa, Fuad Paşa, Ahmed Çevdet Paşa** and **Mithad Paşa**, attempted to drag the empire into the modern era by abolishing the old "millet" system whereby its different nationalities more or less governed themselves. Instead they tried to forge a true **Ottoman identity**, with a new flag and national anthem, and universal conscription for males of all religions. They were only partially successful in their modernizing endeavors, and the Tanzimat era effectively came to an end in 1876.

Gülhane Decree

The Sublime Porte

This drawing shows Bab-ı Ali on the left and the Parade Pavilion on the right.

Across the road from the Parade Pavilion stands the **Bab-ı Ali**, a dramatic canopied gateway dating back to around 1840. Today it gives onto mundane government offices but this was once the **Sublime Porte** through which guests were admitted to the inner sanctum of the grand viziers, men who held an office somewhat akin to that of a prime minister today. The first grand vizier to build himself a palace here was **Sokollu Mehmed Paşa** who moved in in 1564. As time passed and more and more Ottoman business was conducted here the Sublime Porte came to symbolize the government, especially as many visitors were not allowed to venture beyond it.

So ambassadors would be said to be accredited to the Sublime Porte rather than to the Ottoman Empire just as they are said to be accredited to the Court of St James rather than to the British government today. In 1839 the grand viziers moved up the road to what is now the Governor's Office but the old name lingered on to refer to the empire.

Parade Pavilion (Alay Köşkü)

Heading downhill following the tramlines and Gülhane Park's outer wall, you will pass an imposing mansion which now houses the Faculty of Political Sciences of Istanbul University but which was originally built in 1875 to serve as a **military college**. Across the road and jutting out from the walls as they make a sharp turn to the right is the graceful Parade Pavilion, a gazebo from which the sultans would watch ceremonial processions, including the **Processions of the Gilds**, a colorful feature of life until the 18th century vividly described by the 17th-century travel writer Evliya Çelebi who makes them sound a bit like an Ottoman version of the Notting Hill carnival in London, UK. No doubt it was more than mere coincidence that the location of the gazebo also enabled the sultan to keep an eye on what was going on across the road at the Sublime Porte, the home of their grand viziers. The original gazebo was probably built for **Sultan Mehmed II** although the current version only dates back to 1819 and the reign of **Mahmud II**. A long stone ramp just inside the park gate enabled people to ride their horses right up to its door.

03

Oriental Business District

Sirkeci and Eminönü

Sirkeci railway station is renowned as the terminus for the old Orient Express trains, and it remains the starting point for train services to Europe and one of the stations of the Marmaray Project. A short walk away is the Main Post Office, a building so beautiful that it's worth visiting as much to take a look around as to post a letter. The Main Post Office dates back to the start of the 20th century and was built in a style that came to be associated with the young Turkish Republic which can also be seen in the First Vakıf Han and in the Fourth Vakıf Han in surrounding Eminönü.

Sirkeci Harbor in the past

The narrow streets of **Eminönü** between the New Mosque and Sirkeci were substantially rebuilt in the 19th century, and since then more and more businesses have been shoehorned into the limited space. This is a good place to come in search of cheap electronic goods, as well as low-budget meals in the many small kebaberies. In Turkish, Eminönü means "in front of justice", a name it may have taken from the **courts** or customs houses associated with the docks. **Sirkeci** means "vinegar-seller" in Turkish although there don't seem to be any records of vinegar being sold here! In fact the name is probably a corruption of the Greek "Strategion", meaning "**the place of the commander**".

Tomb of Abdülhamid I

Opposite the Fourth Vakıf Han in Hamidiye Caddesi stands the lovely **tomb** of **Abdülhamid I** (1774-1789), buried in a small precinct along with his son, **Mustafa IV** (1807-1808), whose short reign became particularly blood-thirsty as he struggled to contain a Janissary revolt. Beautifully restored, it features some especially wonderful 18th-century **tiled calligraphy**. A set of Mohammed's footprints are also preserved in a niche in the wall.

Nimet Abla (1899-1978) was Istanbul's most famous lottery ticket agent

The façade of Sirkeci Station was restored in 2012.

Sirkeci Station (Istanbul Gar)

Sirkeci Station was designed in Oriental-Gothic style in 1887-1889 by the German architect **August Jasmund**, who was also responsible for the Deutsche Bank building (see p. 34). It was specifically intended to serve the needs of passengers arriving from Europe on the **Orient Express**, but unfortunately access to the railway concourse is via a mundane modern entrance while the fine original façade, with its circular stained-glass windows, is hidden by the building. The Sirkeci Station Building, which is a station of the Marmaray Project (see p. 219) also serves as a terminal for train services to Europe. Inside the original part of the building a small **museum** contains pictures of what the station originally looked like, as well as souvenirs of the Orient Express in its heyday. Scenes shot for the film of Agatha Christie's famous thriller "**Murder on the Orient Express**" bring to life the colorful hustle and bustle that once took place on the platforms.

Tel: 0212 527 12 01, closed Sundays and Mondays.

Murder on the Orient Express author Agatha Christie's room in the Pera Palace Hotel.

The incomparable Orient Express

Surely one of the world's most famous and glamorous train services, the Orient Express first steamed out of London heading for Istanbul via Paris in 1888. At that time the journey took nearly three days to complete but the train was equipped with every modern comfort to suit its upscale clientele. The journey was immortalized by **Agatha Christie** in her crime novel "Murder on the Orient Express", starring the Belgian detective **Hercule Poirot** and filmed in 1974, 2001 and 2017.

Pera Palace Hotel

Hobyar Mosque

Frequently overlooked to the rear of the post office is the small hexagonal **Hobyar Mosque**, also by Vedat Tek and also adorned with Kütahya tiles although the roof of the minaret looks to have stepped straight from Syria. This was the only mosque designed by the architect.

Main Post Office

Main Post Office (Büyük Postane)

This imposing building, given added gravitas by the stone steps leading up to it, was designed between 1905 and 1909 by **Vedat Tek**, one of the stars of the First National Architecture movement. The small domed rooms at each end were an attempt to meld a newly emerging **Turkish national style** with more familiar Western elements, while the **Kütahya tiles** used to decorate the façade were chosen in an attempt to breathe new life into a faltering industry.

Philatelists will love the small **museum** inside the post office that contains some of the original wooden furnishings and a collection of old postboxes and stamps. It's mainly interesting, though, as a chance to see the lovely staircase, ceilings and other interior design details. A five-year restoration and organization plan at the museum was initiated in 2018.

The Hobyar Mosque is called a mescid in some sources.

Vlora Han

Detail from the Vlora Han

Vlora Han

If you stand on the steps of the post office and look to your right you will see the fine Art Nouveau **Vlora Han**, its façade adorned with stone roses like those on the better-known **Casa Botter** on İstiklal Caddesi.

A short walk down Yeni Postane Caddesi brings you to a fine newly restored building in First National Architectural style that was created for the **Yapı ve Kredi Bank**. Immediately facing it is a far more austere Teutonic building designed to house the **Deutsche Bank** by **August Jasmund** in 1890.

Old Deutsche Bank building

Old postcard showing sebil in front of Türkiye İş Bankası Museum on right and part of Fourth Vakıf Han on left.

First and Fourth Vakıf Hans

In the 1910s architect **Kemaleddin Bey**, the second of the main movers behind the First National Architecture movement, built four large hans that were really Istanbul's first modern office blocks in the streets between Sirkeci and Eminönü. **The Fourth Vakıf Han** is the more obvious of the two surviving buildings as it stands opposite the famous **Ali Muhiddin Hacı Bekir** shop where **lokum** (Turkish delight) was first created. After **the First World War** it served as the headquarters of the French army, before going into a long decline during which it became the haunt of glue-sniffers until finally being rescued and turned into the World Park Hotel. Like the Post Office building, it has domed rooms at each corner. There's also an original hamam in the basement.

First National Architecture

This was the name given to a style of architecture characteristic of the first half of the 20th century that pulled together elements of the Selçuk and Ottoman to create something entirely new. Features include overhanging roofs, thick lancet windows, panels of tiling on the façade, and obtruding semi-spherical ornaments. Its two leading lights were **Vedat Tek** (1873-1942) and **Kemaleddin Bey** (1870-1927) whose moustachioed face now peers out of the 20TL note. Aside from the **Main Post Office**, other fine examples include the **Land Registry** and **Rectorate buildings** in the Hippodrome, the **Four Seasons Hotel** in Sultanahmet, and the **Sütlüce Convention Center**.

Detail of façade of Liman Han

Architect Kemaleddin Bey's portrait appears on the back of the TL 20 banknote.

Türkiye İş Bankası Museum

Between the Main Post Office and the New Mosque several fine 19th and early 20th-century buildings house branches of major banks. The Türkiye İş Bankası building dates back to 1898 and was originally used first as the post office and then as a parcel sorting office. In 1928 it passed into the care of Türkiye İş Bankası and now boasts a small state-of-the-art **museum**. The paperwork on display may be of interest only to true banking devotees, but children will enjoy being able to go inside the **basement vaults** with their enormous doors, and peeking inside **safe-boxes** to see what sort of things people valued enough to store in them. You might also want to spare a glance at the elegant **Garanti Bank** building across the road, another fine example of the First National style of architecture.

Garanti Bank building

www.muze.isbank.com.tr
Tel: 0212 511 13 31
Closed Mondays.

Liman Han

Harbor Building (Liman Han)

If you cut up Yalı Köskü Caddesi from the waterfront you will see on the right the huge Liman Han designed by **Vedat Tek** in 1907, with its beautiful tiled façade. At the end of the road is the **Hidayet Mosque**, designed by **Alexandre Vallaury**. Dating back to 1887, it stands on the site of an older wooden mosque.

Today the Eminönü waterfront is a ferociously busy transport interchange. Until the late 19th century though this was where the fish market stood, and before that it was where the Venetians and the Amalfians had their trading colonies.

New Mosque (Yeni Cami)

The large mosque that dominates the waterfront has the apparently perverse name New Mosque, even though it dates back to 1591, which makes it very old by most people's standards. Foreigners have a hard time understanding why this mosque is called "**new**" but in Turkey those which are older than a thousand years are "**historical**", while the ones that are younger are "new". Work on the mosque was started by **Safiye Sultan** (1550 -1605), at a time when this was a predominantly Jewish neighborhood occupied by tall wooden apartment blocks called Jeweries. The Jews were relocated to **Hasköy** on the far side of the Golden Horn, but progress on the mosque was slow because Safiye Sultan lost her power on the death of her son **Sultan Mehmed III** in 1603. Like so many modern buildings in Turkey, the mosque was left incomplete and eventually caught fire. It was only completed in 1633 by which time **Hatice Turhan Sultan**, the mother of **Sultan Mehmed IV**, had taken charge of things. Her architect, **Mustafa Ağa**, completed the work in 1663 using the plans drawn up by the original architect, a pupil of Sinan's called **Davud Ağa**.

Restoration of the Sultan's Lodge attached to the New Mosque won a Europa Nostra award in 2010.

Courtyard

The mosque, one of the last such large buildings to be completed in the classical Ottoman style, boasts two minarets, a flurry of 66 domes, and a secluded courtyard centered on an attractive şadırvan (ablutions fountain). Tiles and calligraphic inscriptions decorate the courtyard walls. Unusually, the mosque has open galleries on each side of the exterior, while the minarets each boast triple balconies which meant that in the days before loudspeakers half a dozen müezzins could give the call to prayer at the same time. When it was first completed, the mosque would have stood right on the shore with the water lapping at its steps.

Internally the mosque is very elegant, its walls covered with tiles that, while not of the finest quality, are nevertheless very pretty, its windows filled with richly colored stained glass. The **minbar** (pulpit) and **müezzin mahfili** (muezzin's pew) are of marble, and the **kürsü** (imam's prayer seat) is of wood inlaid with mother-of-pearl. Above the windows verses from the Koran were beautifully inscribed by **Mustafa Çelebi**.

Attached to the shore side of the mosque is a brick-and-stone structure accessible via a ramp to the rear. This is the newly restored **hünkar kasrı (sultan's lodge)** which housed private quarters for the sultan offering direct access to the mosque's interior. The restoration won a Europa Nostra award in 2010. Across the road on the inland side is a small precinct that contains the **tombs** of **Hatice Turhan Sultan**, her son **Sultan Mehmed IV**, and those of sultans **Mustafa II, Ahmed III, Mahmud I, Osman III** and **Murad V**. Facing it across the street, a now derelict **time-keeper's lodge** is built into the walls of the mosque.

A little further along the road on the same side as the tombs, the elaborate **sebil**, or water dispensary, that formed part of the mosque complex was badly damaged by a fire that destroyed the surrounding buildings in the late 19th century. Its restoration was originally supervised by **Osman Hamdi Bey**, the archeologist who founded the Istanbul Archeological Museum. It has recently been restored again, although sadly today the water is dispensed from a mundane machine plonked down beside it.

Pampered pigeons

In front of the New Mosque stands a row of kiosks from which licensed retailers sell small trays of birdseed for visitors to feed the many appreciative pigeons. This is a common sight outside Turkish mosques since pigeons are revered here rather than treated as pests. The reason lies in a story often told about the Prophet Mohammed who had taken refuge from his enemies in a cave. A spider wove a web across the entrance and a pigeon nested in front of it, thereby putting pursuers off the scent and guaranteeing its descendants a lifetime of pampering.

Spice Market (Mısır Çarşısı)

When you stand on Galata Bridge and look inland you will see a small but sturdy multi-domed building immediately to the right of the New Mosque. This is the Spice Market or Egyptian Bazaar, which was built in 1660 and took its name from the fact that goods from the **Far East** and **India** arrived here from Egypt on the so-called **Mısır Kervanı (Egyptian Caravan)**. L-shaped in layout, the bazaar nurtures almost 100 shops beneath its vaulted ceilings plus two restaurants above the main entrances: the famous Pandeli and less well-known Bab-ı Hayat. The Spice Market, together with a hamam that has since been lost, was originally built so that its shops could provide financial support for the neighboring mosque.

Main entrance

The Spice Market gained its hauntingly romantic nickname because at one time the majority of its shops sold herbs and spices. Today you can still come here to shop for cooking ingredients, although you will have to search harder for them amid the more prominent souvenir tea sets and trays of lokum (Turkish delight) aimed at tourists. A few of the shops have given up selling foodstuffs altogether and now sell much the same sort of things as you could find in the **Grand Bazaar**. Outside, however, it's a different story. The surrounding streets still stock a wide choice of staple foodstuffs: cheeses, fruit and vegetables, and meat, on one side; pet food, flowers and leeches on the other. On the side of the bazaar closest to the New Mosque an attractive outdoor market primarily sells seeds and plants as well as a rather disheartening selection of animals and birds in overcrowded cages. Here, too, you will find plastic bottles full of leeches that are still used in traditional medicine. On the side facing **Tahtakale** you'll find a mouth-watering array of local cheeses, jars of honey, and mountains of fresh fruit and vegetables. To the rear of the bazaar a string of small shops sell kitchenware and other basic household goods. The bazaar was originally part of the complex attached to the New Mosque, although today they are completely separate.

Some shops still retain a traditional atmosphere, others cater to tourists.

Kurukahveci Mehmet Efendi

For beautiful bags with modern designs drop into Tuğra at No. 70 (Tel: 0212 527 67 01)

Pandeli

In business since 1901, Pandeli is housed in a set of exquisite turquoise-tiled rooms over the bazaar's main entrance. It's wonderfully "oriental", and the views of the Golden Horn, if you can land a front-window table, are unforgettable. The food is also pretty good. Everday it's open from noon until 7 pm.

Tel: 0212 527 39 09
www.pandeli.com.tr

05

Bridging the Old and New

Galata Bridge

Until the 19th century the old Byzantine city of Constantinople was completely separated from Galata and Pera by the Haliç or Golden Horn, the stretch of water that cuts inland at the point where the Sea of Marmara and the Bosphorus meet. Several bridges have been built across it over the centuries. The current Galata Bridge is the fifth on the site.

Adorning Istanbul's third hill above the Galata Bridge, the Süleymaniye Mosque's four minarets symbolize that Sultan Süleyman the Magnificent was the fourth sultan after the conquest of Istanbul, while its 10 galleries symbolize that he was the Ottoman Empire's 10th sultan since its foundation.

As long ago as the reign of the **Emperor Justinian** there had been attempts to bridge the Golden Horn, and there are known to have been early bridges upstream at Ayvansaray and Kağıthane. However, both were destroyed during the disastrous Fourth Crusade that diverted to Constantinople in 1204.

Renaissance polymath **Leonardo da Vinci** came up with a design for a new bridge, but it wasn't until 1836 that a permanent crossing of rafts was strung out between **Unkapanı** on the southern shore of the Horn, and **Azapkapı**, to the north. Since then there have been several more Galata Bridges culminating in the current model that links **Eminönü** on the southern shore with **Karaköy** to the north. This latest incarnation is not especially beautiful although it has an iconic status, famous as much for the myriad fishermen who dangle their rods over its sides whatever the weather as for its engineering. The line of fish restaurants nestling beneath it make great places to watch the sun go down over the Horn.

Waiting for the fish to bite.

Leonardo's Bridge

So obvious was the need for a bridge across the Horn that both Leonardo da Vinci and Michelangelo came up with plans that they submitted to the sultan. Leonardo's drawing, completed in 1502 for Sultan Beyazıd II, has received the most publicity, and in 2001 a scale model of it was constructed in Aas in Norway as part of the Leonardo Bridge Project. Instead of using Da Vinci's ideas, a modern bridge is being built as part of the Marmaray Project. It will cross between the existing Galata and Unkapanı bridges.

www.leonardobridgeproject.org

Leonardo's Bridge as constructed at Aas in Norway.

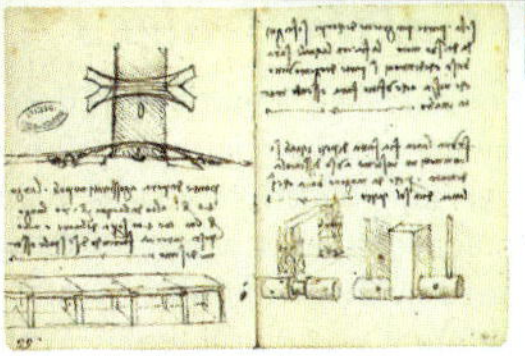

Nostalgic photo of shoeshine boys on the bridge.

Most Famous Galata Bridge

When people murmur nostalgically about the old **Galata Bridge** they are usually referring to the elegant 1912 version which served the city faithfully for 80 years and whose underside was festooned with picturesque fish restaurants. Just before it was due to be decommissioned in 1992, this bridge caught fire. However, as soon as its replacement was in position, it was speedily repaired. The nostalgic bridge was completely removed in 2016 after having served for pedestrians between **Sütlüce** and **Eyüp**.

Earlier bridges

Inconceivable as the idea seems now, it wasn't until the mid-19th century that there was a proper permanent bridge across the Golden Horn; until then, people made do with boats that served as water taxis. In 1845 **Bezm-i Alem Valide Sultan**, the mother of Sultan Abdülmecid I, paid for a permanent bridge to be built across the Golden Horn to facilitate access to Galata. Her bridge had several different names: **Yeni Köprü** (New Bridge), **Cisr-i Cedid** (New Bridge), and **Valide Köprüsü** (Queen Mother's Bridge) in honor of its founder. In 1863 **Ateş Ahmed Paşa** paid for a new bridge, which was, in turn, replaced in iron in 1875 and 1912; in 1878 restaurants and teahouses were added to its underside. Many writers, including **Edmondo de Amicis**, have left vivid descriptions of the colorful throng that was forever passing over what became known as "**the most wonderful pathway of Europe**". In 1910 a new wood-and-iron model, the most famous of all the Galata bridges, was built. This was designed in such a way that it could be opened to allow larger ships to pass from the Bosphorus into the Golden Horn. The latest concrete version opened in 1994.

Why the Golden Horn?

Many reasons have been given for how the Golden Horn acquired its picturesque name. Some focus on the horn shape created by the two streams – the **Alibey** and **Kağıthane rivers** – that flow into it from the west, others on the way that the setting sun is reflected on the water. Yet others suggest that it acquired its name because of the quantity of gold tossed into the waters by the Byzantines as they confronted defeat at the hands of the Turks in 1453. In fact the name is a translation of the Greek word "**chrysokeras**" whose precise derivation is unclear. The Turkish name for this stretch of water, **Haliç**, is not a translation of "Golden Horn" but an abbreviation for the less romantic **Haliç-i Dersaadet**, meaning "Bay of Istanbul" in Osmanlı, the language of the Ottoman Empire.

Cruising the Golden Horn

It costs almost nothing, but one of the most enjoyable things to do on a trip to Istanbul is cruise up or down the Golden Horn. An hourly ferry leaves from Karaköy and criss-crosses the Horn, calling in at Kasımpaşa, Fener, Balat, Hasköy, Ayvansaray, Sütlüce and Eyüp. Amongst the buildings most easily seen from the boat are the Naval Command Office (Bahriye Nezareti) and Istanbul Naval Hospital at Kasımpaşa, and the Greek High School at Fener.

www.sehirhatları.com.tr

Haliç Metro Bridge

The Metro bridge project was first begun in 2004. In 2009 UNESCO issued a report detailing its harmful effect on the silhouette of the Süleymaniye Mosque and recommended another project for a flat bridge to replace it. The ongoing work was discontinued briefly and the project was revised. The towers, which were first planned at 82m, were reduced to 65m. The bridge was opened for service in 2014 as the connection line for the Hacıosman-Yenikapı metro line.

The bridge behind bridge

The Galata Bridge must be the only bridge in the world to have bestowed its name on a card game. According to a 1901 guide to this quintessentially British game, it was originally dreamt up by a group of British soldiers who were based in Galata during the Crimean War. Every evening they would walk across the Galata Bridge to coffeehouses in the Old City where they could play the game, so when pressed to come up with a name for it they called it simply "bridge".

"The Bridge"

Geert Mak's best-selling book "The Bridge" lifts the lid on the underside of life in Istanbul through interviews with the men and women who eke out a living on and around the Galata Bridge.

06

Beyond the Chain

Karaköy, Perşembe Pazarı and Azapkapı

The easily overlooked area north of the Galata Bridge is called Karaköy after the Karaite Jews who used to live here in the 19th century. It's a bustling, commercial district where ferries arrive from Kadıköy and Haydarpaşa, cruise ships dock from all around the world, and a colorful fish market takes place. The maze of narrow streets between the waterfront and busy Necatibey Caddesi is dotted with forgotten churches. Bankalar (Voyvoda) Caddesi is lined with wonderful 19th-century office blocks, most of them once occupied by banks. At Azapkapı a fine Sinan mosque stands beside an exquisite fountain.

Karaköy Harbor

Nordstern Han

Karaköy Square ①

The Karaköy tram stop deposits its passengers in Karaköy Square, the rather messy area immediately north of Galata Bridge that was once the heart of Genoese Galata, a virtually independent, walled trading colony that flourished under the Byzantines. At its height it stretched all the way from Azapkapı, where the Atatürk Bridge now stands, to Tophane, and uphill as far as the Galata Tower.

Standing on the tram platform it's possible to admire, amid the chaos of traffic, the **Karaköy Palas** building which was designed by the Italian architect **Guilio Mongeri** in 1920 in a style that mixes and matches Byzantine, Selçuk and Ottoman features. It now houses branches of a bank. Facing it across the tramlines is the **Nordstern Han**, also apparently designed by an Italian architect.

Karaköy Palas

Port Area ② ③

Heading down towards the Karaköy ferry you pass, on the corner, the imposing Neoclassical façade of the **TC Ziraat Bankası**, built immediately before the First World War to house the Vienna Bank. Its parapet supports two statues, the female said to represent **commerce**, the male **industry**. Alternatively the figures may be of **Master Hiram** from the Old Testament and his **widowed mother** (characters, incidentally, who crop up in Masonic ritual). In either case they are very early instances of figurative sculpture in the city.

Today the Ziraat Bankası occupies what was once the Vienna Bank.

Strolling along the waterfront you will have a fine view across to **Sarayburnu** and **Topkapı Palace**, and to the pretty little **Basketmakers' Pavilion** at Eminönü. In 2008 the ferry landing stage sank in heavy winds. Facing it, the **Uğurlu Han** is a fine example of First National Architecture, as is the tiny health center next door. A third example of the style at the end of the harbor was beautifully restored in 2010.

The old ferry landing stage.

Decorated (previously Voyvoda) Police Station from reign of Sultan Abdülaziz

Turkish Maritime Lines Building 4

At the far end of the harbor stands the sturdy **Deniz Yolları Building**, the former headquarters of the Turkish Maritime Lines company. It was built between 1912 and 1914 in grand, if eclectic, style. The building is one of the two structures which were not demolished as part of the Galataport Project.

Christos Kremastos Monastery

The picture on the left shows this ancient Byzantine structure in 2005, while the one on the right shows it in 2010. By that time parts of it had been demolished to make way for a car park which is a bit like demolishing parts of Hagia Sophia. Let's see how well the rest of it survives the test of time.

Underground Mosque 5

One of Karaköy's more unexpected treasures is this small underground mosque hidden amid the workaday shops of Kemankeş Caddesi. It's thought that a **tower** originally stood on this site; to it was attached the **chain** that was strung across the Golden Horn to close it to intruders (stretches of this chain still survive in the Naval (see p.86) and Military museums). After the tower was demolished following the Ottoman conquest of Istanbul, the site was used to house a **gunpowder depot**. Later a shrine was built inside the cellar after, in 1640, a şeyh (religious leader) of the Nakshibendi sect claimed to have found the bodies of two men killed during the **Arab siege of Byzantium in the 7th century**. In 1757 Grand Vizier Köse Mustafa Paşa paid to have the shrine upgraded to a mosque. The novelty of its being underground aside, the mosque is of no great architectural significance.

Fountain in front of Kemankes Mosque

Underground Mosque (Yeraltı Camii)

Tomb of Arab warrior

Zülfaris Synagogue 6

Tucked away in Perçemli Sokak, just round the corner from the Tünel entrance, you'll see the redundant **Zülfaris Synagogue**, is easy to miss, and, when you find it. There had been a synagogue on this site since the 17th century, but the current building was paid for by the wealthy **Kamondo family** in 1890. It became redundant in 1985 and reopened as Jewish Museum in 2001.

In the courtyard a statue called "**The Soaring Flame**" welcomed the guests. The statue by Nadia Arditti commemorated the Turkish Jews who died in different parts of the world. The restoration of the synagogue had fully revived its neoclassical grandeur. The main body of the museum housed what was once the prayer hall. However, the fate of the synagogue was repeated and its doors were closed again in 2015. The Turkish Jewish Museum was moved to the **Neve Shalom Synagogue** in Galata. The building today serves as a center of culture, art and events.

Kemankes Mosque (1642)

Zülfaris Synagogue

Who were the Karaite Jews?

The Karaites are non-Orthodox Jews who reject the Talmud and the rabbinaical tradition, accepting only the Tanakh (Bible) as a source of authority. Unlike most Jews, they are patrilineal (i.e. if the father is a Jew so is the child). They worship in **underground synagogues** of which there is a single example in Hasköy, the **Bene Mikra**, that was rebuilt in 1800 after a fire. Karaite Jews appear to have arrived in Byzantium some time in the 8th century. Others arrived from Russia and were settled in the Karaköy area by **Sultan Mehmed II**. Their numbers were further augmented in the late 18th century when the Russians seized Crimea and its Karaite population fled. Nowadays perhaps around 30-40 remain in the city.

The elongated interior of the Arab Mosque is very striking.

Arab Mosque (Arap Camii) 7

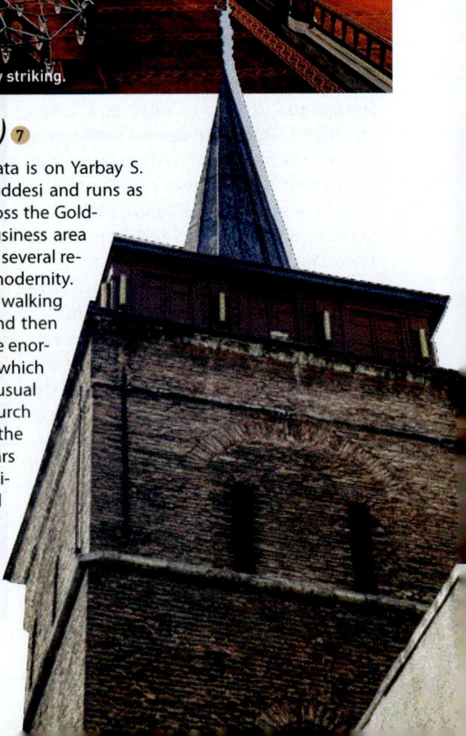

The entrance to the Tünel leading up to Galata is on Yarbay S. Evren Caddesi which continues as Tersane Caddesi and runs as far as Atatürk Köprüsü, the second bridge across the Golden Horn. Although this is predominantly a business area known for its many **hardware shops** there are several reminders of the distant past mixed in with the modernity. The finest of these reminders can be found by walking along the road as far as Sırmalı Nafe Sokak and then turning right along this road until you reach the enormous Arab Mosque (*Galata Mahkemesi Sokak*) which dates back to 1323-1337 and features an unusual square bell tower topped with a **spire**. The church was apparently built by **Dominican friars** on the site of an earlier church of St Paul, and appears to have been used by the **Genoese** community since excavations in the nave uncovered many Genoese tombstones. In the early 16th century it was taken over by **Moors** who had been expelled from Spain, hence its current name, the Arap (Arab) Camii. Inside, the elongated space immediately suggests that the building started life as a church.

Ancient hans continue in use today.

Rüstem Paşa Hanı

Karaköy Hans 8

On the water side of Yarbay S. Evren Caddesi are two early Ottoman hans. The first is the picturesque, vine-shaded **Rüstem Paşa Han** (also called the Kurşunlu Han) which was built by **Sinan** for the Grand Vizier Rüstem Paşa between 1544 - 1550 on the site of the old Genoese Cathedral of St Michael. Its two courtyards are separated by a double flight of steps leading up to the upper storey whose brick arches are ogival in shape. A little further along a cluster of nine domes bestrides the roof of the old **Bedesten**, also known as the **Fatih Han**, that almost certainly dates back to the reign of **Sultan Mehmed II**.

Perşembe Pazarı

For a glimpse of what **18th century Galata** might have looked like, cut inland off Yab. S Evren Caddesi along the street called Perşembe Pazarı (Thursday Market), where a series of old brick houses with corbelled upper storeys perpetuate an architectural style that probably passed straight from the Byzantines to the Genoese and then to the Turks.

Azapkapı Mosque 9

(Sokollu Mehmed Paşa Mosque)

Azapkapı Mosque

Right at the end of Tersane Caddesi and overshadowed by the busy Atatürk Bridge stand the Azapkapı Mosque and the newly restored and regilded **fountain** paid for by **Saliha Valide Hatun**, the mother of **Sultan Mahmud I**, in 1733. The mosque itself is a work of the famous Ottoman architect **Sinan** who designed it for **Sokollu Mehmed Paşa**, Grand Vizier to Sultans Süleyman the Magnificent, Selim II and Murad III, in 1577. It stands on a raised platform which would once have been filled with **shops** whose profits would have supported the mosque. Interestingly, it also has a **detached minaret** which is linked to the rest of the building by an arched corridor over the porch. In the 1930s the mosque was narrowly saved from demolition to make way for the bridge by public protests.

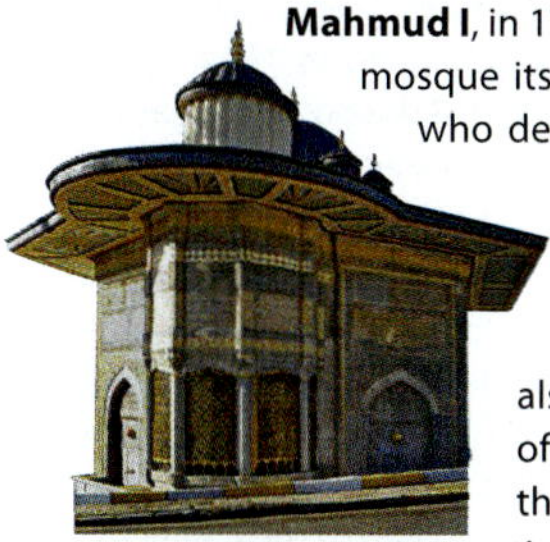

Saliha Valide Hatun Fountain

Bankalar (Voyvoda) Caddesi

10

Often overlooked by visitors who prefer to take the Tünel rather than climb the hill from Karaköy to Pera, Voyvoda Caddesi was one of the most important streets of 19th-century Istanbul, and many banks and insurance companies set up their head offices here, hence its nickname "Bankalar Caddesi". To find the street look for the colorful **Minerva Han** building which stands at the junction with Yüksek Kaldırım Caddesi, the road that leads directly to the Galata Tower. Newly restored, the Han boasts a blue-tiled façade adorned with cherubs that dates back to 1911-1913 when it may have been designed by the architect Basile Couremenos.

At first glance Bankalar Caddesi has something of the look of the City of London about it, an impression created by the serried ranks of imposing buildings that line both sides of the street. In particular look out for the **Assicurazioni Generali Han** that was designed by **Giulio Mongeri** in 1909, and for the **Hezaren Han** designed by **Alexandre Vallaury** (the man responsible for the Pera Palas Hotel) in 1902. Between 1890 and 1892 Vallaury also designed the splendid building that houses the Ottoman and Central Banks in a style that has been described as "**Banker's Renaissance**". Today the Ottoman Bank has ceased to exist and the building contains the **SALT Gallery**, which accommodates a museum of banking history as well as several art workshops.

The street fell quiet when most of the banks moved their headquarters to Ankara after the founding of the Turkish Republic in 1923. Today the city's main banking districts are Levent and Maslak.

@salt_online, Tel: 0212 334 22 00, www.saltonline.org, closed Mondays.

Minerva Han

Minerva Han when it housed the Deutsche Bank

Kamondo Steps

Kamondo Steps

Midway along Bankalar Caddesi are the curvaceously lovely **Kamondo Steps**, which were photographed in 1964 by **Henri Cartier-Bresson** and feature in British crime writer **Barbara Nadel's** novel "Pretty Dead Things". They are named after the Jewish banking family that is thought to have paid for their construction by an unknown architect in the 1880s. They provide a short cut for getting up to the Galata Tower.

Yüksek Kaldırım 11 12

Just to the north of Bankalar Caddesi a second road climbs up to Pera by a more direct and steeper route. This is Yüksek Kaldırım (High Pavement), originally a street of 118 stone steps which connected with what is now **Galipdede Caddesi**. Not surprisingly once the funicular railway opened, traffic on this street slackened off – one look up it and you'll understand why. This was always a very **cosmopolitan area**, with all sorts of interesting shops. Today the shops mainly sell electrical appliances, the steps have been replaced with asphalt, and the colorfulness reported by many 19th century visitors has completely drained away. To get an idea of what it might have looked like, peer up nearby Hacı Ali Sokağı which still retains its steps.

Ashkenaz synagogue, off Yüksek Kaldırım

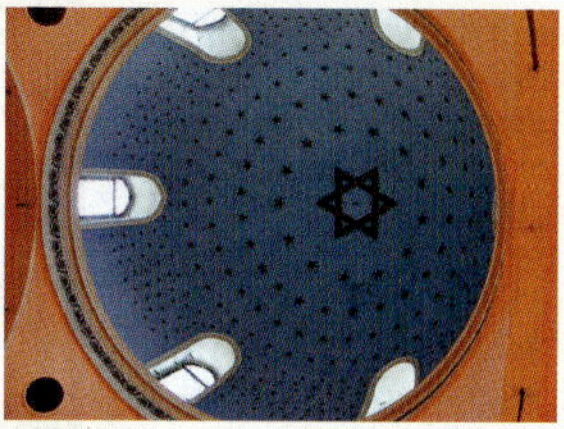

Ashkenaz synagogue

Greek Orthodox Primary School on Kemeraltı street

St Benoit High School (13)

There's a chapel right beside St. Benoit High School.

On Kemeraltı Caddesi a long wall closes off an L-shaped building that houses the St Benoit High School. Its most prominent feature is a **bell tower** dating back to 1427 when **Benedictine monks** founded the church of St Benoit (Benedict) here. In 1583 **Jesuit missionaries** established a school for Greek and Jewish boys on the site; when the Jesuit order was abolished in 1773, it was given to the Lazarist sect instead. In 1839 a school for girls was added to the complex. In 1987 the two parts of the school merged and became co-ed. It's not normally open to the public even though what is now the school chapel contains the **tombs** of several early French ambassadors to the Ottomans.

Surp Krikor Lusavoriç Armenian Church

Karaköy's forgotten churches (14) (15)

The most visible of Karaköy's many churches is the huge **Surp Krikor Lusavoriç (St Gregory the Illuminator) Church** which stands right beside Tophane Caddesi. Greatly in need of a spring-clean, it is still an imposing building with the raised dome and blind arcading typical of Armenian architecture. A church seems to have stood on this site since 1431 when the Armenians bought the land from the Genoese. However, the original building was damaged by a series of fires in the 18th century, and was then demolished when the road was widened in 1958. So, despite its appearance of great age, the current church only dates back to 1966 when it was rebuilt by **Bedros Zobyan**, basing the design on that of the church in **Echmiadzin in Armenia**. Access to the church is via a side entrance which passes under the belltower.

Surp Hisus Pırgiç Church.

Right next door to St Benoit High School is the Armenian Catholic **Church of Surp Hisus Pırgiç (Jesus Christ the Savior)**, product of a breakaway group of Armenians led by an early 18th-century monk called Mekhitar from Sivas who thought salvation could be found in union with Rome. The Armenian Catholics took to speaking French, and their church, built in 1834, has an unexpected whiff of Italy about its decoration. I never found it open. You may be luckier.

The Turkish Orthodox Patriarchate

Church doorknocker

Tucked into the back streets in Ali Paşa Değirmen Sokak you will eventually stumble upon the **Church of Panagia Kafatiani (Church of St Mary)**, the only functioning church belonging to the obscure and controversial Turkish Orthodox Church, which broke away from the Greek Orthodox Patriarchate in 1922. The original church on the site dated back to the 16th century, although this particular version was built in 1840. In 1924 it was occupied by **Papa Eftim I** as the headquarters of his new movement. The present patriarch is **Papa Eftim IV** who succeeded to the position in 2002. Today the church is in the possession of the Erenerol family, its only congregation. Normally only the narthex is open to the public who will find small silver ships hanging from the ceiling, offerings placed there by mariners in thanks to **St Nicholas** for a safe voyage. The pretty courtyard is lined with 19th-century tombstones.

St John the Baptist Church

Russian Orthodox churches (16)

The most extraordinary of Karaköy's forgotten places of worship are four rooftop **Russian Orthodox churches**, complete with cupolas, which were originally built as chapels above hostels, called "podvoriyes", where **Russian pilgrims** en route to Mt Athos (Greece) or Jerusalem could break their journeys; the clergy would stay on the floor immediately beneath the chapel, everyone else on the lower floors. The first to go up in 1870 was the St Andrei Podvoriye. It was followed in quick succession by the St Panteleimon Podvoriye in 1878, the St Ilya (Elijah) Podvoriye in 1879 and the Triotskoye (Trinity) Podvoriye in 1880. All four were officially linked to Russian monasteries on **Mt Athos**.

The chapels were at their busiest between 1920 and 1924 when **White Russians** fleeing the Bolshevik advance into Crimea flooded into Istanbul. By then at least two of the churches already boasted bright blue walls and murals in the style of the Russian Symbolist painter **Mikhail Vassiliyevich Nesterov** (1862-1942).

Of the four churches, St Pantaleimon in Hoca Tahsin Sokağı is the prayer-house of choice for most modern Russians; in the past a handful of elderly White Russians used to attend St Andrei's, the most beautiful of them all, in Galata Mumhanesi Caddesi while the other two chapels are effectively derelict.

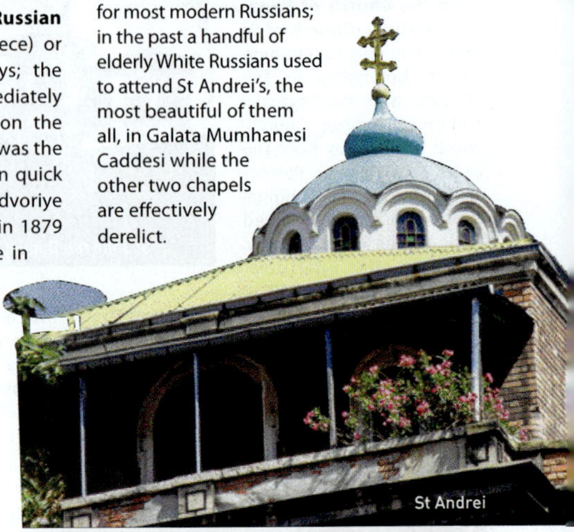

St Andrei

The lady in the photograph above was one of the last remaining White Russians. She has sadly also passed away.

St Andrei Church

This photograph was taken from a restaurant by Madeline Albright's (USA's first female Secretary of State) daughter, Katie, during a family dinner.

07

Art and the Arsenal

Tophane and Kabataş

The district running along the shores of the Bosphorus between Karaköy and Dolmabahçe is called Tophane (Cannon Foundry) after the Ottoman foundry that used to stand here. Throughout the 20th century this was a part of town with many warehouses as a result of its proximity to the port at Karaköy. It acquired a new lease of life when one of the warehouses was converted into the Istanbul Modern art gallery. The Galataport project is planned to breathe new life into the neighborhood with its renewed living spaces.

Kılıç Ali Paşa Mosque.

Istanbul Modern

Istanbul Modern, opened in 2005, is the first Turkish museum opened specifically to exhibit works of art of the 19th and 20th centuries. In addition to its rich collection, Istanbul Modern is also occasionally home to exhibitions of art and photography. The museum, related to all fields of art with its rich library and movie theatre, also has a restaurant and a gift shop. The museum is also very attractive for families with children. There are art workshops in another department to enable children to spend their time with art.
Modern Turkish art is not perhaps as well known as it deserves to be, and the Istanbul Modern has gone a long way to rectify the problem. It shows both paintings belonging to its own permanent collection and other pieces that are on loan, which means that you can visit again and again and still find something to surprise and delight you. Particular treats to home in on include "Village Women" by **Nuri İyem** (1915-2005), "Woman Knitting" by **Nurullah Berk** (1906-92), and "Child Fishing" by **Orhan Peker** (1927-78). It's also worth looking out for works by **Burhan Doğançay** (1929 - 2013), and **Fahrelnissa Zeid** (1901-1991), the wife of a Jordanian prince whose paintings hang in some of the world's most important galleries.Other names to conjure with include those of **Fausto Zonaro** (1854-1929) who was court painter to the sultans from 1891 to 1910, **Abdülmecid Efendi** (1868-1944), the son of Sultan Abdülaziz, who ended his life in exile in Paris (see p.511). Şeker Ahmet Paşa (1841-1907), **Osman Hamdi Bey** (1842-1910) and **Süleyman Seyyid** (1842-1913) were three men who studied abroad and went on to become professional artists, while **İbrahim Çallı** (1882-1960) and **Hamit Görele** (1894-1980) were leading lights in more modern times whose work tends to reflect trends in art on the international stage.
After the warehouse number four, which was the first house of the museum in Tophane for fourteen years, was demolished as part of the Galataport Project, the museum continues to greet art lovers in Meşrutiyet Street until the construction of its new building.

@istanbulmodern, Tel: 0212 334 73 00,
www.istanbulmodern.org,
closed Mondays.

The museum is open for visitors in Beyoğlu, near Pera Palace Hotel until its new building is completed as part of the Galataport project.

Village Woman, by Nuri İyem.

Contemporary artists

Those keen to know where Turkish art has been going over the last 30 years should look out for works by Kutluğ Ataman, Gülsün Karamustafa, Hale Tenger, Sarkis, Taner Ceylan, Hussein Chalayan, Leyla Gediz, Hüsamettin Koçan, Mithat Şen and İpek Duben.

Admission to the Istanbul Modern is **free on Thursdays** when the gallery stays open until 8 pm. Free guided tours, only held in Turkish, are organized on Thursdays and Sundays at 5 pm. Private tours, customized for individuals or group tours can be organized every day except on Mondays, for a fee per person. Tours are 45 minutes in duration and are available in Turkish and English. Guided tours must be reserved in advance. Audio guides, geared towards adults, are available in English and Turkish, with a duration of approximately 45 minutes.

Istanbul Biennial

Since 1987 Istanbul has been hosting a lively modern art jamboree every two years. The Biennial spreads itself out through venues all over town, some of them indoor, some of them out, and it has acquired a reputation for spotlighting unexpected locations.

@iksv_istanbul, www.iksv.org/bienal

Galataport

Today, as you walk from Karaköy to Fındıklı, the whole coastline looks like a building site. The reason for this is the Galataport project, which was initiated in 2015 with the aim of uniting historical and daily living spaces. The project covers a coastline of 1.2 km and includes many historical monuments and important spaces for Istanbul. Once the project is completed, the Karaköy coast will be used as a port and it will also be open for pedestrian traffic. The project also includes culture and art centers, and hotels and covers an area of 30 decares. The nargile cafes, which long dominated the area, were the first to be demolished. I await the results with impatience.

Tophane Fountain opposite Kılıç Ali Paşa Mosque

Interior of Kılıç Ali Paşa Mosque

Kılıç Ali Paşa

Kılıç Ali Paşa Mosque

Immediately opposite the Tophane tram stop is the Kılıç Ali Paşa Mosque which was built by the great Ottoman architect **Sinan** in 1580 for **Vice Admiral Kılıç (The Sword) Ali Paşa**. Ali seems to have been an Italian who was seized by pirates and then joined his captors in their Mediterranean marauding. Later he worked in the Istanbul shipyard, before going on to serve in the navy under **Turgut Reis**, after whom Turgutreis on the Bodrum Peninsula is named. Kılıç Ali then became governor general in Tripoli in Libya, and later took part in the disastrous naval engagement at **Lepanto** in 1571 when the Ottoman fleet was defeated off the coast of Greece, an event that marked a turning point in the Empire's fortunes. Kılıç Ali was the only commander who managed to retreat without his ships being wiped out, whereupon he was promoted to the post of vice admiral. He then returned to an earlier occupation and developed the **Royal Shipyard** so that it would be able to turn out larger vessels.

The Kılıç Ali Paşa Mosque was supposedly built on **reclaimed land** after bureaucrats had objected to giving Ali land to build on, saying that "All the seas are yours. What business do you have on the land?" Sinan was in his nineties when he designed it and he seems to have taken **Hagia Sophia** as his model. Today the entire külliye (complex) still survives, complete with a **tomb** and a **medrese**. Restoration of the entire mosque complex was finished in 2011.

Tophane Fountain

Facing Kılıç Ali Paşa Mosque across Tophane İskele Caddesi is a magnificent free-standing baroque fountain with overhanging roof that was built for **Sultan Mahmud I** in 1732. It is decorated all over with naturalistic images of fruit and flowers, and has **mukarnas** (stalactites) carved in the corners, a characteristic of early 18th-century fountains. The fountain was badly damaged by fire in the mid-18th century and rebuilt in 1957. Recently it was restored and regilded, making it once again a distinctive feature of the area. Hard though it is to believe it now, the surrounding area once accommodated the city's thriving **fruit** and **vegetable market**. Before that it was a **military parade ground**.

Tophane Fountain in old engraving

The Arsenal (Tophane)

The original arsenal at Tophane was apparently built in the 15th century for **Sultan Mehmed II** and expanded by **Beyazıd II**. It was then replaced with a new arsenal by **Süleyman the Magnificent** who needed to stockpile ammunition for his wars against the **Holy Roman Emperor**. In turn that building was replaced in 1803 by **Selim III**, and it is this multi-domed structure that you see today standing on the inland side of the road across from the Tophane tram stop and forming part of the modern **Mimar Sinan University**; look up towards the top corners of the building to see two tiny carved cannons that serve as a reminder of its history.

The Arsenal and the small adjacent building are sometimes used for temporary art exhibitions. Beyond it, a string of ruins heading up towards **Cihangir** were part of a barracks attached to the foundry.

Cannon relief on Arsenal building

Tomtom Neighborhood

These days a momentous transformation is taking place in Tomtom Neighborhood. Once the richest and most splendid neighborhood, it is now reviving its past glory. The buildings are being restored and brand-new designer boutiques, stores, art galleries and cafes are being opened. The Tomtom Neighborhood holds a very special place in Beyoğlu's history. Adjacent to Çukurcuma between Karaköy and Galatasaray, it is a unique oasis surrounded by consulates, schools, palaces and large gardens. It rapidly evolved into a design neighborhood similar to Soho in England, Meatpacking in New York and Marais in Paris. Once the Galataport project is finalized, the pedestrian and tourist traffic in **Boğazkesen**, the connecting axis street between **Karaköy** and the **Istiklal Street**, is likely to increase.

The legal cases of French citizens under the protection of the French embassy were held in the yellow-colored French or Capitulation Court located at the end of **Tomtom Kaptan Street**. Next to the court is the **Venetian Palace**. The **French Palace**, with a deep-rooted history, is located just across the court. The architect of the French Palace, which assumed its present condition after the great fire of Pera, is the Parisian architect **Pierre Lauracisque**. The palace building with its plain façade is currently used as the residence of the consul general. It has an air of a separate city in the heart of Beyoğlu with its church, school and institute. The residence of the old Franciscan nuns, dating back to the 1850s, and the adjacent buildings were harmonized with the European palaces on the same street after a series of restoration works started in the 2000s.

There are numerous addresses like galleries, craft workshops, design stores and restaurants awaiting discovery along Boğazkesen Street in the Tomtom Neighborhood. The street is an essential destination for local and foreign tourists who are in love with photography. The **Zanaat Atelye**, located in the historical **French Orphanage** dating back to 1850, is a papier-mâché museum and a cafe. You can admire the original plaster models of many historical spaces and enjoy your time in its garden.

Named after its green gardens, there is an ongoing project at the heart of the Tomtom Neighborhood: **Tomtom Gardens**. Last year it was awarded the "**Best Residence**" as part of the Sign of the City Awards. It is a spectacular restoration project with seventeen buildings around three different courtyards. The first courtyard of Tomtom Gardens is located on the Tomtom Kaptan Street. The project was carried out with an Italian landscape architect and has achieved an extraordinary result. Art and design spaces are also in operation here.

The second phase of Tomtom Gardens, located on Boğazkesen Street, neighbors the French Orphanage and also sports a splendid courtyard. The third phase is located just across the Tomtom Kaptan Mosque on Boğazkesen. **Architect Han Tümertekin** will design a very beautiful building and a modern courtyard on an indoor parking space. Some historical buildings such as the **Yugoslavian School, Austria-Hungary School,** the **Baltazzi Apartment** and **Hotel Italia Dakar** will be restored.

Tomtom Gardens's courtyard

Çukurcuma

Just across the Tomtom Kaptan Street, Çukurcuma is the place where you can find some of the best antique shops in Istanbul. The best way to discover this place is to get lost among its narrow streets... It is possible to get surprised by the distant and serene atmosphere of this location just adjacent to the hubbub of Istiklal Street.

Innocence in Çukurcuma

The Museum of Innocence in Çukurcuma is named after Turkey's first Nobel Price-winning author Orhan Pamuk's 2008 novel dedicated to his daughter. The museum inspired by the novel was opened in 2012. As the first city museum in Istanbul, it is located in a three-story building dating back to 1897 in Çukurcuma.

Tomtom Gardens is located right across from Italian High School

Tophane Pavilion

The cute little green pavilion standing a little way along the road from the fountain was built as a base from which **Sultan Abdülmecid** (1861-1876) could inspect his troops. It was designed by **William James Smith** who was also responsible for the British Embassy (now the consulate) in 1852. The sultans received many foreign statesmen here, and the pavilion was also the setting for several international conferences and meetings. After the 1923 Treaty of Lausanne ended the Turkish War of Independence, the **Bosphorus Commission** met here to agree arrangements for using the strait. Today it houses part of the **Mimar Sinan University**.

Nusretiye Mosque and Arsenal in old picture

Interior of Nusretiye Mosque

Nusretiye (Victory) Mosque

Hünkar Mahfili

Sultan Mahmud II commissioned the Turkish-Armenian architect **Krikor Balyan** (1764-1831) to build this fine mosque in a style midway between the baroque and imperial styles. It was given its name to celebrate his **victory** over the troublesome **Janissaries** in 1826. Building work took place between 1822 and 1826, and almost immediately the overly thin minarets fell down and had to be rebuilt. For the Nusretiye mosque Balyan abandoned the traditional courtyard and instead built what looks almost like an apartment over the entrance, a feature which was reproduced in the **Dolmabahçe Mosque**, just down the road. Inside the **hünkar mahfili** (sultan's pew) is shielded by a screen so fine that it looks almost like lace.

The grand if grubby **sebil** beside the mosque originally stood across the road but had to be moved when the road was widened. It bears a fine calligraphic inscription by **Yesarizade İzzet Efendi**.

Clock Tower

As you visit the mosque, make sure to look out for the little **clock tower** standing at the back of the grounds. Dating back to 1848-1849 and probably a work of **Bali Balyan**, it was the city's first such clock tower and used to stand beside Tophane Pavilion until it was moved during road-widening in the 1950s.

Molla Çelebi Mosque (Fındıklı Mosque) and around

Continuing north along the coast road towards Dolmabahçe Palace, you will pass the **Meclis-i Mebusan Building**, a pair of Balyan-designed buildings, once called the twin palaces, that were built in 1856 for **Münire Sultan** and **Cemile Sultan**, the daughters of Sultan Abdülmecid. After the declaration of the Republic they hosted sessions of the Grand National Assembly. Today they house the **Mimar Sinan University**. Next you will come to the **Molla Çelebi Mosque**, another work of **Sinan** which dates back to 1561-1562 and was built for poet and **Chief Justice Mehmed Efendi**.

Fındıklı Park

Hekimoğlu Paşa Fountain

Koca Yusuf Paşa sebil serving as a café

Right beside the Molla Çelebi Mosque is the free-standing **Hekimoğlu Ali Paşa fountain** which dates back to 1732 and is a plainer version of the one at Tophane. It was restored in 2008. Across the road is a pretty little **sebil** which was paid for in 1787 by **Koca Yusuf Paşa**, Grand Vizier to Sultan Abdülhamid I; it's now occupied by a small café. Continuing towards Dolmabahçe Palace there's a second **sebil** at the junction of Meclis-i Mebusan Caddesi, the coast road, with Dolmabahçe Gazhanesi Sokak, which climbs uphill towards Taksim. This sebil was paid for in 1741 by **Hacı Mehmed Emin Ağa**, whose tomb is inside it. Members of his family are buried in the small adjoining graveyard.

In Ottoman times sebils were **staffed fountains** where water and sherbet drinks would be dispensed to passers-by in contrast with **çeşmes** which were self-service fountains. Look out for snack shops and drink stands around town with names such as Café Sebil or Sebil Büfe, and you'll be looking at a slice of water distribution history.

Hekimoğlu Paşa Fountain

Did Cervantes work in Istanbul?

Picasso sketch of Don Quixote and Sancho Pancho

Could Cervantes, the world-famous author of **Don Quixote,** have had a hand in the building of the Kılıç Ali Paşa Mosque? Cervantes had been wounded during the battle of **Lepanto** in 1571, and recent research in the mosque archives suggests that he was taken captive by the Ottomans and that his handiwork can be detected in the building. More mainstream opinion, however, has Cervantes returning to military life after a lengthy sojourn in hospital.

Kabataş Pier

Despite objections, the old Kabataş pier was demolished as part of the arrangement of the Kabataş Square and the transfer center project. The "Martı (Seagull) Project" as named by the public in reference to the shape of the new pier to be built, will integrate the pier with the 4 large piers and the Kabataş-Funicular line, Bağcılar-Kabataş Tram line and the new Mahmutbey-Kabataş metro line. By building the land road underground, the square is planned to integrate different means of transportation.

08

Baroque Beauty of the Bosphorus

Dolmabahçe Palace

By the mid-19th century the Ottoman sultans were obsessed with all things Western and decided to move out of Topkapı Palace and into the Dolmabahçe Palace on the southern shore of the Bosphorus. The palace consists of one large main building divided into two separate wings along with a couple of smaller pavilions and extensive gardens. It's a riot of lavish baroque ornamentation, which will come as a shock to those who like their décor minimalist.

Straight ahead from the garden is the entrance to the Administrative Section.

Unlike Topkapı Palace, which was, like the Byzantine Great Palace, a collection of relatively small buildings, the Dolmabahçe Palace conforms more closely to Western ideas of a palace as a single large structure although Islamic tradition still decreed that there must be two separate sections, one to show off the public face of the state, the other for the private life of the sultan. The fact that **Sultan Abdülmecid** chose to have it built on the far side of the Bosphorus also indicated a mental break with the past; Topkapı harked back to Byzantine times not just in its layout but also in its location; Dolmabahçe in contrast was built on the side of the Bosphorus more usually associated with Westerners.

In Turkish Dolmabahçe means "**filled-in garden**", a reference to the fact that the land on which the palace was built had been reclaimed from the Bosphorus (the area now covers 110,000 square meters). Until 1614 there had been a port here, but under first **Sultan Ahmed I** and then **Sultan Osman II** it was slowly filled in to provide space for a park and cirit ground as well as for the wooden Beşiktaş Palace, a complex of buildings like Topkapı Palace that increasingly came to serve as the sultans' summer residence.

The present Dolmabahçe Palace was designed by **Garabet** and **Nikoğos Balyan** who came from a celebrated family of Ottoman Armenian architects. Work started in 1843. When it was finally completed in 1856 the main building contained **285 rooms, 43 halls and six bathrooms**. The palace was even equipped with its own 600-meter-long quay since most visitors would have arrived by water. The entire complex stretches all the way from Kabataş in the south to Beşiktaş in the north although not all of it is open to the public.

The **last six sultans** lived for varying amounts of time in the Dolmabahçe although Sultan Abdülhamid quickly retreated to the greater security of the Yıldız Palace. The last of the imperial family to live here was **Abdülmecid Efendi**, the caliph-artist who was forced into exile in 1924.

Time management

Allow an hour for the tour of the Selamlık and another hour for the Harem. Unfortunately, you may have to wait in line to buy a ticket before going into the grounds, and there may be further waits for guided tours in the appropriate languages. If your time is limited, stick with visiting the Selamlık.

The palace's **interior decoration** was the work of a Frenchman called Charles Séchan who also designed the Paris Opera. It's all very over-the-top, with Baccarat and Bohemian crystal, Sevres and Yıldız porcelain, and Hereke carpets the order of the day. Some of it could certainly do with a good dust, and the rushed guided tours make it hard to take in the excess of detail.

Tel: 0212 236 90 00/1359
www.dolmabahce.gov.tr
closed Mondays and Thursdays
guided tours in English and Turkish

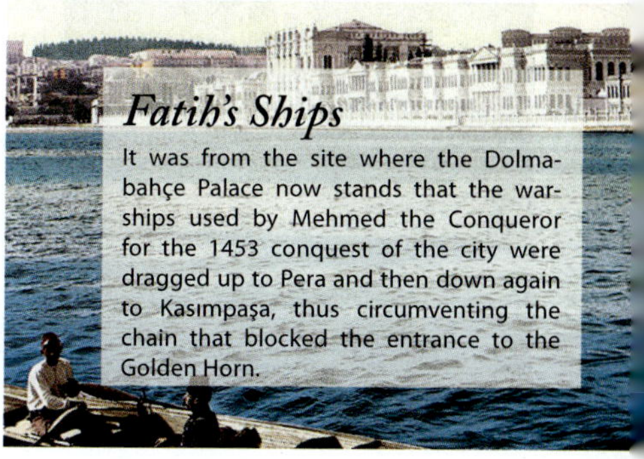

Fatih's Ships

It was from the site where the Dolmabahçe Palace now stands that the warships used by Mehmed the Conqueror for the 1453 conquest of the city were dragged up to Pera and then down again to Kasımpaşa, thus circumventing the chain that blocked the entrance to the Golden Horn.

Dolmabahçe Mosque

Restored in 2009, the mosque near the entrance to the palace was built in baroque style by **Garabet Balyan** for Sultan Abdülmecid's mother **Bezmialem Valide Sultan**, and completed after her death in 1855. It's adorned with two minarets, but its most conspicuous features are the **huge arches** studded with windows that provide supports for the dome on four sides. Those same large windows allow light to flood into the interior from the Bosphorus, making it especially delightful. The original courtyard and sebil were sadly sacrificed to road-widening. From 1956-1960 the mosque was used to house the Naval Museum, returning to religious duty in 1967 when the museum moved down the road to Beşiktaş.

The palace exterior

Baroque architecture is not to everybody's taste, but the white sandstone exterior of the Dolmabahçe is certainly impressive, especially when viewed from the water. The monumental scale of the building combined with the lavish decoration of the exterior marks it out from the Topkapı Palace; the harem of the Topkapı, for example, is richly decorated on the inside but extremely plain on the outside.

Administrative Section

The clock tower

The path to the palace runs past a 27-meter-high, four-storey clock tower erected by Sarkis Balyan for Sultan Abdülhamid II in the 1890s. Its four faces are still inscribed with **Arabic numerals**, and the ground floor is adorned with two thermometers and two barometers.

Clock Tower

The gates

Modern visitors enter the complex via the **Administrative Gate** that was used by politicians and civil servants. In the past the most important visitors would have arrived at the **Shore Gate**, stepping onto the quay from their caiques. Traffic on busy Dolmabahçe Caddesi whisks past the imposing **Ceremonial Gate** that was used by the sultan and grand vizier when they processed to the nearby mosque for Friday prayers.

Saltanat (Ceremonial) Gate in an old postcard

The gate as it is today.

The Selamlık (Administrative Section)

Visitors enter the palace up stairs from the garden into the huge **Reception Hall** where guests would wait to be received. The 60-branch chandelier, the fine Hereke carpet, and the fireplaces with shimmering glass panels above them were all designed to create a grand first impression. On the seaward side of the hall are the rooms that were occupied by the most important officials; members of parliament had offices on the inland side; the grand vizier had a room just beside the entrance on the seaward side. The Reception Hall was the scene of meetings convened by **Atatürk** in 1928 to devise a **new Latin alphabet** to replace the Arabic one that had been used to write Ottoman Turkish.

On the landward side of the entrance was a room to store the gifts that the sultan as caliph sent to Mecca every year at the time of **the Haj (Pilgrimage)**. The sultans were never able to perform the Haj themselves because of the length of time it would have taken, but every year a camel train weighed down with gold would set out to make the journey in their stead; **"The Sürre Procession"**, a huge painting by the Italian artist **Stefano Ussi** (1822-1901) hanging in one of the clerk's rooms beyond the reception hall, vividly portrays it pressing on from Cairo. The painting is the largest canvas in the palace's extensive art collection.

The tour moves past rooms occupied by the secretariat into the **Entrance Hall** that was used by the sultan when on short excursions; doors opened into the back garden so that he could leave by carriage and into the front garden so that he could leave by boat.

As is the case throughout the palace the Reception Hall is completely symmetrical

The Sürre Procession by Stefano Ussi, 1873

Crystal Staircase

Süfera Salonu (Ambassadors Hall)

Ambassadors Hall's entrance

Zülvecheyn Salonu (Privy Chamber)

Crystal Staircase

One of the most spectacular features of the Selamlık is the **Crystal Staircase**, a double flight of stairs lined with crystal banisters that winds up to the second floor, passing beneath an enormous Baccarat chandelier. It leads to the vast and elaborately decorated **Süfera (Ambassadors) Hall**, which was used to host formal receptions and where gifts to the sultans, including a pair of bearskins given by **Tsar Nicolas II**, are displayed. Small rooms opening off from the front of it were used as waiting rooms and are decorated with paintings of sea scenes by the Crimean artist **Ivan Konstantinovic Ayvazovski** (1817-1900), who visited Istanbul eight times and was a particular favorite of **Sultan Abdülaziz**. In one of them you can also see a table inlaid with images of Napoleon and 12 famous European women including his wife, the Empress Josephine, Queen Marie Antoinette and the murderer Charlotte Corday.

Fausto Zonaro

Privy Chamber

A corridor from the Süfera passes a guest room on one wall of which can be seen Fausto Zonaro's wonderful **painting** of Kaiser Wilhelm II arriving at the palace in 1898. It then opens into a glorious **Reception Room**, better known as the Red Room because of its dramatic red and gold decoration. Here ambassadors would wait again before finally being admitted to the sultan's presence. The corridor then dodges past a pair of rooms set aside for the crown princes before re-crossing the Süfera to reach the huge **Privy Chamber**, with its elaborate parquet floor. This was used for **religious ceremonies** especially during Ramadan, and for **wedding parties and banquets**, with an orchestra providing music from the stairwell; its alternative Arabic name "Zülvecheyn", meaning "double-fronted", refers to its

Caliph Abdülmecid's Library

location midway between the selamlık and harem quarters. A door leads into **Caliph Abdülmecid's Library**, which overlooks the Bosphorus; as well as many leather-bound books, it contains a self-portrait of the caliph who was an artist of considerable ability. Also opening off it is a **Music Room**, equipped with a grand piano and a pair of cellos.

Sultan's Reception Room

The tour skips through a small sitting room containing another Fausto Zonaro painting, "Women Getting into a Rowing Boat", before reaching the exquisite **Hamam**, the sultan's private Turkish bath which came complete with marble floors and walls of translucent, honey-colored Egyptian alabaster. The last room in the Selamlık is the **Memorial Room**, which contains paintings and photographs of four sultans. A corridor then winds round **Muayede** (the Ceremonial Hall) (see p. 81) to the Harem. It's lined with **paintings** by, among others, **Şeker Ahmed Paşa**, **Osman Hamdi Bey** and **Fausto Zonaro**, including the latter's colorful and much reproduced set of four images portraying **Sultan Mehmed II** and the conquest of Istanbul in 1453; it's also pierced with windows that allowed the women of the harem to observe the goings-on down below without being seen themselves. The corridor ends at the **Sultan's Reception Room** in the Harem, a lovely room also called the Crimson or Domed Room after the most conspicuous features of its décor, which was where the sultan would receive his wives and children.

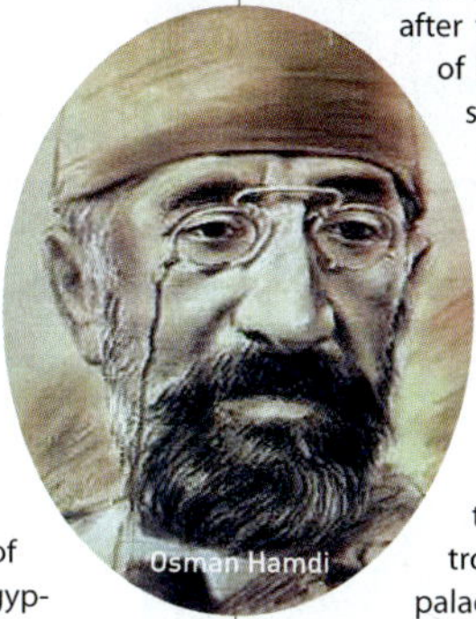
Osman Hamdi

Blue Hall

Another short corridor furnished with an organ concealed in a wooden case and a portrait of his wife by **Abdülmecid Efendi** leads to the grand **Blue Hall** with its trompe d'oeil columns where the palace women would assemble to celebrate religious holidays. It was also used by the queen mother or the principal wife to entertain **visiting head of states**, and as the years passed, some important male guests were also greeted here. In 1937 an elevator was inserted into the room so that it could be used more comfortably by **Atatürk** whose study, just off it, is almost equally elaborate.

Sultan's Hamam

Atatürk's office.

10 November 1938

At 9.05 am on 10 November 1938 **Mustafa Kemal Atatürk** died in the Dolmabahçe Palace. His body lay in state in the Ceremonial Hall for three days, and all the palace clocks have shown the time of his death ever since.

Atatürk's deathbed.

Ceiling above Caliph's Staircase

Palace paintings

The Dolmabahçe Palace contains a collection of around 500 paintings including masterpieces by the court artist Fausto Zonaro, the maritime specialist Ivan Konstantinovic Ayvazovski, the orientalist-archeologist Osman Hamdi Bey, and the caliph-artist Abdülmecid Efendi. It's a shame that the rushed guided tours make it hard to appreciate any of them.

Atatürk's deathbed

The tour then passes through one of the most important rooms in the palace, which is the one in which **Atatürk** died in 1938. His bed is draped with the Turkish flag in perpetuity, just as all the clocks in the palace are permanently stopped at the time of his death. Across the corridor is Atatürk's bathroom fitted out with a private pharmacy of medicaments.

Next you will enter the **Pink Hall**, once the living room of the queen mother where she received special guests and celebrated important occasions. A telescope is poised to take in a view of the Bosphorus which would have been so much less built-up in those days. The tour then passes a couple of pretty guestrooms and another hamam before returning through the **Blue Room** to glance at Sultan Abdülaziz's bedroom. The beautiful **Caliph's Staircase**, illuminated by another wonderful chandelier, then leads back down to the ground floor and the entrance hall to the harem that was guarded by the head maid in her room right beside it. The importance of her position is suggested by the fact that her room is not much less elaborately furnished than the guestrooms.

The tour then makes a circuit of what was once a dining room for some of the sultan's servants but now houses selected items of **glass, porcelain** and **silver** from the palace's collection. Perhaps the single most amusing item on display is a set of decanters that could be concealed inside what looked like a set of leather-bound books.

Ceremonial Hall

Finally the tour winds up in the most astonishing room of the entire palace, the breath-taking **Ceremonial (Muayede) Hall,** which stands right in the center dividing the selamlık from the harem. Thirty-six meters high, it's topped with a **dome** that is invisible from the exterior, and is supported by 56 columns; it is apparently the largest throne room in the world. The room is so large that it required a silk Hereke carpet covering 124 square meters, and a Bohemian crystal chandelier weighing 4.5 tons and requiring 664 lightbulbs, a gift from **Queen Victoria** of Great Britain. It took three months just to install it. A form of central heating could be piped up the columns but required a full three days to take effect.

Ceremonial Hall (Muayede Salonu) with sultan's throne at the back

The hall was used for all the most important imperial ceremonies including those associated with the holiday following Ramadan. At that time the sultan's glittering **250-kilogram throne** would be brought from the treasury at Topkapı and set up against the west wall. The ambassadors would line up in the gallery facing him, with other guests to the left and the orchestra to the right; the space above the sultan would be left empty since no one but Allah could be positioned above him.

Several important events took place in this room. In 1876 the coronation of **Sultan Murad V** was staged here instead of at Topkapı. It was also here that the **first meeting of the Ottoman parliament** was held in 1877, an event that contained within it the seeds of the end of the Empire. Later, it was here that **Atatürk** gave his first speech as president of the Republic of Turkey; a copy is on display in the room.

A reception in the Ceremonial Hall.

The Tour of the Harem

Young Woman Combing Her Hair, by Osman Hamdi Bey

The Ceremonial Hall marks the dividing point between the public part of the palace and the private part where the sultan's family lived. Today you must enter the harem from a separate entrance to the rear.

No matter how Westernized the palace looked on the outside the way of life on the inside continued much as it had at Topkapı, with the **Valide Sultan (Queen Mother)** at the apex of a hierarchy of women who were still closely guarded by **black and white eunuchs**.

The tour of the harem starts in the **Entrance Hall** whose ceiling cornices are painted with images of Istanbul scenery. From here you ascend to the first floor and bypass several rooms before arriving at the **Hall of the Royal Women** that was used to celebrate religious occasions and also the more private achievements of the sultan's children; the decoration of the room, while still elaborate, is toned down a little in comparison with the Selamlık. The same is true of the **Hamam of the Royal Women** which in no way compares with the beauty of the sultan's alabaster bath in the Selamlık.

The tour continues through a rather more sparsely furnished **Hall of the Royal Women** and continues to the **Japanese Salon** that was used by the queen mother and features fabrics decorated with sunflowers alongside more overtly Japanese motifs. Next to it is the **Bedroom of the Sultan's Mother** that was furnished for Sultan Abdülaziz's mother **Pertevniyal Valide Sultan** with a French-style cream lacquer bedroom suite. There follow a series of guestrooms fitted out in a variety of styles, some with throne-like beds, others with iron bedframes. The tour then passes back through the Hall of the Royal Women to visit a suite of rooms typical of those that were assigned to the senior women of the harem; it comes with a little lobby equipped with a piano and a sitting area off which open a small bedroom, sitting room and bathroom. Here can be seen **Osman Hamdi Bey**'s lovely painting **"A Young Lady Having her Hair Combed"**. You then bypass a room decorated as it might have been if the head maid had been occupying it, before arriving at a second similar suite of rooms.

The tour then returns through the main Hall of the Royal Women, which gives you a chance to peek into the **Circumcision Room** where the royal princes would have rested and received well-wishers after their *sünnet* (circumcision). You will also get a chance to peek in on a child's **playroom** with a photo of Sultan Abdülmecid's grandson İbrahim Tevfik Efendi on the wall before returning to the Entrance Hall to leave.

Conservatory of Glass Pavilion

Main room of Glass Pavilion

Glass Pavilion (Camlı Köşk)

Attached to the outside wall of the palace and so visible from Dolmabahçe Caddesi is the Glass Pavilion, which many may think the most delightful room in the whole palace. Luxuriantly decorated in red, gold and blue, it's furnished with a piano with crystal legs and features a ceiling cornice painted with images of particularly mild-looking wild animals; four gilded eagles fill in the corners. A conservatory-like room focused on a crystal fountain is attached to it at an L-shaped angle and lets light flood in from one side. The suite served as a private rest room for the sultan apart from the hustle of the main palace building.

The gardens

The palace gardens provided the gardeners with a wonderful opportunity to show off, and they're exceptionally beautiful in the summer when a fountain adorned with stone swans plays as a centerpiece amid lawns on which stone lionesses frolic with their cubs. All sorts of exotic plants can be seen here. The grounds also contain an **aviary** that has recently been brought back to life, with peacocks, chickens, guinea fowl and ornamental pheasants ambling around amid the shady cypress and plane trees.

Imperial gardens

Dolmabahçe by night

The National Palaces' Clock Museum

This collection housed in a garden museum mainly consists of 19th -century French and British clocks that were used in the palace. While Western clockmaking was the preserve of philosophers and mathematicians, Ottoman timepieces were crafted by mosque officials, most of them senior members of the Mevlevi sect, whose chief duty was to determine the time for the call to prayer. The museum includes examples of clocks crafted by such masters as **Eflaki Dede, Mehmet Şükrü** and **Mehmet Muhsin**.

Palace of the Crown Princes (Istanbul Painting Museum)

Glance through the gates at the Beşiktaş end of the palace gardens to see the façade of this completely separate building that now houses the **Museum of Painting**.
It was designed by the Balyans in a mixture of Empire, Baroque and Rococo styles in 1856. In 1937 Atatürk had the **Istanbul Fine Arts Academy** (now the Mimar Sinan University) founded here. It was the first such establishment in Turkey. It contains a notable collection of 19th-century Turkish paintings, including three by Osman Hamdi Bey (1842-1910), and was a favored haunt of the young Orhan Pamuk, as described in his "Istanbul: Memories of a City".

Tel: 0212 261 42 98, www.millisaraylar.gov.tr, Closed Mondays

09

Barbarossa's Backyard

Beşiktaş

Frequently overlooked by visitors, Beşiktaş is a frantically busy part of town, with major interchanges for buses and ferries. The most obvious attraction is the Naval Museum right on the waterfront beside Barbaros Square, but it's also worth venturing into the back streets to find the pretty little Ihlamur Pavilion and the lovely Art Nouveau Şeyh Zafir complex. Akaretler were once the living quarters for staff at the Dolmabahçe Palace.

In Turkish Beşiktaş means "**cradle stone**", a name which commemorates a claim that a piece of Jesus' cradle was brought here from Bethlehem by early Christians and stored in a local church. It's possible that it was then taken to Hagia Sophia, only to be stolen by the Fourth Crusaders in 1204.

Like Kadıköy, Beşiktaş is a busy shopping area, its streets crammed with ordinary people shopping on ordinary budgets in contrast with more upscale Nişantaşı, just a short distance away. At the heart of a tight-knit network of shopping streets to the west of busy Barbaros Bulvarı an undercover **fish market** is ringed with neighborhood fish restaurants. Two **eagle monuments** nearby commemorate the hundredth anniversary of the much-loved local football team Beşiktaş ("the Black Eagles") whose stadium is in nearby Dolmabahçe.

Cihanüma Virgin Mary Greek Orthodox Church

Köyiçi Greek Orthodox Church of the Virgin Mary

Amongst other scant reminders of a past more cosmopolitan lifestyle is the 19th-century **Church of Cihanüma Meryemana (St Mary)** which stands behind high walls opposite Bahçeşehir University on the main road.

Eagle Statue in Beşiktaş Market.

The Black Eagles in numbers

- Founded in 1903, Beşiktaş was Turkey's first sports club. In the 1936 Olympics in Berlin it was also the first club to showcase a female athlete.
- 14 times Turkish top-tier league champion.
- 9 times winner of the Turkey Cup.
- Beşiktaş was also the first team to score 10 goals in an official game, against Adana Demirspor in the 1989-1990 season.

Tulumbacis (early fire-fighters)

Naval Museum

An important port of call for crusty sea-dogs everywhere, the **Naval Museum** honors the important role the navy played during the heyday of the Ottoman Empire. Many of the exhibits are of fairly specialist interest, although most people will love the **caiques**, the graceful, gondola-like boats that were used to move people and their belongings around the Bosphorus. Most came equipped with 13 pairs of oars, although the number of oars increased or decreased with the importance of the passengers. The finest caiques were the ones reserved for the imperial family and used to convey the sultan to Friday prayers. These imperial caiques have small enclosed kiosks at the stern; those intended for the sultan bear his coat of arms and decorative weaponry, while those intended for the women of the harem are decorated with fruit and flowers. Many also have an eagle carved like a ship's figurehead at the bow end. The oldest and biggest imperial caique in the collection dates back to the 17th century; it required 24 pairs of oars to convey **Sultan Mehmed IV** about town. Most of the other caiques date from the 19th century.

On the ground floor the **Atatürk Room** preserves the first Turkish president's cabin from the state yacht Ertuğrul, while across the hall a room shows off a collection of souvenir handkerchiefs. Upstairs is a length of the **chain** used in Byzantine times to close off the Golden Horn from the Bosphorus, along with paintings of the many different types of boat that used to ply the strait. One room shows off the different uniforms worn by the Turkish navy over the centuries, while on the landing a glass-case contains the green ensign removed from the tomb of Barbaros Hayreddin in the square outside.

www.denizmuzesi.dzkk.tsk.tr
Tel: 0212 327 43 45, closed Mondays

Tomb of Barbarossa

Barbaros Square

Barbaros Hayreddin Paşa

Beside the Naval Museum is Barbaros Square, a rather bleak expanse of concrete much loved by skateboarders that is home to a **statue** of Barbaros Hayreddin (c.1478- 1546), a famous pirate turned admiral known as **Barbarossa (Redbeard)** to the Europeans. It was Barbarossa who established the Ottoman control of the Mediterranean that lasted until the **Battle of Lepanto** in 1571. During the reign of Süleyman the Magnificent, he was not just in charge of the Ottoman navy but also governed Algeria and parts of Greece. He left a book of memoirs which detail his many campaigns and formed the basis for **M. Ertuğrul Düzdağ**'s novel "**The Mediterranean Was Ours**". Across the square from the statue stands the two-storey octagonal **tomb** designed by Mimar **Sinan** for Barbarossa in 1541. Before setting off on naval engagements sailors still salute the great admiral by firing shots outside the mausoleum.

The statue of Barbarossa is inscribed with rousing words by the poet **Yahya Kemal Beyatlı** (1884-1958):

"Whence on the sea's horizon comes that roar?
Can it be Barbarossa now returning
From Tunisia or Algiers or from the Isles?
Two hundred vessels ride upon the waves,
Coming from lands the rising Crescent lights:
O blessed ships, from what seas are ye come?"

Sinan Paşa Mosque

Across the road from the square stands the brick-and-stone striped **Sinanpaşa Mosque**, another work of Mimar Sinan dating back to 1555-1556 and built for the admiral Sinan Paşa (1506-1596), a brother of Grand Vizier Rüstem Paşa.

Beşiktaş jetty

Beşiktaş ferry terminal in an old photograph

Beşiktaş ferry terminal

The **shore** in front of the square hosted Istanbul's busiest quay in the mid-19th century, and it was here that the first stone jetty was built for the Bosphorus ferry company, **Şirket-i Hayriye**, which started business in 1854. When catching the ferry to Üsküdar be sure to take a look at the cute little ticket office designed by architect **Ali Talat Bey** (1869-1922) in 1911 in First National Architectural style. It was one of the first buildings in Istanbul to use reinforced concrete although you are more likely to admire the dinky little tiles on the façade.

Akaretler means "rentable property"

Old appearance of Akaretler

Akaretler

Fausto Zonaro

Just inland from the main coast road at Beşiktaş is the district called Akaretler. You can find it by walking along Süleyman Seba Caddesi, pausing to inspect the small **Milli Emlak Dükkanları (National Estate Agency Shops)**, an attractive minor work by architect Vedat Tek which serves as a branch of a bank, on the corner. Akaretler is where the Armenian architect **Sarkis Balyan** designed a set of row-houses to accommodate the workers from the Dolmabahçe Palace in the 1870s. They have now been restored to form a hotel complex (see p. 91) whose presidential suite once served as the studio for the Ottoman court artist **Fausto Zonaro** (1854-1929), some of whose work can be seen in the **Pera Museum** and **Dolmabahçe Palace** (see p.74). From 1914-1918 Atatürk's mother Zübeyde and sister Makbule lived in a house that now forms part of the hotel complex.

Palace Collections Museum

This was opened as a store museum in 2006 in the **Matbah-ı Amire** (Palace Kitchens) buildings to exhibit the works kept in the Dolmabahçe Palace warehouses. The museum exhibits daily objects used mainly in Dolmabahçe Palace and at the Ottoman palaces during the 19th century.

Tel: 0212 236 90 00, www.millisaraylar.gov.tr
Closed Mondays

Şeyh Zafir complex

In Yıldız Caddesi, just off busy Barbaros Bulvarı, the unusual and newly restored Şeyh Zafir complex (also known as Ertuğrul Lodge) includes a tomb, fountain, and library. It was designed by **Raimondo d'Aronco** in 1903-1904 for the leader of a dervish order who had also been a spiritual advisor to **Sultan Abdülhamid II**. It's a wholly unique and beautiful building – you'll find nothing else like it in Istanbul.

Şeyh Zafir Türbesi

Abbasağa Mosque

Surp Asdvadzadzin (Virgin Mary) Armenian Church

Ali Paşa Fountain

Abbasağa Park

Martyrs for democracy immortalised in Abbasağa Park.

To the west of Barbaros Bulvarı the hillside Abbasağa Park features a group of statues of men and women who have died in the struggle to bring greater democracy to Turkey: Uğur Mumcu, Ümit Yaşar Doğançay, Abdi İpekçi, Ahmet Taner Kışlalı, Asım Bezirci, Bahriye Üçok, Bedrettin Cömert, Çetin Emeç, Doğan Öz, Muammer Aksoy, Onat Kutlar and Orhan Cavit Tütengil. Continuing downhill from the park you will come to the small **Abbasağa Mosque**, dating back to the mid-17th century but restored in 1834-1835 at which time it acquired an unexpectedly delightful wooden ceiling and galleries. It is completely outstripped in the size stakes by the vast Armenian **Church of Surp Asdvadzadzin (St Mary)** nearby with a redundant school facing it across the road. Designed by **Garabet Balyan** in 1838, it has a **false dome** that is invisible from the outside to comply with the law which at the time forbade the minority populations to indulge in such ostentation.

Pavilion of the Linden Trees (Ihlamur Kasrı)

By the 19th century the shores of the Golden Horn were falling from favor as a place for recreation, and Ihlamur, a wooded valley close to the new palaces on the Bosphorus, quickly attracted the attention of **Sultan Abdülmecid I**. After the Dolmabahçe Palace was completed in 1856 he commissioned **Nikoğos Balyan**, a member of the family responsible for its design, to build him a lodge where he could stay overnight when traveling between Beşiktaş and the shipyards of the Golden Horn, or between the various Bosphorus palaces. Today the two pavilions at the northern end of Ortabahçe Caddesi (*closed Mondays*) still stand in a pleasant small garden, now hemmed in by traffic but once part of a much larger park; the landscaping, complete with ornamental pool, reflects the western style favored at the time.

The larger **Ceremonial Pavilion** (Mabeyn Köşkü), with its elaborately carved ceilings, porcelain fireplaces imported from Britain, and indigo-colored glass door panels, would have been used by the sultan and his guests. Once reserved for the harem and the rest of their entourage, the **Entourage Pavilion** (Maiyet Köşkü) now serves as a simple café. The elaborately carved façades of both buildings mark a move away from traditional Ottoman design that focused all its decorative efforts on the interiors of buildings. With Beşiktaş' registry office just across the road, the steps of the Ceremonial Pavilion now form a popular backdrop for **wedding photos** especially at weekends.

Tel: 0212 236 90 00, www.millisaraylar.gov.tr
Closed Mondays

Mabeyn Köşkü (Ceremonial Pavilion)

Kaymakçı Pando (the Clotted Cream Seller)

A description of Beşiktaş would be incomplete without mentioning Pando the Cream Seller, who was one of the symbols of the Beşiktaş Çarşısı (Bazaar) and who passed away soon after he was removed from his shop. I fondly commemorate Pando with his delicious breakfasts with honey and clotted cream as Istanbul loses all her past colors from the old days.

Kaymakçı Pando

Fire Brigade Mu

The museum, which was fi
by the Metropolitan Municip
Cistern since 2013. The museu
hibits fire extinguishers as old as 2
years, water pumps and costumes o
fire brigades.

Tel: 0212 259 91 24
Closed on Saturdays and Sundays.

Beşiktaş JK Museum

The museum which is part of the Vodafone Park, home to Beşiktaş JK, is Turkey's first sports museum of sports history and culture. The museum had first been opened in the İnönü Stadium. After the stadium was demolished, it was renovated and reopened in 2017 with a perspective of modern museology. This museum is an enjoyable destination for sports-lovers from all ages.

www.bjk.com.tr, Tel: 0212 948 19 03, closed Mondays

ast Retreat

ark, and Palace

First there was the Eski Saray (Old Palace) on the Third Hill, near Beyazıt Square. Then came Topkapı Sarayı at Sarayburnu (Seraglio Point). Then there was Dolmabahçe Palace on the Bosphorus waterfront. Finally the Ottoman sultans withdrew to the Yıldız (Star) Palace as their empire gradually slipped away from them. Today Yıldız Park acts as one of the lungs of the city, a vast open space adorned with mature trees and shrubs, and dotted with historic buildings in an otherwise very built-up area.

The wooded slopes of **Beşiktaş Hill** were left untouched well into Ottoman times when **Sultan Ahmed I** finally had a *hasbahçe* (royal park) laid out around a small hunting lodge here. Covering 500,000 square meters of hillside, what is now Yıldız Park was originally laid out in the early 19th century for **Mihrişah Sultan**, the mother of **Sultan Selim III**, on land that had originally formed the gardens of the Çırağan Palace. Over the course of the 19th and 20th centuries the park was slowly developed until it consisted of a complex of buildings and gardens of varying dates and styles more reminiscent of the layout of the Topkapı Palace than the Dolmabahçe. Several of the buildings are now open to the public, who can, in any case, come here just to explore the many paths and driveways, and to walk around a lake where wild animals were once kept on the islands (seen from above, the lake turns out to be shaped like **Abdülhamid II**'s "*tuğra* (**monogram**)"). In the 1980s the park was rescued and restored by the tireless Turkish Touring and Automobile Association although it has now passed back into municipality hands.

The last Ottoman sultan to wield absolute power, **Abdülhamid II** was nonetheless terrified of everyone and retreated to Yıldız Palace from the waterside palaces fearing an attack from the Bosphorus. Even then he was unable to relax. The men who carried out the building work on the palace were not allowed to discuss the plans with each other, and the sultan had some of the corridors blocked with stones to slow the progress of intruders. Finally he was deposed in 1909 and **exiled to Salonica** whereupon the palace was plundered of many of its valuables. When Salonica fell to Greece in 1912, the ex-sultan was brought back as a prisoner to **Beylerbeyi Palace** (see p.242) where he died in 1918. The last days of this unhappy man who was reduced to spying on his subjects through a telescope are vividly evoked in **Brian Unsworth**'s marvelous novel **"The Rage of the Vulture"**.

View of a parade in front of Mabeyn Pavilion at Yıldız Palace in an old etching

The world's largest Hereke carpet covers the floor of the Reception Hall.

The Chalet and museums are all closed on Mondays.
Tel: 0212 259 32 92
www.millisaraylar.gov.tr

Yıldız Chalet

Despite its cohesive look, the graceful two-storey Yıldız Chalet was actually built in three stages. The oldest part dates back to the 1870s when it was designed as an **official guesthouse** completely separated from the imperial complex by a high wall. In 1889 it was expanded by **Sarkis Balyan** for the state visit of **Kaiser Wilhelm II**, the first such visit ever hosted by the sultans. The Kaiser visited again in 1898 when a third section, designed by **Raimondo d'Aronco**, was added for his benefit. Amongst the many other visiting dignitaries to be accommodated here were the British prime minister **Sir Winston Churchill**, the French president **Charles de Gaulle**, and the Romanian dictator **Nicolae Ceaucescu**.

The most impressive room in the 60-room Chalet is the huge **Ceremonial Hall**, which measures 30 by 15 meters and is home to the **largest Hereke carpet** ever woven; 60 weavers worked on this single piece of floor covering that spreads out over 400 square meters

The splendor of the palace rooms.

of ground. During the early years of the Republic the hall was turned into a luxurious **casino**. After the Marmara earthquakes of 1999 then US president **Bill Clinton** was guest of honor at a cocktail party held here.

More decoratively interesting is the **Banqueting Hall**, also called **Sedefli Salon** (the Mother of-Pearl Room), a grand dining room with Moorish ceilings and doors inlaid with mother-of-pearl that were transferred here from the **Çırağan Palace**. It's set up today as if anticipating diners at any moment.

Ultimately Abdülhamid ended up living in the Chalet guesthouse rather than in the State Apartments, as did the very last of the Ottoman rulers, **Mehmed VI**, who finally fled to Malta in secret with his family in 1922. He died and was buried in Syria.

Yıldız Palace in an old photograph.

"Dolmabahçe Sarayı Rıhtımında Kayzer Wilhelm," 1890, Fausto Zonaro.

The first visit of **Kaiser Wilhelm II** to **Sultan Abdülhamid II** was immortalized in a painting by the Italian-born court artist **Fausto Zonaro**. It's on display in the Dolmabahçe Palace.

Malta Pavilion

Park and Mansions

Yıldız Park is a wonderful place to while away a few hours. Many of the trees and shrubs are labeled to help you identify them, and you'll see squirrels foraging for nuts, and hear green parakeets screeching overhead.

The park contains two beautiful pavilions, both designed by the ubiquitous **Balyan brothers**. The finer of the two, the lovely **Malta Köşkü (Malta Pavilion)**, was built during the reign of Sultan Abdülaziz and became a **prison** for Sultan Murad V and his mother after Murad was deposed in 1876. It now houses a restaurant with stunning painted ceilings and great views out over the Bosphorus. Centerpiece of the ground floor is what would once have been a magnificent **indoor pool**, its central fountain adorned with marble fish and swans; two more fountains against the wall have matching swan motifs. Even the ladies' restroom is impressive as it retains the original marble washbasin; you can also examine, although not use, the original marble toilet.

Warning!

It is not possible to pass directly from Yıldız Park and the Şale to the Yıldız Palace buildings.

Despite its demure exterior, the **Çadır Köşkü (Çadır Mansion)**, right beside the lake, has rather a grim history since it was here that Abdülhamid had the Grand Vizier Mithad Paşa and his associates tortured in an attempt to prove that they had murdered Sultan Abdülaziz. It now houses a café and restaurant too.

Çadır Pavilion

Mithad Paşa

Described as the father of the 1876 constitution, Mithad Paşa (1822-1884) was a would-be reformer and two-times grand vizier who found himself battling against the obduracy and/or incompetence of the later Ottoman sultans. Accused of complicity in the possible murder of **Sultan Abdülaziz** in 1876, he was tortured in the **Çadır Köşk**; only foreign intervention saved his life. There's a bust of Mithad Paşa in front of the old TC Ziraat Bankası building in **Cağaloğlu**.

Mithad Paşa

A Tragical End

By the time Abdülhamid II was forced into exile in Salonica there were some 230 women aged between 15 and 50 in his harem, almost all of them Caucasian. Telegrams were dispatched to their families, and some fathers and brothers arrived to reclaim their daughters who were then officially freed from slavery. For others there was to be no such happy ending as no trace could be found of their families. This story forms the backdrop for **Ferzan Özpetek**'s lavishly beautiful 1999 film "**Harem Suare (The Last Harem)**".

Yıldız Palace Buildings

State Apartments (Büyük Mabeyn)

The heart of the last imperial complex, the **Büyük Mabeyn (State Apartments)** were completely rebuilt in 1866 by **Sarkis** and **Agop Balyan** but are not currently open to the public. It was allocated to the Presidency in recent years. The German Prime Minister **Angela Merkel** was one of its famous visitors.

Just to the east of the state apartments are three small museums. **İBB Şehir Müzesi** (The **City Museum)** houses a collection of **Yıldız porcelain** as made at the factory in the Park (see p.99), as well as examples of the sort of **wooden toys** once sold at Eyüp, and some fine paintings by **Şevket Dağ, İbrahim Çallı, Hamit Görele** and **Bedri Rahmi Eyüboğlu** among others. The adjoining **Yıldız Palace Museum** displays miscellaneous items from the palace in Marangozhane (the old Carpentry Workshop) where Abdülhamid himself used to work. There are also some magnificent examples of Art Nouveau furniture here too.

Facing the museums across the courtyard the **Silahhane (Armory)** is not currently open to the public. Another work of Raimondo d'Aronco, the **Yaveran Dairesi (Assistants' Apartments)**, used to house the sultan's aide-de-camp.

In a separate courtyard behind the State Apartments is the gorgeous d'Aronco-designed **Yıldız Palace Theatre and Turkish Performing Arts Museum,** a private entertainment center where Sultan Abdülhamid would come to watch plays sitting all alone in a box over the entrance – the stalls below him could not be used since no subjects could sit with their backs to the sultan. Amongst the performers he would have seen in action was the French actress **Sarah Bernhardt**, a habitué of the Markiz Pastanesi on İstiklal Caddesi. The theater is decorated in blue and gold, and the dome is adorned with **stars** ("yıldız" is Turkish for star).

City Museum

The museum at the **Gedikli Cariyeler** (Regular Concubines) building adjacent to it exhibits costumes of the Palace Theatre, archival documents of the traditional and westernized Turkish theatre and some personal belongings of famous artists.

Yıldız Palace Museum

Yıldız Hamidiye Mosque built by Sultan Abdülhamid II after a suicide attack at the Friday Salute

Clock Tower

Interior magnificence of the Hamidiye Mosque.

The mosques

Abdülhamid was far too paranoid to travel far for Friday prayers, so in 1886 he had the **Hamidiye Mosque** built close to the palace on Barbaros Bulvarı (and even worked on carving the minbar himself). The calligraphy above the main entrance is especially fine. The three-storey **clock tower** beside the gate was completed in 1890.

He would have had rather further to walk to the delightful, Balyan-designed **Küçük Mecidiye Mosque**, near the park's lower entrance opposite Çırağan Palace, which dates back to 1848 and the reign of **Sultan Abdülmecid**. Its complex incorporated a school, medrese and caravanserai. Soil brought from Mecca was used in creating the walls which are decorated with pretty swags of flowers rendered in white plaster.

Küçük Mecidiye Mosque

Imperial Porcelain Factory

At the top end of the park stands a factory, designed by the Italian architect **Raimondo d'Aronco** to resemble a medieval castle from Europe. This began turning out **Sevres-style porcelain** in 1896, possibly as a cost-cutting measure to reduce the expense of importing popular European dinner services for the palace. Production stopped between 1909 and 1911 and had only just recommenced when the factory was taken over to produce insulation materials for use in the **Turkish War of Independence**. From 1920 to 1957 it once again ceased production. Since 1995 it has been operating as a **museum-factory** churning out decorative china for export and sale in its gift shop.

Çadır Mansion

Malta Mansion

11

Phoenix of a Palace

Çırağan Palace

Today one of Istanbul's most beautiful and exclusive hotels with an infinity swimming pool stretching right to the edge of the Bosphorus, the original Çırağan Palace was erected in 1856 on the site of a series of older palaces and is intimately linked to events in later Ottoman history. Like so many Istanbul landmarks it was destroyed by fire in 1910 and the site stood abandoned until the 1980s when the palace was restored and turned into a hotel. Across the road are the shrine of Yahya Efendi and Yıldız Park.

Entrance hall of Çırağan Palace.

The site of the Çırağan Palace has a long history dating back to the reign of **Sultan Ahmed I** (1603-1617) when it was part of the royal Kazancıoğlu Gardens. Later Ahmed III's Grand Vizier **Damat İbrahim Paşa** had the Ferahabad Palace built here for his wife, Fatma Sultan. It became the setting for many of the lavish **Tulip Era parties** for which he was famed and this included the **candle-lit soirees** after which the district is believed to have taken its name (in Persian "cereğan" means "full of light").

When **Ahmed III** was overthrown in 1730, the palace fell into disuse until **Sultan Mahmud I** started to use it to entertain foreign ambassadors. Towards the end of the 18th century it was replaced with a new summer palace intended for Sultan Selim III's sister, **Beyhan Sultan**. During the reign of Sultan Mahmud II the Turkish-Armenian architect **Garabet Balyan** expanded the palace and made it habitable in winter; what was called the "**Beyaz Sarayı (White Palace)**" then started to play a big part in imperial life, as home to **Sultan Abdülmecid I; Sultans Murad V, Abdülhamid II** and **Mehmed V Reşad** were all born here. However, once the larger Dolmabahçe Palace was completed, Abdülmecid moved there, and in 1856 the White Palace was torn down to make way for a new building.

Sultan Abdülaziz employed the **Balyans** to complete the work on the new palace, asking them to incorporate Moorish details into what was otherwise a typically "Western" design; architects were sent to inspect the **Alhambra** and other Moorish buildings

Çırağan Palace in 1839 in an old engraving.

in Spain but still the sultan is said to have interfered so frequently with the plans that they had to be redrawn 20 times. Work on the palace was finally completed in 1874, and the sultan moved in, only to move straight out again, complaining that it was damp (although others think that he had been scared away by rumors that ill luck would come to those responsible for moving a dervish lodge that had stood on the site). The sultan died less than two years later in suspicious circumstances; some believe he killed himself, others that he was murdered. He was succeeded by his nephew **Murad V** who proved too mentally unstable to govern, and was deposed after 93 days in favor of his brother, **Abdülhamid II**.

Sultan Abdülaziz

Murad was then imprisoned in the Çırağan Palace where, in 1878, there occurred an event known as **"the Çırağan Incident"** during which **Ali Suavi**, a teacher at the Şehzade Mosque, led a band of insurgents in an unsuccessful assault on the palace from the Bosphorus, hoping to rescue Murad and reinstate him on the throne. Soon afterwards the ex-sultan was moved to the **Malta Pavilion** in Yıldız Park which was thought to be more secure (the park is connected to the Çırağan Palace via a marble bridge). Ultimately Murad stayed a prisoner for 28 years until his death.

Sultan Murad V

When he died in 1905, the building was abandoned, only to spring to life again briefly as a home for the new **Turkish Parliament** that was elected in 1908. Then in 1910 disaster struck and the palace burnt down in a mere five hours, taking with it many priceless antiques and historic documents. The site then languished for decades, playing a walk-on part in **footballing history** as a temporary pitch for Beşiktaş before the construction of their stadium at Dolmabahçe. It wasn't until the 1980s that it was rebuilt to form the centerpiece of a new **Kempinski Hotel** which opened in 1990. The hotel was restored again in 2007, and has played hosts to many famous guests including **John F. Kennedy Jr, Pavarotti, Sting, Bill Clinton, Kofi Annan,** and **Oprah Winfrey**.

Çırağan Palace on fire in 1910.

The Feriye Palaces. On the left the building used as Galatasaray University, on the right the one used as Kabataş High School.

Shrine of Yahya Efendi

Just a short uphill walk across the road from the hotel is a delightfully secluded and much revered shrine which houses the remains of Yahya Efendi (1495-1570), one of Sultan Süleyman the Magnificent's brothers-in-law. It was built by **Sinan** in around 1570, and became a popular place with sailors who would visit it to give thanks for their safe return from a voyage. Several minor members of the imperial family are buried here, including one of Sultan Süleyman's daughters.

Shrine of Yahya Efendi.

The Feriye Palaces

At one time the part of the coast extending from **Beşiktaş** to **Defterdarburnu**, the headland at Ortaköy just beyond the Bosphorus Bridge, was reserved for the summer palaces of the nobility, and on either side of the Çırağan Palace stand lovely old waterside mansions whose workaday modern uses disguise their previous importance. The one that was closest to Beşiktaş is now the **Four Seasons at the Bosphorus Hotel**, the one that was furthest from Beşiktaş is what was the **Hatice Sultan Palace** in Ortaköy. In the middle of Palace Row was what now houses the **Kabataş High School** in which Sultan Abdülaziz died in 1874. Many of the buildings belong to Galatasaray University whose language department is housed in one of the finest. Unfortunately, the wooden building built in 1871 was burnt down together with the documents and archives in it during the fire in 2013. The restoration of the building started in 2016 after it stayed in its derelict state for 3.5 years. Security for all these palaces was provided by the grand 19th-century **Feriye Tabya (police station)** that now houses the Feriye Lokantası. Across the road stand the **Zaptiye Barracks**, which have been restored recently.

Çırağan Palace Kempinski Hotel

12

Clubber's Paradise

Ortaköy

From the Bosphorus, Ortaköy is one of the least missable suburbs, partly because it sits right beside the First Bridge on the European side and partly because its mosque stands on a promontory jutting out into the water. This is one of Istanbul's more happening suburbs, with a cluster of restaurants hugging a small waterside square, a lively Sunday handicrafts market, and a string of fashionable nightclubs on the outskirts. Amid all this fun and games a few reminders of the past – churches, synagogues and hamams – often get completely overlooked.

Ortaköy (Middle Village) has a history dating back to Byzantine times when there were several monasteries here. By the 17th century Evliya Çelebi was able to report a large mixed population of **Jews, Greeks** and **Muslims** living side by side; the village had already established a reputation as a place with a lively nightlife as he reports that there were "a great number" of taverns here. Today that reputation is well-earned and on summer evenings the traffic on the coast road around Ortaköy can be murderous as well-heeled nightclubbers head and other entertainment hotspots.

The focal point of daytime life remains the waterside square which is overlooked by a collection of old houses, most of them now housing cafes and restaurants. Lost amid the weekend melee is a wonderful 18th-century **fountain** erected by **Damat İbrahim Paşa**, son-in-law and grand vizier to Sultan Ahmed III (1713-1730).

Ortakoy Square.

Dome of Ortaköy Mosque.

The interior of Ortaköy Mosque is absolutely breathtaking.

Ortaköy Mosque (Büyük Mecidiye Camii)

Sitting on **Defterdarburnu**, a promontory right beside the First Bridge, the light-filled, baroque style Ortaköy Mosque was designed by **Nikoğos Balyan** for **Sultan Abdülmecid** in 1854-1855 on the site of an earlier 18th-century mosque (he was also responsible for the Dolmabahçe Mosque (see p.76) and there are similarities between the two buildings). Attached to the rear a two-storey pew for the sultan was designed so that he could enter it directly from his caique without having to walk round to the main entrance. Inside the dome is decorated with painted clouds floating between columns, a touch of whimsy that fits with the Bosphorus setting. It was restored in 2012.

The Kethüda (Steward) Turkish Bath

Mimar Sinan

The bath is one of the four monuments in Beşiktaş designed by Architect Sinan. It is located where the traffic is at its most dense and it is known as the first monument to be built after the Turks settled in Ortaköy. Also known as the Ortaköy Turkish Bath, the building was used a restaurant, a night club and a design office after its restoration. It currently functions as a cultural center of the Beşiktaş Municipality. It is thought to have been built for Hüsrev Kethüda, a steward to the Grand Vizier Sokullu Mehmet Paşa in the 1570s. The internal layout is unusual, with four doomed rooms replacing the usual single chamber of the hot room. I hope the building will be used as a Turkish bath.

The road linking Beşiktaş to Ortaköy.

18 houses whose occupants are thought to have been Jews.

Etz Ahayim Synagogue.

Churches and synagogues

Almost invisible behind the shops stands the huge Greek Orthodox **Church of Hagios Fokas**. It only dates back to 1856 although a Byzantine church with the same dedication originally gave its name to the surrounding area. Look out for the small belfry perched above the gate that leads into the courtyard from the main road.

Not far away is the **Etz Ahayim (Tree of Life) synagogue**, which dates back to the 14th century although the current building mainly dates from 1813 and 1941. Behind it lies a long story of fires and more fires, the congregation having been considerably expanded in the early 17th century after a conflagration drove them out of the Grand Bazaar.

Along Dereboyu Caddesi you'll see the Armenian **Church of Surp Krikor Lusavoriç**, built in 1839.

Hagios Fokas Greek Orthodox Church.

On the right is Hagios Fokas belltower

Fehime Sultan Yalı

Hatice Sultan Yalı

Waterside mansions

Just past the Ortaköy Mosque, its impossible to miss the stone-built remains of the **Esma Sultan Yalı**, built for the fun-loving sister (1778-1848) of Sultan Mahmud II who had been widowed at the age of 25 and went on to make the most of her wealth and connections.

Hatice Sultan and her daughter Selma Sultan

As time passed the mansion became first a school, then a tobacco warehouse and finally a coal depot before a terrible fire in 1975 reduced it to a ruin. In the 1990s the shell was bought by the Marmara hotel group. It's now used for **social events**, including high-society weddings.

At Defterdarburnu beneath the First Bridge stand the charred remains of the **Fehime Sultan Yalı**. This was originally given by Sultan Abdülhamid II to **Gazi Osman Paşa**, the hero of the battle of **Plevne**, in 1883. After his son Kemaleddin Paşa married the sultan's daughter Naime Sultan they lived in the yalı, so that it is sometimes confusingly called the **Naime Sultan** or even **Gazi Osman Paşa Yalı**. In 1910 it was given as a present to Fehime Sultan, one of the daughters of Sultan Murad V, and went on to house a secondary **school**. It burnt down in 2003.

Almost next door to it, the **Hatice Sultan Yalı** had been given to Fehime's elder sister Hatice Sultan. After serving time as an orphanage and primary school, it then housed a sports center. To add to the confusion there had also been an earlier palace here that was designed for another Hatice Sultan, the sister of Sultan Selim III, by the Dutch architect **Antoine-Ignace Melling** (1763-1831) who left a beautiful drawing of it. Work to convert both mansions into a **hotel** began in 2009.

Forbidden love

Hatice Sultan (1870-1928) was one of history's many female victims. The daughter of **Sultan Murad V** who was deposed, she was still unwed at the age of 31, and pleaded with her uncle, the new sultan **Abdülhamid II**, to let her marry. The husband he found for her was an ugly old man, so, perhaps to get her own back, Hatice embarked on an affair with her cousin Naime Sultan's husband, **Kemaleddin Paşa**. Inevitably, Kemaleddin was forced to divorce his wife and was sent into exile. When Abdülhamid was, in turn, deposed, Kemaleddin returned and proposed to Hatice who refused him in favor of an ordinary but handsome man called **Rauf Hayri Bey**. Hatice's grandson, Kenize Murad, told the story in his book "Saraydan Sürgüne (From the Palace to Exile)".

The Taut House on the Ortaköy hillside

Taut House (Taut Evi)

As you drive across the Bosphorus Bridge towards Ortaköy you may glimpse a house on the right-hand side of the hillside that looks rather like a burgundy-colored pagoda. This was the home of the German architect **Bruno Taut** who said that he had designed it to "express the Orient's spiritual values…in a modern house".

Taut lived in Istanbul from 1932 to 1938

Who was Bruno Taut?

A German Jew born in Königsberg in 1880, Taut had already made a name for himself as an architect especially with some Modernist housing estates in **Berlin** which are now listed as a world heritage site when he was forced to leave the country in 1932. After spending time abroad, he was made a professor of architecture at what is now the **Mimar Sinan University of Fine Arts** in 1936. He lived in Turkey until his death in 1938 and was responsible for several buildings in Ankara and Trabzon. As his final commission he designed the **catafalque** used for Atatürk's state funeral in Ankara in November 1938.

Sarkis Balyan Yalı

13

Waterside Art Nouveau

Kuruçeşme and **Arnavutköy**

Arguably the most beautiful of the Bosphorus suburbs, Arnavutköy is distinguished by its magnificent wooden houses, a reminder of what many of the villages must have looked like in the past. Famed at one time for its vineyards, Arnavutköy came to be better known for the strawberries introduced here in the early 19th century. On the hillside above the lovely houses stands the modern incarnation of the famous and influential Robert College. The nightlife of Ortaköy is slowly spreading towards Kuruçeşme, an upscale suburb to the east. There are also a growing number of excellent restaurants in this part of town.

The Arnavutköy promenade is perfect for a stroll.

Kuruçeşme

Kuruçeşme (Dry Fountain) was probably named after the 17th-century **Köprülü Hemşire Fountain** attached to the **Tezkireci Osman Efendi Mosque**, although the area may originally have been called Koruçeşme, meaning "the Fountain of the Woods" because at that time it was lush and green, and the fountain well supplied with water. Then it dried up and the name had to be changed. Given how fashionable the area is now, it's surprising to learn that until recently it was an industrial zone where coal and sand were stored. Almost the only reminder of that these days is the bus stop named "Kömür Tevzii (Coal Distribution Point)". Kuruçeşme is a pretty place to take a waterside stroll, with a newly laid promenade along the Bosphorus from which you can admire the tethered yachts of the wealthy and gaze across at the fairy-tale building that houses **Kuleli Military High School** (see p.263).

Tezkireci Osman Efendi Mosque.

Kuruçeşme wooden houses with Art Nouveau details.

Also known as the Ayvaz Paşazade Yalı, this building was sold by its Armenian banker owner to a Cretan called Ali Vafi Bey after whom it was renamed the Ali Vafi Mansion.

There are a number of churches in Kuruçeşme, including the **Surp Haç (Holy Cross)** Armenian church, a rectangular brick-and-stone building designed by **Garabet Balyan** in 1881, that stands on the site of a much earlier structure. It's on the left as you head inland along Kırbaç Sokak. At the top of some steps at the end of the same road is the **Church of Hagios Demetrios** (St Demetrius), which was built in 1798. The latter is especially interesting as it was here that the contentious theological school now on **Heybeliada** started out in 1804. Those signing up to train for the priesthood used to stand on the symbol of a double-headed eagle inset in the ground just inside the entrance and vow to observe the teachings of the Church. At the back of the church a **tunnel** runs uphill to the **Hagios Sotiros ayazma (sacred spring)** whose source is a cave some 40 meters away. The continual dripping of water over the last hundred years or so has caused the walls to calcify so that they now look like the inside of a cave. It's a minor but rather remarkable sight. Finally, the small **Church of Ioannis Prodromos (John the Baptist)**, with its round wooden turret, is half-hidden behind high walls at the point on the Kuruçeşme-Arnavutköy Yolu where Kuruçeşme meets Arnavutköy.

Surp Haç Armenian Church

Hagios Demetrios Church

Ioannis Prodromos Church

Hagios Sotiros sacred spring

Galatasaray Island AKA Suada (Water Island)

Just offshore at Kuruçeşme is a **small island** that was given to the Armenian architect **Sarkis Balyan** by **Sultan Abdülhamid II** in 1880 as a reward for his work on the nearby Esma Sultan Yalı (see p.107) and **Çırağan Palace** (see p.100). Of the two-storey yalı he built on the island and in which he carried out physics experiments there remains no trace. Later the island became a walled garden and then a water sports center. Today it belongs to **Galatasaray Sports Club**. All the buildings on the island, which was home to a complex of restaurants and night clubs for a long time, were demolished in 2017 on the grounds that they were not consistent with the zoning plan. I don't know what the fate of the deserted island will be.

Robert College

In 1871 an American College for Girls affiliated to the boys' college at Bebek was founded on the hilltop above Arnavutköy. In 1971 the two colleges amalgamated, and the new co-ed establishment retained the famous Robert College name. Ex students include the writer **Halide Edip Adıvar** and ex-prime minister **Tansu Çiller**.

Halet Çambel (Red) Yalı

On the waterside heading north towards Arnavutköy the **Halet Çambel Yalı** is a rusty-brown (Ottoman rose) mansion built for an Armenian who was a gardener for Sultan Mahmud II in the 1830s. Educated in the girls school beside the house, Halet Çambel was the archeologist who excavated the Hittite site at Karatepe-Aslantaş near Osmaniye. She was married to the award-winning, self-taught architect **Nail Çakırhan**. She donated it to Bosphorus University.

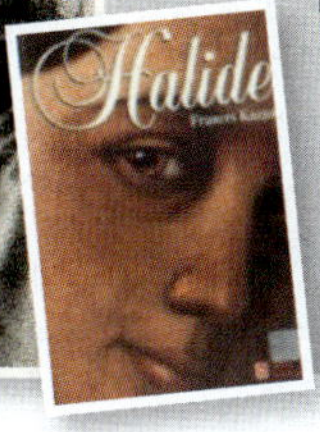

Who was Halide Edip Adıvar?

Born in 1884, Halide Edip Adıvar was a Turkish novelist and feminist who became a lecturer in literature and then went on to fight in the **Turkish War of Independence** (1919-1922). Later she traveled in France and Britain before returning to become a professor of English literature at **Istanbul University** and, briefly, a **member of parliament**. She died in 1964, and there's a **bust** in her memory behind the Milion in Sultanahmet. Her 1926 autobiography, "The Memoir of Halide Edip", describes her years in Arnavutköy. Her childhood also formed the basis for **Frances Kazan's novel "Halide's Gift"**.

Old Arnavutköy ferry terminal

Arnavutköy

A short walk north of Kuruçeşme, Arnavutköy ("Albanian Village") is named after the **Albanian builders** who were brought here by Sultan Abdülmecid in the 19th century to lay sidewalks for Istanbul. At one time it had a large population of Greeks and Jews. Today a few Greeks remain but the Jews are all gone.

Arnavutköy's back streets are full of wooden houses

The former Greek Primary School now serves as a kindergarten

Cruising along the Bosphorus, it's impossible to miss Arnavutköy where a dense cluster of wooden houses still adorn the waterside. That's all that most visitors get to see. However, if you disembark at the landing stage and wander inland you will discover even more fine houses climbing up the hillside, some of them designed with an **Art Nouveau** flair. Most of these houses probably date back to the early 20th century, and although to modern eyes they appear both beautiful and individual, experts believe that the **Art Nouveau** twists were often just additions to preexisting buildings, the patterns being mass produced rather than individually designed. An exception is the house at **4 Dulkadiroğulları Sokak** which was almost certainly designed by an architect rather than being put together by a builder from standard patterns.

Yalıs lined up along the coast road.

Heading inland from the Tevfikiye Mosque near the water you will come to the huge late 19th-century **Taksiarkhes Church**, built beside a sacred spring. Its central dome looks exactly like those of the larger mosques, although it has a bell tower over the entrance too. Inscribed on the bell tower are Jesus' words "Come to me".

Taksiarkhes Church

At the westerly end of the waterfront the **Arnavutköy Mosque** dates back to 1832 and the reign of Sultan Mahmud II. Beside it stands a fine 19th-century **Karakol (Police Station).**

Tevfikiye Mosque

If driving between Etiler and Arnavutköy along Sekbanlar Sokak, you might want to divert briefly along Körkadı Sokak to see the pretty little 19th-century **chapel** built over an ayazma sacred to Elijah. Its dome is especially attractive. The chapel is kept locked after several thefts but the caretaker may be willing to open it for you (he lives in a house in the cemetery across the road).

Hagios Elias Chapel

Akıntıburnu

At the eastern end of Arnavutköy the coastline juts out into the Bosphorus and the current becomes so powerful that it is not always possible for small boats to pass. In the past porters on the shore would have had to tow some of the more fragile boats around Akıntıburnu, the **Cape of the Current**. According to the 16th-century French writer Pierre Gilles, the paving stones here had been worn down by the passage of crabs that came ashore and walked around the cape rather than risk the current.

Bayraktar Holding has its headquarters in the İzzeabad Mansion between Arnavutköy and Bebek.

Türkan Saylan

A doctor of medicine, academic, writer and an educator... Of course all these titles are not sufficient to describe Türkan Saylan, one of the old residents of this neighborhood. Her name is more often associated with **Çağdaş Yaşamı Destekleme Derneği** (the Association for Supporting Contemporary Life, ÇYDD) as one of the association's founders and president. The association contributed significantly to the education of girls and their participation in modern life. The World Health Organization issued a report about the "significant reduction of leprosy" in Turkey thanks to the country-wide work of this idealist woman, who came to be the first woman to be awarded with the Gandhi Award in India. I very much hope that her house on the Beyazgül Street will one day be reopened as a museum to inspire women in Turkey and in the world.

The stylite lifestyle

Back in the days when Kuruçeşme was still the Byzantine settlement of **Anaplous,** it was home to two of those extraordinary **Christian hermits** called stylites, or men who sat on top of pillars. From 433-460 **Simeon the Stylite** perched atop a perch overlooking the Bosphorus, and from 460-493 **St Daniel the Stylite** did likewise. So impressed by this was **Emperor Leo I** that he supplied Daniel with a second column linked to the first by a beam so that he could stretch his legs. Later he even added a shelter against the wind and rain which Daniel reluctantly agreed to use. Not surprisingly, the crowds flocked in to stare at them.

14

Beautiful "Baby"

Bebek

Midway along the western shore of the Bosphorus, Bebek (Baby) is an unabashedly upscale suburb set round a pretty harbor and dominated by the academic might of the Bosphorus University. It's centered on an attractive waterside park and filled with alluring shops and restaurants where the well-heeled can be seen going about their business. Both Rumeli Hisarı and Arnavutköy are within enjoyable walking distance along the waterside promenade.

Where Bebek gets its peculiar name from is unclear. Some people think it was taken from the Turkish expression "**beautiful as a baby**", while others think it was named after the Turkish official **Mustafa Çelebi** who was **nicknamed "Bebek"** because of his good looks and who was put in control of this part of the Bosphorus after the Ottoman conquest of 1453. The area first acquired importance in the early 18th century when **Sultan Ahmed III** had the **Hümayünabad Palace** built here, spurring many other members of the nobility to build luxurious homes nearby. The palace was destroyed in the reign of **Abdülmecid I** (1839-1861) who is said to have been incensed when it was suggested that it would outlive many sultans.

Today Bebek is arguably the trendiest of the Bosphorus suburbs, a place where female fashionistas can feel comfortable strolling around in shorts, and where some of the cafes cater unashamedly to the see-and-be-seen crowd. It's also a notorious traffic bottleneck especially at weekends.

Bebek (Hümayunuabad) Mosque

Across the park from the Egyptian Consulate building, this small and not especially distinguished mosque right next to the site of the old **Hümayunuabad Palace** was built by architect **Kemaleddin Bey** in 1912. Although he was one of the leading lights in the **First National Architecture movement**, the mosque is fairly classical in its design. However, some of the interior woodwork is very impressive.

Bebek Mosque, by İbrahim Çallı

Bebek Kahve

Egyptian Consulate

The single most impressive building in Bebek is a huge Art Nouveau mansion with a mansard roof right on the waterfront that was designed for **Emine Hanım**, the mother of the last Egyptian Khedive, **Abbas Hilmi Pasha**, in 1902. For that reason it is also called **Hıdiva Sarayı** (Palace of the Female Khedive). Although it is often listed as a work of **Raimondo d'Aronco**, it was probably designed by one of two Austrian architects, Fabricius or Antonio Lasciac. The Khedive used the mansion as a summer house until he was deposed in 1914 whereupon it was bequeathed to the Egyptian government on condition that it was used as an embassy (a consulate after the embassy was moved to Ankara in 1923). In 2010 it was completely renovated, which returned some of the original coloring to the stonework.

The photos of Egyptian Consulate were taken by Koray Erkaya.

Beautiful straircase

One of the buildings' elaborately decorated painted ceilings.

The Art Nouveau architectural style is reflected most elegantly in the decorative wrought-iron stairwell railings.

Khedive's mother Khediva Emine Valide Paşa and her private orchestra.

Amongst the buildings commissioned by the khedives appointed Governors of Egypt during the Ottoman era were: the **Khedive's Villa** (see p.320) in Çubuklu, and the **Mısır Apartments** and **Hıdivyal Palas** on İstiklal Caddesi. The State Production Farm in Dalaman belonged to Khedive Hilmi Abbas Paşa who wanted to commission a hunting villa in Dalaman and a train station in Alexandria and came to an agreement with French architects. Somehow the projects got switched round and today Dalaman still has a train station without a railway, while a farm building was constructed in Alexandria!

Splendid details of the building.

Buildings being restored as part of Bebekoy project.

Don't forget to pass the Pink Mansion in March when the magnolia is in bloom.

Hagios Haralambos Greek Orthodox Church

French Orphanage

Churches and Mansions

The **Lazarist Church of Sacre Coeur** in Mektep Sokağı dates back to 1908 when it formed a vast complex with a school which is now closed; the **Old French Orphanage (Eski Fransız Yetimhanesi)** adjoining it was built in 1856 and now serves as a summer school for **St Benoit High School** in Karaköy. A **second orphanage**, also on the hillside, was taken over by the state and given to a company which turned it into Bebekoy, a luxury housing development.

Nearby in İnşirah Sokak, the hill road that leads to Etiler, stands the Greek Orthodox **Church of Hagios Charalambos**, dating back to 1830. The bell tower was added in 1962. Immediately opposite it is a fine white mansion with a magnificent magnolia tree in its garden. When the tree is in flower in March it's almost worth coming to Bebek just to see it.

If you continue along the same road you will come to the Armenian **Kavafyan Mansion**. Built in 1751, it is one of Istanbul's oldest (and largest) surviving **wooden houses**, originally built for Christian shipowners in classic konak style with the rooms opening off a central hall (sofa). Unfortunately it has been locked up for years so we were unable to discover whether it retains its original painted ceilings. It is slowly fading away before our very eyes, at perpetual risk of fire from a carelessly discarded match.

Kavafyan Mansion

Hand-drawn mural detail

Old photo shows Kennedy Lodge housing a canteen for teaching staff.

Bülent Ecevit

Tansu Çiller

Robert College and Bosphorus University

Cyrus Hamlin

Robert College, the first American college to be opened outside the United States, was founded in 1863 by the American missionary **Cyrus Hamlin** who had worked in Florence Nightingale's hospital at Selimiye. It took its name from that of his financial backer, Christopher R. Robert. In 1971 the college land was given to the Turkish Ministry of Education who founded **Bosphorus University** (Boğaziçi Üniversitesi) on the site. The college itself reopened on the site of the Robert College for Girls in Arnavutköy. Past alumni include two ex-prime ministers of Turkey: **Bülent Ecevit** (1925-2006) and **Tansu Çiller** (1946 -), Turkey's first – and so far only – female prime minister. As you walk from Bebek towards Rumeli Hisarı you will see the entrance to the university beside the bus stop. Inside the path winds up through the woods and passes **Manzara**, a viewpoint from which there is a spectacular Bosphorus view ("manzara" is Turkish for view). Before you leave from the Etiler Gate at the top of the site you might want to try one of the campus restaurants. **Yenice** offers home-cooking, while **Wonderland** has very reasonable prices.

Foundation Sciences Faculty Building

Albert Long Hall

Lazarist Sacre Coeur Church

The Lazarists

The Lazarists (also known as the Congregation of the Mission) are a Roman Catholic order of secular clergymen dating back to the 17th century who are **followers of St Vincent de Paul**. Their curious name was acquired from one of the first properties they owned, the Priory of St Lazare in Paris. In 1783 Lazarist missionaries arrived in Turkey. Grateful for having found exceptionally fertile ground in Poland, it was the Turkish Lazarist community that provided the land for Polish settlers in what is now **Polonezköy**.

City Secrets

In my opinion if you fancy a short tour of the Bosphorus you could hardly do better than take the ring ferry from Bebek. You'll have it to yourself and the locals, and you can stop off for coffee or a light meal in Kandilli or Kanlıca on the opposite shore before returning.

Who was Fuzuli?

Fuzuli was the pen name of the much-admired Iraqi poet **Mohammed bin Süleyman** (1480-1556), who wrote in Azerbaijani Turkish, Persian and Arabic. After the Ottomans captured his home town in 1534 he became a court poet to Sultan Süleyman the Magnificent. Despite his posthumous fame, he always struggled to make a living and eventually died of cholera or the plague. The mystery is why he should be commemorated here.

Yılanlı Yalı

As you head out of Bebek towards Rumeli Hisarı you will pass turnings to the **Ayşe Sultan** and then **Arifi Paşa Woods** before coming to the **Kayalar Mescidi**, a rare surviving 17th-century wooden chapel.

Beside it is a fine wooden mansion which is a reproduction of the **Yılanlı Yalı** (Snake Mansion) built here in the 18th century. Its curious name came about after **Sultan Mahmud II** showed too much interest in the house; a quick-witted official distracted him by claiming that it was so full of snakes that it was virtually uninhabitable. Unfortunately the original building burnt down in 1964. In 1989 one half of it was faithfully reconstructed by its new owner. The other half is an ugly concrete apartment block which has had the cheek to misappropriate the original name!

Snake Mansion

Kayalar Mescid

Backstory of the Yılanlı Yalı

The late businessperson **Aydın Bolak** (1925-2004) was the son of **Mehmet Vehbi Bolak**, who was a member of the Ottoman Parliament and briefly Minister of National Education. A founding member of the Hürriyet Party, he was, like his father, elected MP for Balıkesir and was amongst the founders and directors of foundations such as **Turkish Education** and **Türkpetrol**.

The two brothers who owned the Yılanlı Yalı let Cevher Özden, AKA **Banker Kastelli**, have the yalı but got it back again thanks to a legal battle fought by **Aydın Bolak**. Later, they sold the yalı to Bolak on condition that he would partition off a part of it for them. In the photograph, the portion on the right belonged to the family that previously owned the yalı. The overhanging part is supported on dramatic angle braces. Inside it was a dining room with a banqueting table to seat 24.

The part beneath the overhanging section was reserved for Aydın Bolak's collections of weapons, rosaries and Yıldız glassware. Behind this imposing structure the garden contains a grove of lemon trees. A pool sits on one of three terraces, while another was used as a vegetable garden while the Bolak family resided here. Eventually they sold the yalı to a family of industrialists from Bursa.

A picture taken during the restoration of the Yılantı Yalı.

Main hall

Bebek Türkan Sabancı Park

Join the locals for a stroll in **Türkan Sabancı Parkı** which is equipped with a large children's playground, exercise machines, fountains, and a dog-running compound. Many of the plane trees here have preservation orders on them, and you may see (or hear) green parakeets roosting in their branches. Right in the middle stands a statue of the poet **Fuzuli**.

Bebek and Egyptian Consulate from Kandilli

15

The Conqueror's Castle

Rumeli Hisarı and Aşiyan

As you sail along the Bosphorus you can hardly miss the enormous fortifications that make up Rumeli Hisarı (European Castle) lurking just beside the Second Bridge. Rumeli Hisarı may not be the largest but it is certainly the most impressive castle along the Bosphorus. The suburb that grew up around it is well-known for its many pleasant waterside cafes and restaurants.

Wooden houses inside Rumeli Hisarı in the 19th century

Having determined to conquer Constantinople, in 1452 **Sultan Mehmed II** built a vast castle on the European shore at the point where the Bosphorus is at its narrowest, and where it would be facing the considerably **smaller castle**, Anadolu Hisarı (Asian Castle), built by his grandfather, Beyazid I, on the Asian shore. Even though the building of the castle has been described as "tantamount to a declaration of war", the Byzantine **Emperor Constantine XI Dragases** was forced to give him the land on which to build, apparently on the same spot that **Darius the Great**, the king of the Persians, had watched while his army of 700,000 men crossed the Bosphorus using a bridge of boats on their way to attack the Scythians in 512 BC. In a stupendous feat of speed-building, Mehmed employed 1,000 craftsmen and 2,000 laborers to complete work on the fortress, which he had designed himself, in a mere four months. His three grand viziers, **Halil Paşa, Zağanos Paşa**, and **Saruca Paşa**, were put in charge of work on the three main towers that now bear their names. Once the castle was built, Mehmed was able to prevent supplies of grain being shipped from the Black Sea to Constantinople, weakening the city and making its defeat more likely. Only one **Venetian ship** attempted to breach the blockade; it was sunk and its crew impaled for their pains.

Once Constantinople had fallen, Rumeli Hisarı had served its purpose and became a **customs collection point**. In time even this function was lost to Rumeli Kavağı further north (see p.188), and parts of the castle were used as a **gaol** for foreign prisoners of war.

The castle was badly damaged by an **earthquake** in 1509, and the floors of two of the towers were lost to fire in 1746. Sultan Selim III had the castle restored but by the 19th century it had been completely abandoned and some locals even set up home inside the grounds. Drawings made at that time show the tall main towers capped with witch's hat roofs rather like the Galata Tower. In 1953 to celebrate the **500th anniversary** of the conquest of Istanbul the castle was completely restored but with flat roofs to replace the pitched ones.

Emperor Constantine XI Dragases

Bird's eye view of Rumeli Hisarı

The Castle

Built on a slope, the castle had one large tower near the shore (the Halil Paşa Tower) and two others on the hillside above. In between the sturdy walls were broken up with 13 smaller towers; in all the walls enclosed an area of more than 31,000 square meters. Sultan Mehmed had a **mosque** built inside the walls over a cistern, although it has since vanished, with only the stump of the minaret to mark its passing. The castle was one of the first in Europe to be built with the use of cannons in mind. As so often in Turkey, close inspection of the walls reveals that they were constructed reusing material from much older structures. You can walk along some stretches of the walls which offer great views, although parents should be warned that there are no safety railings. The **fountain** set into the sea-facing wall is one of only two 15th-century examples known to survive in the city.

Tel: 0212 263 53 05, closed Wednesdays

Cannon

Dragging the boats

In 1453 when **Sultan Mehmed II** determined to seize Constantinople he faced a serious problem because the Byzantine Emperors had always been able to prevent access to the Golden Horn by stringing a heavy metal chain across it. To solve this problem Mehmed had 80 special flat-bottomed boats built. These were then dragged from **Tophane**, over the **Galata heights** and down into the Golden Horn at **Kasımpaşa**, thereby circumventing the chain and making it possible to attack the great sea walls of Fener and Balat. It was an event memorably immortalized by the Italian court artist **Fausto Zonaro** whose painting "**The Siege**" hangs in the Selamlık of the Dolmabahçe Palace (see p.77).

Fatih Sultan Mehmed Gives Orders to the Fleet, by Fausto Zonaro

The castle's names

Rumeli Hisarı has gone under many guises over the years, including Kulle-i Cedide (New Castle), Yenice Hisarı (Quite New Castle) and Boğazkesen Kalesi (Bosphorus-dividing Castle).

The size of a cowhide

The 17th-century travel writer Evliya Çelebi reported that after Fatih Mehmed decided to build a castle here he approached the Byzantine Emperor for a piece of land big enough to create a hunting lodge. The emperor agreed, specifying that the building should not exceed the size of a cowhide. The sultan then had a cowhide cut into fine strips which were stitched together and spread out to create the huge space now covered by the fort. Since this is the same story as is told about Queen Dido and the founding of Carthage in what is now Tunisia, it's probably fair to assume that it's apocryphal.

Aşiyan (Nest) Museum

Was there ever a bedroom with a more beautiful view than this? On the hillside as you leave Bebek heading for Rumeli Hisarı stands the small house built by the poet and anti-government rebel **Tevfik Fikret** (1867-1915) who had been a professor of Turkish literature at Robert College and who was reinterred here in 1961. In 1945 his house was turned into a museum which displays many of his possessions as well as a superb painting entitled simply "**Sis (Mist)**" by **Abdülmecid Efendi**; beside it hangs the Fikret poem of the same name that had provided his inspiration. Also here are reminders of **Abdülhalk Hamid** and **Nigar Hanım**, two other members of the Edebiyat-ı Cedide (New Literature) movement associated with Fikret. From the benches outside you can gaze out on the **Küçüksu Palace** and the twin streams that used to form the **Sweet Waters of Asia** (see p.297).

Between the house and the road stretches the peaceful **Aşiyan Cemetery** where local notables including the poets **Orhan Veli** and **Yahya Kemal Beyatlı**, and the playwright **Ahmed Vefik Paşa** are buried. Nearby there's a **statue** of Orhan Veli being eyed up by the seagull who features in one of his best-known poems.

@asiyanmuze
Tel: 0212 263 69 86,
Closed Sundays and Mondays

Statue of Orhan Veli

The Aşiyan Museum was restored in 2012.

Tevfik Fikret

Sis (Mist) by Abdülmecid Efendi

Surp Santuht Church

Hacı Kemaleddin Mosque

Mosques and churches

The conspicuous and pretty **Hacı Kemaleddin Mosque** may date back to the reign of **Sultan Mehmed II**. However, it was completely rebuilt in 1746 by Sultan Mahmud I, which is when the fountain in front of it was added. The much less conspicuous **Ali Pertek Mosque** dates back to the mid-17th century although it was largely rebuilt in the 1960s and restored in 2009.

There seems to have been an Armenian community in Rumeli Hisarı since the days of Mehmed the Conqueror, but no trace remains of their original wooden church. The present hillside Church of **Surp Santuht** was built in 1856 and is still in use today.

The Paşa's Library

Ahmed Vefik Paşa

Today it's private property and concealed from view behind a steel gate, but the Paşa's Library with the to-die-for view that plays a leading role in **Maureen Freely's** revisiting of the tense political scene of the 1970s in her 2007 novel "**Enlightenment**", really does exist. It was built for **Ahmed Vefik Paşa** (1823-1891), a politician, playwright and compiler of the **first Turkish dictionary** who eventually sought a retreat from the world here. He originally owned the land now occupied by Bosphorus University but lost it on account of his debts. In 1902 his "birdcage" was given a makeover by Levantine architect **Alexandre Vallaury**. The African American writer James Baldwin (1924-1987) completed one of his novels while a guest in the Paşa's Library.

Photos of the library reproduced with permission of the Tek-Esin Foundation.

Yusuf Ziya Paşa (The Fairy) Mansion

If you stand in front of the Rumeli Hisarı landing stage and look up to the right you will see a stepped and turreted red-brick building in front of the bridge. Left unfinished by the death of its original owner, **Mısırlı (Egyptian) Yusuf Ziya Paşa**, aide-de-camp to **Khedive Abbas Hilmi Paşa**. Yusuf Ziya Paşa lived here with his second wife, Nebiye Hanım, and the three daughters from her first marriage until his death in 1926. It was completed recently with results that don't seem to please everybody. It's better known locally as the **Perili Köşk** (the Fairy Mansion). After the restoration, the mansion was rented by **Borusan Holding**. The mansion is used by the offices and administration of the holding during weekdays, and welcomes art-lovers as a museum on weekends. This makes it the first "**office museum**" in Turkey. Apart from the permanent collection, which focuses on works of contemporary art that are shaped by technology, it also hosts temporary exhibitions all year round. The museum also has a nice café that is ideal for a break by the Bosphorus.

@borusancontemporary
www.borusancontemporary.com
open Saturdays and Sundays

Field Marshal Zeki Paşa Yalı

A rare example of a stone yalı, this fine stone mansion standing right beside the bridge was designed by **Alexandre Vallaury** for the wealthy field marshal **Zeki Paşa** some time in the early 20th century. Zeki Pasa was intensely loyal to Sultan Abdülhamid and for 17 years he was in charge of the arsenal at Tophane. Later the yalı passed into the ownership of **Sabiha Sultan**, the daughter of **Mehmed VI**, the last Ottoman sultan, and her husband **Ömer Faruk Efendi**, a son of the last caliph **Abdülmecid Efendi**. Their eldest daughter Neslişah Sultan was born in the house, and the family continued to live here until the whole family was sent into exile. The building, which has 24 rooms, now belongs to the Baştımar family. It was for sale for $ 100 million.

Mediha Sultan Palace

Baltalimanı

Just past the 2nd Bridge lies the suburb of Baltalimanı which is named after **Admiral Baltaoğlu Süleyman Bey**, the man responsible for building the boats that Fatih Mehmed used for the assault on Constantinople. "Balta" means axe in Turkish; the admiral acquired this nickname because of the vast quantity of trees he had cut down to build the ships.

Mustafa Reşid Paşa

The most impressive building here is what started life as the pink-painted waterside **Palace of Mediha Sultan** and is now an orthopedic hospital. It was designed in the mid-19th century by **Sarkis Balyan** for **Mustafa Reşid Paşa** who held the office of grand vizier under Sultan Abdülmecid no less than six times and who kickstarted the **Tanzimat** reform movement. Later it was occupied by his son Galip Paşa who had married Abdülmecid's daughter Fatma Sultan. Later still it became the property of Damat Ferit Paşa who renamed it for his wife. It was here that a **trade treaty** between the Ottomans and the British was signed in 1838. It eased the restrictions on foreign traders and encouraged a mini economic boom.

Japanese Garden

In an easily accessible spot of Istanbul, in Baltalimanı, this park quietly welcomes visitors. Those who are interested come to see the Japanese cherry blossoms in March and April. When 2003 was declared the Turkish Year in Japan, one of the first steps taken was declaring Shimonoseki and Istanbul twin cities. A Turkish garden was created in Shimonoseki while a Japanese garden was created in Istanbul. When you visit the park, you can see details of Japanese landscaping with bridges, ponds and plant arrangements. The importance of tea in Japanese culture and the tea ceremonies also find place in the garden with a tea house. The entrances to the 6137-square-meter garden are free. Since the opening hours change in winter and summer, make sure to check before you go.

16

Tulip Fever

Emirgan and Boyacıköy

One of the most delightful of the Bosphorus suburbs, Emirgan is centered on a very pretty main square where inviting tea gardens nestle beneath ancient plane trees. Just inland are the Emirgan Woods, once the playground of the Egyptian Khedive İsmail Paşa, now a public park with a lake and three inviting cafes housed in 19th-century mansions. In spring the park is full of tulips, making it one of the most beautiful spots in the whole city.

Yellow Pavilion

Small lake in front of Yellow Pavilion

Emirgan was originally called Emirgune after **Emir Güne Han**, an Iranian nobleman who had surrendered the castle of **Yerevan** (now in Armenia) to Sultan Murad IV without a fight in 1635. In return for this, the Sultan brought him to Istanbul, renamed him Yusuf Paşa, and gave him what were then the Feridun Bey Gardens and are now the 500,000-square-meter Emirgan Woods. For a long time, the sultan and noble remained friends and passed many a drunken night together in the gardens which are described in lyrical terms by the contemporary Ottoman traveler **Evliya Çelebi**. After Murad's death, his successor **Sultan İbrahim I** had Yusuf executed. In the 19th century **Sultan Abdülaziz** gave the woods to the Egyptian **Khedive İsmail Paşa** (1830-1895) who built himself a seaside palace and then adorned the garden with Sarı (the Yellow), Beyaz (White) and Pembe (Pink) pavilions. Forced to abdicate under pressure from the French and British in 1879, İsmail, known as the Magnificent despite running up huge debts for Egypt, lived out the remainder of his days in Emirgan as a **virtual state prisoner**. In 1943 the Istanbul authorities bought the Emirgan Woods and turned them into a public park.

Egyptian Khedive İsmail Paşa

It was Khedive İsmail who commissioned Guiseppe Verdi's opera "Aida" to celebrate the opening of the Suez Canal in 1871.

White Pavilion

The pavilions (köşks)

Designed to look like a Swiss hunting lodge by **Sarkis Balyan** in the 1870s, the **Sarı Köşk (Yellow Mansion)** now houses a restaurant and café, while the Neoclassical **Beyaz Köşk (White Mansion)** has a cafe. **Pembe Köşk (Pink Mansion)** was modeled on a townhouse. The oldest of the three, it was restored in 1982 and now hosts – you've guessed it - a café! All three mansions were restored in the 1980s by the Turkish Touring and Automobile Club.

Surp Yerits Mangants Armenian Church

Stained-glass image of Three Holy Children

Boyacıköy

Between Emirgan and Baltalimanı lies the beautiful and barely noticed suburb of Boyacıköy (Dyers' Village), so named because this was where, in the 18th century, a large family of dyers from **Kırklareli** in Thrace were resettled by **Sultan Selim III** to enable them to prepare all the **fezes** needed in the capital. Its pretty back streets conceal the small Armenian **Church of Surp Yerits Mangants (The Three Holy Infants)**, built over an ayazma (sacred spring), which dates back to 1836. It was wholly reconstructed in 1885, and restored again as recently as 2004 even though the congregation is down to the last 10 families.

In Fırın Sokağı stands the Greek Orthodox **Church of Panagia Evangelistria (St Mary)** which dates back to 1834. Round the corner in **Tebdil Eskisi Sokağı** is the attractive double-fronted **schoolhouse** dating back to 1905. With its original cobbles, shady trees and old wooden houses this street looks like a slice of Safranbolu somehow strayed into the metropolis.

Greek Orthodox Primary School

Panagia Evangelistria Greek Orthodox Church

If only the cafes hadn't gotten up so close and personal with the fountain and had given it some space to breathe.

Emirgan Square

Few squares along the Bosphorus are as immediately inviting as Emirgan's where **ancient plane trees** provide shade for a cluster of pretty little **teahouses** right beside a picturesque mosque and a gracefully restored octagonal **fountain** dating back to 1783 and paid for by the wife of **Sultan Abdülhamid I**. There are few better places to while away a few hours in the middle of a hot summer day before heading on to visit the **Sakıp Sabancı Museum** (see p.146), just up the road.

Hamid-i Evvel Mosque

Beautifully restored in 2009, the present mosque was built in 1838 during the reign of **Mahmud II**, but stands on the site of a much older mosque from which only a fountain survives. Jutting out from the side is the room that served as the sultan's private pew, a more prosaic version of the elaborate **hünkar mahfilis** in buildings like the New Mosque. Facing it across the square is what was once the timekeeper's lodge built in 1844 by **Ağa Hüseyin Paşa** (1776-1849), who also paid for the **Serasker fire tower** in Beyazıt.

Hüseyin, Ruler of Mecca

Lawrence of Arabia

Şerifler Yalısı

South of the main square, the graceful 18th-century Şerifler Yalı stands on the probable site of Emir Güne Han's 17th-century palace. Badly damaged and cut off from the water when the coast road was built in 1940, it is still the **oldest surviving yalı** (mansion) on the European shore of the Bosphorus, and belonged at one time to a Şerif (Ruler) of Mecca called **Hüseyin** (1854-1931), who served in the Ottoman parliament before throwing in his lot with **Lawrence of Arabia** in the Arab revolt that led eventually to the creation of Jordan. One son, **Abdullah**, became the Emir of Jordan, while another, **Faisal**, became King of Iraq. In 1924 Şerif Hüseyin proclaimed himself caliph and fled to Cyprus and then Jordan where he eventually died. **Ağa Hüseyin Paşa,** who built the Hamid-i Evvel timekeeper's lodge, also owned the house for a while. It contains fabulous frescoes.

The women's section of the Şerifler Yalı, which was the oldest yalı on the European side of the Bosphorus, was knocked down during the construction of the shore road in 1946. The ceiling decoration of the surviving men's section, seen in this photo, is truly magnificent.

Tulip Festival

The festival has been taking place in Emirgan Woods for decades, but in 2006 Istanbul authorities expanded the idea to take in the rest of the city and remind visitors that tulips originally reached Europe from Turkey and not the other way around. Every winter millions of bulbs are planted, and then in mid-April concerts, exhibitions and other events are organized to coincide with their flowering. The park looks absolutely magnificent at this time, with beds of primulas planted so densely together that they resemble Persian carpets, and the sweet scent of thousands of hyacinths filling the air.

The company operated 79 vessels during its 90 years in business.

The Şirket-i Hayriye (Beneficial Company)

Until the mid-19th century people were ferried about the Bosphorus in slender caiques, with the size and elegance of the boat depending on the importance of its passengers. But gradually the authorities began to think that transporting passengers in caiques was unsafe and the two small steamboats operated by **British** and **Russian** companies proved to be hopelessly insufficient to cope with the rising demand. Thus was born the idea of the Şirket-i Hayriye, a ferry company that was to transform life in the Bosphorus villages.

Supported by **Keçecizade Fuad Bey** and **Ahmed Cevdet Bey, Reşid Paşa** presented **Sultan Abdülmecid** with a plan to establish a company that would carry both passengers and freight up and down the Bosphorus. This company was established in 1851 and was named the **Şirket-i Hayriye** as if to foretell how vital it would become. A delay in the arrival of the first six paddle steamers ordered from England meant that Turkey's first incorporated company didn't actually commence business until 1854. The first captains were salty mariners who could ply the waters of the Bosphorus in their sleep while the ship's crews were generally recruited from the minority populations. The first actual Turkish captain was **Rıza Ömer** of **Beykoz**.

The original services between **Eminönü** and the **European shore** were gradually expanded to include Üsküdar, and the Şirket-i Hayriye was soon contributing greatly to local life. Residents of Istanbul became acquainted with the villages along the Bosphorus, increasing their trade with them and commuting to and from these settlements more frequently. As new services opened and demand steadily increased, the Şirket-i-Hayriye constructed new piers and opened more ticket offices. Dining and entertainment were also laid on, and unforgettable voices such as those of **Denizkızı** ('the Mermaid') **Eftalya** and **Hazım Bey (Körmükçü)** were heard on board.

During the **Italo-Turkish, Balkans** and **First World** wars the state commandeered the steamboats to transport soldiers and supplies although a few dilapidated vessels were still in service when hostilities ended. Until 1929 all the ferries were imported; after that they were built in the **Golden Horn** shipyards.

In 1944 the Şirket-i Hayriye was nationalized, thus bringing to a close a colorful chapter in the history of private enterprise in Turkey.

All the ferryboats were numbered – the 76 in this photo was Sarıyer.

17

Behind The Horse

Sakıp Sabancı Museum

In a superb location high up in a sloping garden on the shores of the Bosphorus close to Emirgan Woods, the Sakıp Sabancı Museum is one of Turkey's finest privately owned museums, with a small permanent collection and a regular program of high-profile touring shows.

Opened in 2002, the Sakıp Sabancı Museum is housed inside an imposing white mansion also known as the Atlı Köşk (Horse Mansion) because of the prominent **statue of a horse** that stands near the gate. It occupies land which **Sultan Abdülmecid** gave to the **Khedive Mehmed Ali Paşa** in the 19th century, and which was later bought by another Egyptian prince who rebuilt the crumbling mansion that stood on it. This came to be known as the Prince Mehmed Ali Hasan Mansion after its new owner, and it was this mansion, complete with its furnishings, that businessperson **Hacı Ömer Sabancı** bought in 1951. On his death in 1966 his son Sakıp moved into the house which remained the family home of one of Turkey's most important families of industrialists until 1998. Apart from the permanent collections, the Sakıp Sabancı Museum hosts regular blockbuster exhibitions, for example, of works of Picasso and Dali.

@sakipsabancimuzesi, Tel: 0212 277 22 00,
www.muze.sabanciuniv.edu
Closed Mondays

One of the sitting rooms

Mae West's lips at Salvador Dali exhibition

The Rooms

Inside the house three ground-floor rooms retain the grandiose 18th and 19th-century **furnishings** in use when this was a Sabancı family home as well as paintings by well-known artists. One sitting room contains a 19th-century Hereke carpet, a Bohemian crystal chandelier, and portraits of Ömer Sabancı and his wife by Bedri Koraman. The hall and stairwell are decorated with seascapes by **Fausto Zonaro** (1854-1929), while a second sitting room contains two paintings of young girls by the last caliph **Abdülmecid Efendi** (1868-1944), and pictures by the Russian artist **Ivan Konstantinovic Ayvazovski** (1817-1900). The corridor features a series of prints of the sultans commissioned by **Sultan Selim III** who had been impressed by the propaganda value of European royal portraiture. They were made in London in 1814 by **John Young** after originals by **Konstantin Kapıdağlı** whose works are also on display in Topkapı Palace.

Rodin'in bir heykeli

The Koran in miniature

One of the museum's prize exhibits is a tiny leather-bound Koran written in 1635 and measuring only 3.5 by 2.2 centimeters, making it too small to be read by the naked eye.

Young Girl Carrying a Pumpkin, by Fausto Zonaro, 1889

The paintings

The museum also contains a fine collection of 19th and 20th-century paintings, including works by the Turkish orientalist artist Osman Hamdi Bey. Other artists represented include Süleyman Seyyid (1842-1913), Hüseyin Avni Lifij (1886-1927), Halil Paşa (1852-1939) and Fikret Mualla (1903-1967).

The Byzantine Horse

The statue of a horse that stands in front of the museum is a copy of one of those from **aquadriga** (chariot group) that used to stand in the **Hippodrome** before it was stolen by the **Fourth Crusaders** in 1204 and removed to Venice. After admiring it while on a business trip, Sakıp Sabancı had it copied to adorn his garden. The original bronze horses had been brought to Constantinople from Chios in Greece in the 5th century.

The calligraphy

The museum also contains a fine collection of Turkish **calligraphy** spanning a 500-year period, including several lovely old **Korans** and many imperial *tuğras* (monograms) and *fermans* (decrees), some of them dating back to the 15th century. Look out in particular for the work of **Şeyh Hamdullah of Amasya** (1433-1520), who was a teacher of Sultan Beyazıd II, and of **Ahmed Karahisari** (1468-1556), who worked at the court of **Sultan Süleyman the Magnificent**. Striking, too, are the *hilyes*, curious calligraphic pictures used to describe the physical attributes of the Prophet Mohammed according to a pattern designed by Hafız Osman in the 17th century.

Calligraphy collection

A second bronze horse positioned in front of the villa was brought here from the Mahmud Paşa Villa (today's Kadıköy Girl's High School) in Moda.

The Garden

The garden contains fine old fountains, and other marble pieces dating back to Roman and Byzantine times. A second bronze **horse** also stands just in front of the museum building; French-made, it was brought here from its original home in Moda (see p.201). From the garden terrace it is possible to gaze across the Bosphorus to **Çubuklu** and the conspicuous flat-topped tower of the **Khedive's Villa** (see p.320).

Bosphorus view from the garden

18

Best of the Yalıs
İstinye and **Yeniköy**

Continuing along the shore of the Bosphorus you come to the largest and certainly one of the prettiest bays at İstinye, and then, beyond that, to the upscale suburb of Yeniköy which is renowned for its fine yalıs, or waterside mansions. Neither suburb has any specific tourist attractions, although they make perfect places to while away a few peaceful hours on a sunny afternoon. The newly-built "castle" that has housed the American Consulate since 2003 is hardly an improvement to the scenery.

İstinye Bay

İstinye

İstinye is said to take its name from a footnote in the tale of **Jason and the Argonauts** (see p.11), it being a possible corruption of the Greek name Sosthenion (Thanksgiving). According to the story, the Argonauts paused here to erect a statue in gratitude for the help given to the hero **Polydeuces** in defeating **Amycus**, the son of Poseidon and king of the Bebryces, who was in the habit of challenging all comers to box with him. Since he used nail-studded gloves he normally succeeded in killing them, but on this occasion he had met his match. A big and attractive bay, it was for many years used as a **dry dock** (hence the bus stop labeled Tersane (Shipyard)), but is now happily full of pleasure boats again.

The ferryboat lines, which have been run between İstinye and Çubuklu to ease the traffic problems since 2017, offer you an escape from the rush in the city and you can enjoy the view.

İstinye Hamam

Opposite the Neslişah Hanım Sultan Mosque, this hamam is one of the few along the Bosphorus and is thought to date back to immediately before or after the conquest of Constantinople in 1453. It has long since lost its women's section but still opens daily for men.

Istanbul Stock Exchange (IMKB)

No. 71 - The Halas

While many countries carefully maintain their old boats, those of the **Şirket-i Hayriye** were casually scrapped. However, a man named **Haldun Simavi** managed to rescue No. 71, the Halas, from such a fate, before restoring it and putting it to use for touristic purposes. He eventually sold it to late **Mustafa Koç** and his wife **Caroline**.

In 2011, the designer **Merzuka İmrahor** contributed towards the renovation of its interior, playing up nostalgia for bygone days. Nowadays, the Halas is tied up next to the **Deli Fuad Paşa Yalı**, awaiting lucky guests. Otherwise, I can only lament all the other boats that disappeared without a trace.

The Halas in the old days.

The Halas in 2012.

Deli (Crazy) Fuad Paşa Yalı

In İstinye the **Deli (Crazy) Fuad Paşa Yalı** was home to Fuad Paşa (1835-1931), a fearless fighter in the **Russo-Turkish War** and a notoriously plain speaker, hence his nickname. Later he plotted against **Sultan Abdülhamid II** and was sent into **exile** in Damascus. It now houses the offices of Turkey's delegation to BSEC, the Black Sea Economic Cooperation Organization.

The mansion on the hill at the far left belongs to Şehzade Burhaneddin Efendi Yalı.

Yeniköy

Immediately to the east of İstinye is **Yeniköy**, the Greek Neohorion which eventually became Nihori and was later Turkified into Yeniköy (New Town). This is a part of town where many rich and famous people, including Tansu Çiller, who was Turkey's first female prime minister, live in magnificent mansions with security systems that wouldn't look amiss in downtown Lagos.

Don't miss the tall and graceful **Mihrişah Valide Sultan Fountain** in the park. It dates back to 1805 and was completely renovated in 2008.

Cavafy's ancestors

The famous Greek poet Constantine Cavafy's mother Hariklia was born in Yeniköy/Nihori and married there at age 14.

Mihrişah Valide Sultan Fountain

Churches, a synagogue and a mosque

On the hillside above Yeniköy's Villa Park, at the northern end of town, stands the wood-faced, Gothic-style Armenian **Church of Surp Hovhannes Mıgırdıç**.

Behind it are the 19th-century Greek **Orthodox Churches of Hagios Georgios** and **Nikolaos**, with a rotting schoolhouse close by. The **Church of Panagia**, dating back to 1837 and with a detached belltower, stands on a slope in the center of Yeniköy just north of Simitçi Salih Sokağı which is lined with picturesque wooden houses.

Yeniköy's small and inconspicuous **synagogue** right in the center of the suburb was built in 1870 by **Abraham Kamondo** who had a summer home here.

The first **Osman Reis Mosque** was built here in 1635-1636 but nothing now remains of it. In 1904 a small new version in the First National Architectural style was built. It stands on the main road in front of the **Afif Ahmed Yalı**.

Surp Hovhannes Mıgırdıç Church

Hagios Nikolaos Greek Orthodox Church

Greek Primary School

Hagios Georgios Church

Panagia Church

Osman Reis Mosque

Yeniköy Synagogue

Of the city's many Greek schools, today only three high schools (Zapyon, Zoğrafyon and Fener) and one primary school are still accepting pupils.

Yeniköy *Yalıs*

ثروت فنون

SERVET-I-FUNOUN

Illustration Ottomane paraissant le Jeudi

AHMED IHSAN

ISMAIL SOUBHI

19me Année — № 976

A page from the newspaper Servet-i Fünun.

Vaniköy, Kandilli, Kanlıca and Arnavutköy aside, Yeniköy retains the largest number of original yalıs, the oldest of them the **Dadyan Yalısı**, built in the late 18th century for the Armenian family in charge of the gunpowder works in Ataköy. Most are hidden from casual sightseers behind lofty walls. The best way to catch a glimpse of them is from a boat on the Bosphorus.

Recaizade Mahmud Ekrem Bey Yalı

The very first building after the İstinye ferry terminal is the **Recaizade Ekrem Bey Yalı**. Recaizade Ekrem Bey (1847-1914) was an important author, and a member of the literary group called **Edebiyat-ı Cedide** (New Literature) around **Tevfik Fikret** who published a magazine called "Servet-i Fünun" (The Wealth of Knowledge). The same family also had a yalı in Vaniköy (see p.269).

The Recaizade Mahmud Ekrem Yalı can be seen near the start of Yeniköy. The writer was forced to abandon the yalı after an informer turned him into Sultan Abdülhamid II.

Faik Bey Yalı

Next to the Recaizade Ekrem Bey Yalı, the **Faik Bey Yalı**, also called "Pakize Hanımefendi Yalı", was built in the 19th century for a governor of Gümüşhane in north-eastern Turkey.

Ahmed Afif Paşa Yalı

The **Ahmed Afif Paşa Yalı**, built at the end of the 19th century in a style that combines elements of eastern and western architecture by **Alexandre Vallaury**, architect of the Ottoman Bank and Pera Palas Hotel, was later bought by Misbah Muhayyeş, who had owned the Pera Palas. When **Agatha Christie** visited Istanbul to write her famous novel "**Murder on the Orient Express**", she stayed here as a guest. It's now owned by a member of the Sabancı family. The tiny **Osman Reis Mosque** in front of it is another work of Vallaury dating back to 1903. This yalı was acquired for approximately $40 million by the Turkish businessperson **Suzan Sabancı Dinçer** who lives nearby in the **Tahsin Uzer Yalı**.

Ebu Bekir Ratip Yalı

Acquired by the Mısırlı (Egyptian) Ratip Family in 1860, this yalı later became the property of **Osman Mardin** before businessperson and founder of Profilo Holdings **Jak Kamhi** bought it in 1972. Today, Kamhi lives in the modern waterside mansion next to the **Mabeyinci Faik Bey** Yalı (see p.248) in Beylerbeyi.

Selahaddin Adil Paşa Yalı

One previous owner of this yalı, **Emir Zeyd**, was the son of **Ruler of Mekke Hüseyin**, the owner of the **Şerifler Yalı** in Emirgan (see p.141). It then passed to **Selahaddin Adil Paşa** and his wife Siret Hanım. In the 1980s the yalı was acquired by the **Gülçelik Family**, partners in the construction and energy company **ENKA Holdings**.

Tahsin Uzer Yalı

Tahsin Uzer commissioned the architect **Sedad Hakkı Eldem** to build this yalı, with its large garden, which stands on the site of the old **Sağır (Deaf) Ahmed Bey Yalı**. The former owner of the Tercüman newspaper **Kemal Ilıcak** later sold it to **Erol Aksoy**, the owner of İktisat Bank. The building proved unlucky for him. When Aksoy declared bankruptcy, the yalı was acquired at auction by businessperson **Suzan Sabancı Dinçer** who also owns Ahmed Afif Paşa Yalı in previous page.

Madenci Arif Bey Yalı

Constructed in an eclectic style, this yalı originally belonged to **Madenci Arif Bey**. It was subsequently sold to **Süreyya Bey** after whom it is sometimes named. Ali Haydar Bey, the son of Sağır Ahmed Bey who owned the Tahsin Uzer Yalı, became its next owner. It served as the summerhouse of the **Sipahi Ocağı Club**, Turkey's oldest horse-riding club, during the 1920s.

Doktor Hulusi Behçet Yalı

Born in this building that is also known as the Çaycı İstepan Yalı, Dr. **Hulusi Behçet** (1889-1948) graduated from the Military School of Medicine and went on to become a professor. **Behçet disease**, AKA Silk Road disease, was named after him. Fully restored in 2012, it belongs to industrialist **Necati Aslan**'s family.

Rasim Ferid Talay Yalı

This white yalı, distinguished from others by its blue-tinted windows, belongs to former Prime Minister **Tansu Çiller** and her husband **Özer Uçuran Çiller**. In 1918 the original owner Rasim Ferid Talay was co-publisher with Atatürk of Minber, a short-lived political newspaper. The yalı was subsequently acquired by shipowner **Şevket Manioğlu**. It was left to his daughters lyricist **Ayşe Manioğlu** and **Gönül Özdoğan**. When the two sisters could not reach an agreement, it was sold to the Çillers in 1981.

Burhanettin Sezerar Yalı

Sultan Abdülhamid's paranoia meant that electricity didn't arrive in Istanbul until after 1912. A lecturer at Istanbul Technical University, **Professor Burhanettin Sezerar** was the man who finally brought it to several important buildings including the Dolmabahçe Palace. When he died in 1952, Burhaneddin Bey bequeathed the yalı to his son, **Faruk Sait Sezerar**. Now housing a cafe and restaurant, the building can be recognized by the carved balconies running along the water-facing façade.

Şehzade Burhaneddin Efendi Yalı

Şehzade Burhaneddin Efendi Yalı

Acquired for Crown Prince **Burhaneddin Efendi**, the son of **Abdülhamid II**, by his uncle Sultan Abdülaziz in 1912, this 64-room yalı is one of the largest on the Bosphorus with one of the longest waterfronts after the **Amcazade** and **Kıbrıslı** yalıs and a large winter pavilion in the back garden. Its décor reflects the taste of the crown prince. Burhaneddin Efendi left Istanbul after **World War I**, settling in New York where he died in 1949. He was father to Ertuğrul Osman Efendi (1912-2009), known as "the Last Ottoman", who is buried on Divanyolu in Sultanahmet. Once **Mısırlı (Egyptian) Ahmed İhsan Bey** bought the yalı, it was also known as the **Mısırlılar Yalı**. The current owners sold it up for $150 million, to a Qatari family.

Hall

From the hall two staircases lead to the first floor.

Saip Özden Yalı

Constructed by an Istanbul Greek in 1851, this yalı was subsequently sold to the Özden family and then to Murat Soner. Featuring large windows on every floor, the building reflects European architecture rather than the prevalent Bosphorus style.

Gazioğlu, Beyazcıyan ve Kara Todori Paşa Yalı

On the far right the **Kara Todori Yalı** was constructed by **Sarkis Balyan** in 1871, using materials left over from the building of the Çırağan Palace (see p.100). It belonged to Alexandros Todori, the son of the Stefenos Todori, director of Turkey's first medical school. It (Kara Todori) is currently owned by **Naciye Koçak**. The Beyazcıyan Yalı (center) is owned by **İzzet Bayraktar**, while the Muzaffer Gazioğlu Yalı (left) is owned by **Mehmet Rüştü Başaran**, owner of HABAŞ, a company with a finger in many pies.

Mısırlı Fuad Bey Yalı

This yalı belongs to the owner of the Son Havadis (Latest News) newspaper, Mustafa Özkan.

Said Halim Paşa Yalı

In 1863 the Aristarhis family paid for a large yalı on the site of an older building. This was later bought by Mehmed Abdülhalim Paşa who commissioned **Petraki Adamantini**, a Çanakkale architect, to rebuild it on a grander scale. When he died one of his sons, **Sait Halim**, bought out the shares of his eight siblings to take over the property. Sait Halim was a Grand Vizier from 1913 to 1917. Despite his efforts to keep the Empire neutral during World War I, it was in his yalı that the Young Turks signed an **agreement with Germany** in 1914 that resulted in Turkey joining the First World War on their side. Later Sait Halim was **exiled** to Malta; he was **assassinated** in Rome in 1921. Sometimes called the Pembe Aslan Yalı (Mansion of the Pink Lions) because of the statues in front of it, the Sait Halim Paşa Yalı burnt down in 1995 and has since been rebuilt to serve as a popular venue for society wedding parties.

One of the grand meeting rooms

There are splendid Bosphorus views from some of the rooms.

An elegant staircase links the two floors.

The photographs of the Said Halim Paşa Yalı were taken by Sinan Doğan.

İhmalyan Yalı

Does this yalı's bad luck stem from its name, which means 'son of neglect' in Turkish? Once owned by **Eyüp Paşa**, it was acquired by **Parsık Ihmalyan** and offers a fine view from its top-floor cihannüma. It is right beside Yeniköy Pier and has stood stood empty for years.

İhmalyan Yalısı

Faik ve Bekir Bey Yalı

The **Faik and Bekir Bey Yalı**, to the right of the Yeniköy ferry terminal, was designed in 1906 by the Italian architect, **Raimondo d'Aronco** who was responsible for the summer residence of the Italian Consulate in Tarabya. As it was built for the twin daughters of Sara Sultan, it was also called the "Twins' Mansion". It was later sold in two separate parts, called the Faik Bey Yalı and Bekir Bey Yalı respectively.

Ali Rıza Paşa Yalı

Constructed by a French family in the late 1870s, this yalı was sold to the army cartographer, Ali Rıza Paşa, who had trained in France. In 1935 he bequeathed it to his daughter, **İclal Karakaptan**, the first woman in the Turkish Republic to gain a doctorate in economics.

Sandoz Yalı

The Surp Hovhannes Mıgırdıç Armenian Catholic church can be seen peeping out from behind the Kalkavan Yalı.

The Austrian Consulate

On the northern outskirts of Yeniköy as it merges into Kalender, the vast Austrian consulate was originally housed in a building called the **Cezayirliyan Yalı** which was given by Sultan Abdülhamid II to the Austro-Hungarian Emperor **Franz-Joseph I** in 1883 at a time when gifts of desirable real estate were seen as a good way to consolidate political alliances.

Franz Joseph I

At the end of the First World War most of its contents were sold to provide funds for citizens of the defeated empire to return home. It was briefly owned by the **British**, before being returned to the Austrians and then given to the Germans during the Second World War. Today the wheel has come full circle and it once again houses the **Austrian Consulate and Cultural Center**.

The Said İbrahim Yalı stands beside the Austrian Consulate.

Some of the yalıs have been turned into apartments.

From left to right, the Sandoz, Dadyan and Hamapulos yalıs standing side by side in Yeniköy Harbor.

19

A Place Called Therapy

Kalender, Tarabya and Kireçburnu

The further along the Bosphorus you travel, the leafier it becomes. At Kalender you can pause to admire the enormous Huber Yalı, then round the bend you arrive in Tarabya, a huge and beautiful bay whose loveliness is diminished only by presence of the ugly Grand Tarabya Hotel. This was where many of the European embassies supported summer establishments so that their staff could escape the suffocating heat of the inner city. The pleasant restaurants suggest that many people are still seeking escape here today.

An old photograph of Tarabya Harbor

Tiny **Kalender** is sometimes said to have been named after a dervish lodge that used to stand here. However, it is more likely that it took its name from the **summer palace** built in the 17th century by Kalender Çavuş, caretaker of the Sultanahmet Mosque. This was replaced in the 18th century by the **Kalender Garden Palace**, another work of Sultan Ahmed III's busy Grand Vizier **Damat İbrahim Paşa**. Although this was restored in the 19th century, nothing now remains of it bar the garden walls.

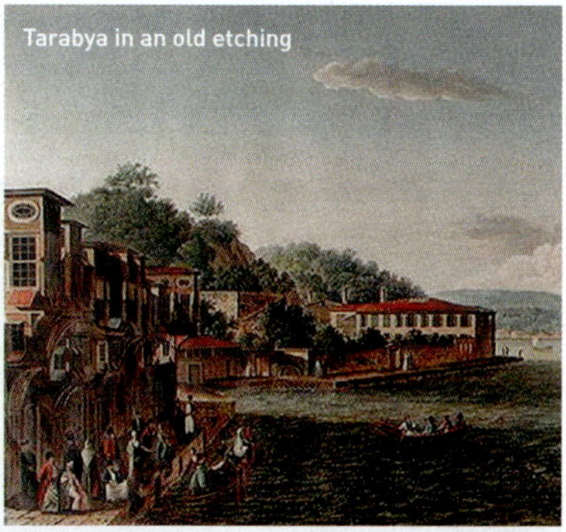
Tarabya in an old etching

The old Huber Mansion is now used as a summer residence for the president.

Auguste Huber's wife

The huge Art Nouveauish Huber Mansion in Kalender, with its wonderful garden, takes its name from its former owner **Auguste Huber** who was the representative of Mauser and Krupp, the company that sold **rifles** to the Ottoman Empire at the end of the 19th century. For some years it was used as a French Catholic girls **school**. Since President Kenan Evren had it renovated in 1985, the mansion has served as a delightful **summer residence** for the presidency. A story claims that the mansion was given as a bribe to the lady-in-waiting of **Empress Eugenie**, the wife of Napoleon III, who was rumored to have had an affair with **Sultan Abdülaziz**. Despite its grandeur, not a great deal is known about the building which may or may not have been a work of **Raimondo d'Aronco**. Tarabya is a much bigger and more impressive place. Its name is said to be a corruption of the Byzantine name Therapeia (Therapy), which some claim had been given to the area because of the **hot springs** with healing properties that could be found here but were apparently destroyed by an earthquake in the 14th century. Others say that Patriarch Attikos gave it the name in the 5th century because of the area's generally **healthy atmosphere**. To confuse matters further, others insist that **Sultan Selim II** bestowed the name on the area after enjoying a fish supper here so much that he had **Grand Vizier Sokullu Mehmed Paşa** build him a palace in the place he dubbed simply "**Tarabiye (Pleasure)**". Tarabya's two Greek Orthodox churches, one of them, at the entrance to the Sümer Woods, dedicated to **Hagia Paraskeve**, and the other to **Hagios Constantinos**, stand as reminders of the large Greek population who used to live here. Tarabya bay is dominated by the high-rise Grand **Tarabya Hotel**. It stands on the site of the summer retreat associated with the historic Tokatlıyan Hotel in Pera that burnt down in 1954.

The old Tokatlıyan Hotel

Summer *Residences*

German Consulate summer residence

In the 18th century several of the **embassies** opened new out-of-town bases in huge houses with gardens in **Büyükdere**. Here their staff could hope to escape the oppressive summer heat. Later Tarabya became a more popular base for the embassies, probably because it was not quite so far away. Many of the **Greeks** from crowded Fener also kept summer homes here, just as some people keep summer houses on the Princes' Islands today. The summer home of the British Embassy burnt down in 1911.

Abdülhamid II passed his adolescence in what later became the summer residence of the **German Consulate** to the south of Tarabya. Later he gave it to **Kaiser Wilhelm II** in return for his re-establishing the Ottoman navy. The mansion was designed by the Belgian architect Cingria who had won a prize in a competition to come up with the best plans. It was restored in 1990 but has lost most of its original internal features. The mansion sits in 45 acres of gardens, and a path through them leads to a small **cemetery** containing 265 graves and an obelisk-shaped war memorial that records the stay of **Sultan Mahmud II** in a military camp here in 1829 and the part played in helping him reform the Ottoman army by **Marshall Helmuth von Moltke the Elder** (1822-1888).

As you head out of Tarabya towards Kireçburnu you'll pass a duo of summer residences. The **Italian Consulate** was housed in a spectacular mansion designed by **Raimondo d'Aronco** and completed in 1908 in a style that mixed and matched Ottoman and Palladian styles of architecture. It was given as a wedding present to **Princess Elena of Montenegro** by Sultan Abdülhamid II, and is currently undergoing particularly slow restoration.

The oldest of the embassies here, the French Embassy had a rather convoluted history. It was housed in a building that had originally belonged to the Phanariot Greek governor of Wallachia, Prince Alexander İpsilanti, who had been executed for treason in 1806. Since the French had helped dissuade the British from attacking Istanbul Sultan Selim III was persuaded to give the building to the Emperor Napoleon Bonaparte. Unfortunately it caught fire in 1913, and only rather mundane portions of the original structure survive.

Kayzer II. Wilhelm

Ural Ataman Classic Car Museum

A stunning collection of 63 vehicles from the days before American car manufacturing hit the bumpers, this small privately-owned museum is only open on Fridays, Saturdays and Sundays but is a great place to bring boys who are tired of historic sightseeing and their dads. It's inland from the coast, across the road from the Metin Oktay sports center.

@uralatamanmuseum
Tel: 0212 299 45 39
www.atamanmuseum.com

Summer residence of the Italian Consulate

There are fine wooden houses along the shore at Kireçburnu.

The poisoner

In antiquity Tarabya appears to have been called Pharmakeus which means "the poisoner" because it was here that **Medea**, abandoned by her lover **Jason** (see p.11), threw away the poison with which she had been intending to kill him. An alternative story claims that a witch poisoned the drinking water as the Argo was sailing past in an attempt to kill its occupants. Her fiendish plot failed because the goddesses Hera and Athene stepped in to clean up the water.

Dikranyan Yalı

Kireçburnu

The promontory just north of Tarabya bay is called Kireçburnu (Lime Point), perhaps because of the past existence of **lime quarries** in the area. But the most important thing about Kireçburnu is that it is here for the first time that you start to be able to see the **Black Sea** straight ahead of you, an enthralling sight were it not for the pylons and electricity wires that disfigure it.

Why Delaware?

As you stroll along the Bosphorus it's impossible not to notice all the Delaware-flagged vessels berthed alongside the promenade. Did they cross the **Atlantic Ocean** just to cruise through the **Bosphorus Strait**, you ask yourself? Delaware may be the second smallest of the 50 US states, but it turns out that 60% of the companies on the Fortune 500 list are registered there because of a corporate tax loophole. Countless vessels either flagged or registered in Delaware cruise the Seven Seas scot free.

Bosphorus obstacles-boats and anglers

While strolling along the Bosphorus you're bound to encounter all sorts of obstacles. In the first place your view may be obscured by the many boats waiting for passengers. More alarmingly, anglers cast their rods in all the best spots, threatening the eyes of passers-by in the process. And that's without mentioning the people who set up smelly barbecues along the shore, let their dogs foul the pavement, and drop litter without a care in the world.

What Happened to the Greeks?

Just as in most of the Bosphorus villages, significant numbers of Greeks used to live in Tarabya. But after the Wealth Tax imposed during the Second World War, the 'Events' of 6-7 September 1955, the deportations of 1963, the Cyprus troop landings of 1974, and the coup of 1980, only some 1,200 to 2,500 citizens of Greek origin still live in Istanbul as of 2012. (It's difficult to ascertain how many more have married Muslims, go back and forth to Greece, or have changed their surnames.) This migration was and still is considered a great loss for Turkey, as is the loss of the other minority populations. The city's erstwhile colorful make-up has faded to grey.

In 2012 there were 231 students enrolled in Istanbul's Greek schools, a surprisingly large number for such a small population. It turns out that many **Arab Orthodox** immigrants from around Antakya send their children to these schools and they are obliged to learn the language in order to be enrolled. Were it not for the children of these southeastern Anatolian Christian families that the Greeks look down upon and call '**Arapis**', their schools would close completely. As for the Greek migration, we will end with a poem entitled 'Leaving Therapia,' which was written in 1882 by the Greek poet, **Constantine Cavafy**, whose mother was born in Yeniköy (see p. 153).

Leaving Therapia

Good-bye to Therapia and the joys of the hotel, Good dinners that make you exultingly swell, Good beds that refresh you from the toil of the day, Fine sights near which you'd wish ever to stay. To all these good things the time is well nigh I must bid a good-bye!

Cavafy's First Poem

When the Cavafy family home was gutted during the British bombardment of Alexandria, Constantine lost his entire library and works. Dated 16 July, 1882, 'Leaving Therapia' is the earliest poem known to survive in his own hand-writing.

The Vikings in Istanbul

During the Byzantine era, the Vikings sailed down the Russian rivers to the Black Sea and thence to Istanbul, which they called **Miklagard** and where they worked for the emperors as mercenaries. It's still possible to pick out the Viking name **Halvdan** on a piece of ninth-century graffiti in the women's gallery of **Hagia Sophia**. The most famous Viking to visit Istanbul was **Harald Hardrada** (1015-1066), the king of Norway and a bodyguard to the emperor. Harald wanted to marry the emperor's niece Maria and abducted her when she refused his proposal. Of course the boat in this photo is not a real Viking longship, but a boat moored at Eminönü from which fried fish sandwiches are sold.

20

Escaping the Heat

Büyükdere and **Sadberk Hanım Museum**

In 1980 Turkey's first privately-owned museum opened in Büyükdere, which comes just before Sarıyer. Resembling a cut-down version of Ankara's Anatolian Civilisations Museum crossed with the Ethnography Museum, it houses the collections of Sadberk Hanım who was the wife of the businessperson Vehbi Koç. Come here to see everything from Ancient Greek pottery to the finest Anatolian embroidery. The museum is housed in two magnificent old yalıs. Several others stand close by.

Promenade of Büyükdere

Büyükdere takes its name from the "büyük dere" (big stream) at the head of the bay where the battalions of the **First Crusade** paused to catch their breath before crossing the Bosphorus into Asia Minor on their way to Palestine in 1096. **Evliya Çelebi** left a breathless description of it as a beautiful wooded place inhabited mainly by Greeks and Armenians in the 17th century. Today, of course, it is very built up, and of the Greeks and Armenians only their churches remain. However, this is still a very charming part of the Bosphorus, where the coast road has been built on reclaimed land a little way in front of the yalıs and where there are still many lovely **wooden houses** surviving in the back streets.

There are many old yalıs and mansions in Büyükdere.

Büyükdere in old photograph

Büyükdere houses

Russian Consulate

Summer retreats

Heading back from the museum towards the center of Büyükdere you come to the magnificent neoclassical summer residence of the **Spanish Consulate** that was built by Franciscan friars and given to the Spaniards in 1783 following a cholera epidemic. It has lost its original gardens to the coast road but acquired in their place some parkland to the rear. The Franciscans also built the **Church of the Immaculate Conception** here in 1866; it's further west, just before the main road running inland rejoins the coast road heading for Tarabya. East of the Sadberk Hanım Museum, what eventually became the **Russian Consulate** was originally built in 1840 for **General Nikolai Ignatiev**, the "shrewd paşa", also known as "the vice-Sultan", who was extremely keen to secure the Bosphorus for the Russians. Since he never succeeded in achieving that his ghost is said to haunt the old consulate building, in any case a sad sight today with its black and white pebble-mosaic path leading through an overgrown garden to an abandoned building.

Spanish Consulate

Greek Primary School and its old sign

Surp Boğos Church

Churches

Originally built as an Armenian Catholic chapel in 1847, the **Church of Surp Boğos**, near the Spanish Consulate, was expanded into a Gothic-style church in 1893; it wouldn't look out of place in Britain or France. A little further inland, the Greek Orthodox **Church of Hagia Paraskeve** stands on the site of a church dating back to the early 17th century. The current model may be far more modern but it stands in a particularly pretty **cobbled courtyard** shaded with huge trees. The old **schoolhouse** with which it was once associated stands derelict at the top of the stairs behind it.

Church of the Immaculate Conception

Hagia Paraskeve Greek Orthodox Church

Ceramics collection in museum

Sadberk Hanım Museum

If this marvelous small museum were in Sultanahmet, it would be heaving with visitors. As it is you may well find you have it to yourself.

The museum is housed inside what was originally the wooden **Azaryan Yalı** built at the start of the 20th century by Manuk Azaryan Efendi who was a member of parliament towards the end of the Ottoman era. It was sometimes called the **Vidalı (Criss-crossed) Yalı** because of the wooden latticework on its façade. In the 1950s the Koç family bought the mansion and turned it into a family home. In 1980 it opened to the public as Turkey's first private museum, expanding to incorporate the next door yalı in 1988.

The original building contains collections related to **Turkish and Islamic art,** and **Ottoman Turkish life**, while the second building houses the **archeological collections** arranged in chronological order. In the first section the rooms set up to show off the rituals associated with circumcision and engagement as well as what the bedroom of a new mother would have looked like are particularly interesting. Also wonderful are the exquisite samples of embroidery, the colorful Ottoman clothing, and some delicate examples of 18th-century **oya** (the embroidery stitched around the edge of women's headscarves) amongst which those shaped like pansies are especially lovely. The museum also houses one of the finest collections of 16th-century **İznik pottery** in the country. Be sure, too, to take a look at the **Beykoz glass** originally produced at the glass-making works on the opposite side of the Bosphorus (see p.328).

Normally the museum also showcases artworks typical of the Selçuk, Mameluk, Safavid and other Islamic styles. However, these are sometimes sidelined in favor of temporary exhibitions. Check Instagram for details.

The archeological section in the Sevgi Gönül wing contains exhibits dating from **Neolithic through to Byzantine times** and includes some wonderful cuneiform tablets, Phrygian bowls, glass perfume bottles, coins and gold jewellery as well as a fine collection of Roman lamps, some of them carved with scenes that are very naughty indeed. Most of the exhibits were collected by the late Hüseyin Kocabaş, although Sevgi Gönül, the daughter of Sadberk Koç, was also responsible for recovering many items that had been removed from the country illegally.

This is a state-of-the-art museum in which every-thing is beautifully presented, with English labeling and explanations to supplement the Turkish. There's an excellent giftshop on the ground floor along with a **tea garden** in the secluded back garden.

@sadberkhanimmuzesi
Tel: 0212 242 38 13
www.sadberkhanimmuzesi.org.tr
Closed Wednesdays

The museum showcases everything from Ancient Greek pottery to old Anatolian embroidery.

Who was Sadberk Hanım?

Sadberk Hanım (1908-1973) was the wife of the hugely successful Turkish businessperson, Vehbi Koç, and an enthusiastic collector, especially of historic fabrics and embroidery. Sadly, she died before she could see the museum that was her dream open its doors.

Floatplanes

Did you know that there were flights from Turkey to Italy in 1924? And with floatplanes that took off from the Harbor of Büyükdere! The flights that were scheduled on two main courses (Istanbul-Athens-Brindisi and Istanbul-Athens-Rhodes) between 1924-1936 were carried out by the Italian Aero Espresso Airlines. The Dornier Wal planes with the passenger capacity of 10 were flown by Turkish and Italian pilots.

Fuat Paşa Yalı

Housed inside a late 18th-century yalı, the 56-room hotel takes its name from a later owner, **Keçecizade Fuat Paşa**, who was a grand vizier to Sultan Abdülaziz in the late 19th century. Not as glitzy as some of its more recently refurbished competitors, the Fuatpaşa still has history and Bosphorus views.

Kocataş ve Sait Paşa Yalıları

Kocataş Mansion, built in the 19th century, was bought by **Necmettin Molla Kocataş**, who served as the Minister of Justice and Deputy Vizier in the Ottoman Government. The neighbouring Sait Paşa Mansion was commissioned by **Mehmet Sait Paşa**, who was the Grand Vizier of Abdulhamid II in the second constitutional era. Both mansions are revived today with the modern touches of Six Senses, while paying regard to their original architecture.

21

Shrine of the Silver Saint

Sarıyer, Rumeli Kavağı, Garipçe and Rumeli Feneri

Towards the far end of the European shore of the Bosphorus lies the bustling suburb of Sarıyer. It still retains something of the feel of a place apart, and is one of many places to come to dine on a fine fish supper. Some people come here to visit the shrine of Telli Baba just outside Sarıyer. Beyond it lie much smaller Garipçe, Rumeli Kavağı and Rumeli Feneri, after which the Bosphorus opens out onto the splendid vista of the Black Sea.

There is some debate as to how Sarıyer got its name which means simply "**yellow place**" in Turkish. Some say that it took it from a yellow-hued local soil, others that Sarıyer is a corruption of Sarıyar meaning "**blonde beloved**", a name it had acquired in memory of one of the sultans' favorites. Yet others suggest that it was named after a local holy man, **Sarı Baba**, about whom nothing is known. Then there is a suggestion that it was named after two **blond soldiers** (sarı erler) associated with Sultan Mehmed II and buried near a town center mosque. In desperation some people have even suggested that it acquired the name because it was a place where people spent many **yellow (gold) coins**. A surprisingly conservative backwater which has acquired a sizeable population of expatriate Iranians and Arabs in recent years, Sarıyer still retains a **fishing fleet** with the accompanying fish market and restaurants serving an array of fresh fish dishes. Right beside the quay a turreted building dating back to 1911 houses the **Naval Officers' Club**; other fine if forgotten buildings lurk in the back streets, including one now owned by Kızılay that must be amongst the finest wooden mansions in all Istanbul. Amid the lovely old wooden buildings hidden in the back streets of **Yeni Mahalle** there is a 19th-century church dedicated to **Hagios Ioannis Prodromos (St John the Baptist)**, although it no longer offers regular services. Above Yeni Mahalle there are great Bosphorus views from **Havantepe**.

Sarıyer Ordu Evi (Army House)

Hagios Ioannis Church

Mansion belonging to Red Crescent

Shrine of Telli Baba

Heading up the Bosphorus towards Rumeli Kavağı you pass the tomb of **İmam Abdullah Efendi**, better known as Telli Baba, an **evliya** or holy man who is thought to be able to help the single find husbands or wives. When pilgrims leave the shrine they take away a piece of **silver wire** which they return to attach to it once they are securely married. The shrine is so popular that whole wedding parties often visit it as part of their celebrations. In the past local fisherman also sought Telli Baba's intercession to protect them on their voyages.

Not much seems to be known about Telli Baba, and the two stories most commonly told about him belong to two completely different periods in time. According to the first, he fought alongside **Sultan Mehmed II** at the conquest of Istanbul in 1453, while according to the second, he was fighting alongside **Sultan Mahmud II** when Cossacks attacked Rumeli Kavağı in the 19th century. He is thought to have been a dervish who established a lodge on the site where his shrine now stands. He may have been a member of the Qadiri sect who adorned their turbans with the same sort of silver threads as were used to decorate bridal veils, hence his nickname Telli Baba (Silver-Threaded Father).

Wooden house overlooking Sarıyer harbor

Bird watcher's paradise

The far end of the Bosphorus is one of the best places in the world for spotting **raptors** as they pass over on their way to and from their winter homes in Africa. To cite just one example, around 40,000 **lesser spotted eagles** pass this way every year, although **common and honey buzzards, marsh harriers** and **steppe eagles** are also familiar sights. The best times and places to observe the birds are at **Rumeli Feneri** in spring, and at **Toygar Hill** in Beykoz, **Otağtepe (Tent Hill)** (sea p.306) in **Kavacık** and **Çamlıca Hill** in autumn.

Rumeli Feneri with Third Bosphorus Bridge behind it.

On the opposite shore Yoros Castle at Anadolu Kavağı can just be seen

Rumeli Kavağı

This last stopping place for the public ferries on the European side of the Bosphorus is little more than a cluster of houses and fish restaurants attached to a fishing harbor, a great place to stop for lunch. Rumeli Kavağı might have been named after the **poplar trees** (kavak) that used to grow here, although it is much more likely that it acquired its name from the secondary meaning of "kavak", which is "control point". Certainly there has been a castle, **İmroz Kalesi**, on the hillside here since the 12th century when Manuel I Comnenos built it to enable him to levy **tolls** on passing ships. This was later occupied first by the Genoese and then by the Ottomans, before **Sultan Murad IV** turned the whole area into a military base to guard the mouth of the Bosphorus.

Garipçe

In ancient times Garipce was **Gyropolis (City of Vultures)**, a place closely associated with the gods of the winds. It may have acquired its modern name as a corruption of "Karibce", meaning "quite near" in Turkish, because of its proximity to the lighthouse at Rumeli Feneri. Today it is little more than a pretty, secluded fishing harbor with a couple of rickety wooden houses interspersed with fish restaurants, and the remains of a castle dating back to 1778, although plans to site the third Bosphorus bridge here would completely destroy its tranquility. Unfortunately, once the abutment of the 3rd Bosphorus Bridge was built here, the place has lost its unspoiled beauty.

Rumeli Feneri

There has been a lighthouse at Rumeli Feneri (European Lighthouse) since at least the 16th century. Just off-shore are a pair of rocks – Kocataş (Great Stone) and Körtaş (Blind Stone) – which the Ottomans called the **Kanlı Kayalar (Bloody Rocks)** because of the hazard they presented to shipping. To the Ancient Greeks these were the Symplegades between which Jason and the Argonauts managed to sail en route to finding the Golden Fleece (see p.11). The current 30-meter-tall **lighthouse** here was built in 1769 and modernized by the British during the Crimean War in 1856. It forms a pair with the one across the Bosphorus at **Anadolu Feneri**. Out on the headland are the remains of a twin-towered castle dating back to 1550 and offering fine views of the Black Sea and the Symplegades from its arched exterior wall.

Rumeli Feneri on the Bosphorus, by Jean Laurens, 1853

Castle

The 3rd Bosphorus Bridge at the mouth of the Black Sea

THE BOSPHORUS

(Asian Shore)

22

Ancient Chalcedon

Kadıköy and **Moda**

Hard though it is to imagine it today, Kadıköy was once a completely separate settlement gazing at Byzantium across the water. This was the Chalcedon of the Megarians which was founded in c. 635 BC, but fell to the Turks long before Byzantium. Of all the suburbs on the Asian side of the city, today's Kadıköy has to be one of the liveliest, with a large student population and plenty of nightlife opportunities especially along its famous "Bar Street". Adjoining Moda is one of Asian Istanbul's glitziest residential suburbs.

Kadıköy shoreline

Arriving by ferry in Kadıköy (the Village of the Judge), its attractions are not immediately obvious – you will find yourself stranded in a shapeless concrete plaza facing onto what looks like an unbroken line of high-rise shop and apartment blocks. The sole building of distinction is the low-rise **Old Market Building (Eski Hal Binası)** on the right which was built to house a wholesale market in the 1920s but is now home to the **Istanbul Conservatory**. Still, appearances can be deceptive, and you only have to delve down the side streets behind the high-rises to find narrow pedestrianized streets lined with interesting shops, enticing restaurants and lively bars that cater to a large local student population; it's a bit like Beşiktaş but with heavy metal T-shirts and attitude. Here, too, are a number of small, discreet churches dating back to the 19th century. 1

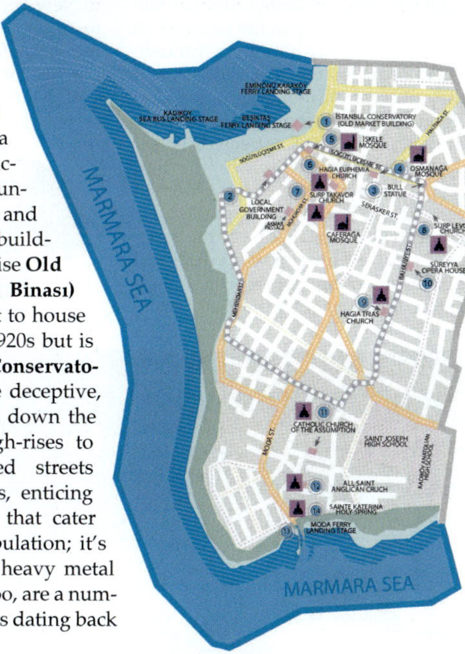

Kadıköy harbor in old photo

Kadıköy is within handy walking or ferry distance of **Haydarpaşa station**, the imposing, German-designed terminal for train services to Asia. To the right of the Eski Hal Binası an unusual **statue of Atatürk** commemorates the changeover from writing Turkish in the Arabic script to writing it using the Roman alphabet in 1928. A huge step forward in enabling ordinary people to learn to read and write, the change had the unintended consequence of cutting Republican Turks off from Ottoman history which was sealed in the archives in suddenly mysterious Ottoman Turkish. Just behind the statue, you will see one of the most important monuments of the **First National Architectural Movement**. It was designed to be used as the Istanbul Şehremaneti Branch (the first municipal organization of the Ottoman period) by the Istanbulite Armenian architect **Yervant Terzian**, one of the assistants of **Giulio Mongeri**, who designed numerous monuments for Istanbul. It is almost identical with the building of the Fatih Municipality, another work by Terziyan. The pier building (Beşiktaş ferry Quay) and Istanbul Şehremaneti Branch were built on a landfill area publicly known as Kumluk. Now it serves as **Kadıköy History, Literature and Art Library** since 2014. It also functioned as **Kadıköy Mayor's Office** and underwent a thorough restoration in 1995. Amid the maze of busy shopping streets there are a couple of landmark monuments to look out for. Just as Wall Street in New York has its monumental bull, so too does Kadıköy. Watch out, too, for the monumental slab with a tiny crocodile perched on the corner and use it to get your bearings inside the market. 2 3

Kadıköy ferry terminal

On the right the Old Market building as it was in the past; on the left how it is now

The Land of the Blind

Fable has it that Byzas, the founder of Byzantium, was advised by the famous oracle of Apollo at Delphi in Greece to build his new town opposite "the Land of the Blind". Arriving at the point where the Golden Horn and Bosphorus met the Sea of Marmara, Byzas gazed across at Chalcedon and decided that its inhabitants must have been blind not to have recognized the advantages of this location as opposed to their preferred spot in Asia. So in 667 BC he went ahead and founded Byzantium on the site that went on to become Constantinople and Istanbul. More than 2,000 years later that inveterate Ottoman travel writer Evliya Çelebi retorted that the truly blind had to have been those who settled across the water and didn't recognize the beauty of Kadıköy!

The Kadıköy crocodile

Deep in the bazaar you may come across a slab of inscribed stone with a tiny bronze statue of a crocodile in the corner. Believe it or not, the 1st-century geographer **Strabo** recorded that people would feed the crocodiles at a spring a little inland from Chalcedon!

The Kadıköy shoreline is a favorite with young people.

Kadıköy History, Literature and Art Library

Kadıköy Market

Churches 6 7 8 9

Facing the small square adorned with the sculpture of a crocodile is the best known of Kadıköy's Christian places of worship, the Greek Orthodox **Church of Hagia Euphemia** that started life in 1694, although the current building only dates back to 1830. As the story goes, Hagia (Saint) Euphemia was a local Christian who rejected the governor's instructions to pray to a pagan god. For her obstinacy she was tortured, before being thrown to a bear in c. 305. Later, it was believed that her spirit intervened at the **Fourth Ecumenical Council**, held in Chalcedon in 451, when two groups of Christians were unable to agree on whether Jesus was possessed of one or two natures. Following her intervention, the Council ruled that Jesus was both wholly man and wholly god (i.e. that he had two natures), a distinction that may seem unimportant today but was, in the fifth century, as contentious as arguments over gay priests today. Hagia Euphemia's remains were removed to Constantinople during the **Persian invasion of Chalcedon** in the seventh century. Today a casket purportedly containing her remains can be seen in the church of the Greek Patriarchate in **Fener** (see p.232). A late 19th-century painting of the Council of Chalcedon can be seen in the narthex.

Nearby is the Armenian **Church of Surp Takavor (Christ the King)**, originally built in the 17th century but only dating back to the late 19th century in its present form. It has a pleasant central dome inset with oval windows.

The basilica-shaped **Church of Surp Levon (St Leo)**, at the start of Bahariye Caddesi, is unusual in that it is an Armenian Catholic church, the sole example in Anatolian Istanbul. The current building dates back only to 1911 although there is believed to have been an older wooden church on the site.

Finally, not far from "Bar Street" in Hacı Şükrü Sokak is the huge **Church of Hagia Trias (the Holy Trinity)**, which dates back to 1902 and boasts an especially colorful dome.

Hagia Euphemia Greek Orthodox Church

Surp Levon Armenian Catholic Church

Hagia Trias Greek Orthodox Church

Surp Takavor Armenian Church

Hemdat İsrael Synagogue

Synagogue

Kadıköy's only synagogue, the **Hemdat Israel (The Thanks of Israel)**, stands between İzzettin and Uzun Hafız Sokaks, a little inland and uphill from the harbor. It dates back to 1899 when many Jews moved into Kadıköy after a fire devastated nearby Kuzguncuk (see p.228).

Mosques 4 5

Unlike nearby Üsküdar, which is dominated by Islamic religious buildings, Kadıköy's mosques keep a relatively low profile. The oldest of them, the low-slung **Osman Ağa Mosque** on Söğütlüçeşme Caddesi, was built during the reign of Sultan Ahmed I (1603-17) for Mısırlı (Egyptian) Osman Ağa who also paid for the decorative fountain nearby. More obvious as you head into the market from behind the ferry terminal is the **Harbor (İskele) Mosque** that dates back to 1760 but was completely rebuilt in 1858.

Historic Tuesday Market (Tarihi Salı Pazarı)

The Historic Tuesday Market has been moved to Hasanpaşa, effectively in the middle of nowhere. There are free service buses from the site of the Eski (Old) Salı Pazarı behind the Fenerbahçe football stadium, but we think you'd have to be feeling pretty desperate for a cheap T-shirt to endure the queues or the traffic along the way.

Süreyya Opera House

Bahariye Caddesi 10

Süreyya İlmen

Pedestrianized Bahariye Caddesi (officially General Asım Gündüz Caddesi but no one calls it that) is the İstiklal Caddesi of the Asian side of Istanbul with a similar old-fashioned **tram** trundling along it en route to Moda. The most striking monument on the street is the grand **Süreyya Opera House** donated to the city by Süreyya and Adalet İlmen in 1924. This was later converted into a **cinema** but was restored to its original function in 2007. The facade is decorated with carvings of the Muses and masks of tragedy, and comedy and many people will find the elaborate interior more than worth the price of a concert ticket. Beside it stands a modern marble sculpture by **Neslihan Pala** called Vodvil (Vaudeville).

There are masses of cheap, delightful bars and cafes tucked away in the side streets. To find Bahariye Caddesi walk up Söğütlüçeşme Caddesi from the harbor until you reach the statue of the bull and then turn right.

www.sureyyaoperasi.org

Süreyya Opera House

Yeldeğirmeni

Once populated mostly by **Greeks** and **Jews**, Yeldeğirmeni is a neighborhood around the streets which trail down to Kadıköy Rıhtım Street. Its churches and its location as home to the only synagogue in Kadıköy is living proof of this. The **Germans** and **Italians** who came to build the **Haydarpaşa Station** often chose to live in this neighborhood and they built nice buildings to remind us of their history. Throughout the years, particularly during the events of 6-7 September and following the Cyprus Operation, Yeldeğirmeni lost its Greek population. For many years it stayed as an unsafe and uninhabited group of streets just next to Kadıköy. But, particularly because the young population are choosing to live in this neighbourhood in ever increasing numbers, new venues have been opened and it has now reassumed its past glory. As a result of this change, the Kadıköy Municipality opened the **Notre Dame du Rosaire Church**, built in 1895 as a monastery, school and church, as Yeldeğirmeni Art in 2014. The church had been used as a gym during the 1980s but was evacuated after the 1999 earthquake.

Baylan

Baylan stands out with its different style among the modern stores as you walk up from the post office building. This is a very old but quite popular patisserie serving its clients since 1961. Its owner was a Greek person and it changed hands in 2010. It offers a great opportunity to relax in the hubbub of the bazaar and to taste the nostalgic flavours which have been preserved for years.

NIGHTLIFE

For a fun night out head straight for **Kadife Sokak** (AKA Bar Street), a street full of old wooden houses which have been turned into bars each with their own distinctive character. **The Nazım Hikmet Cultural Center** offers a program of music, films and art exhibitions.

Tel: 0216 414 22 39, www.nazimhikmetkultur merkezi.org

Moda in an old postcard

Moda 11 12 13

Facing out towards the Sea of Marmara and the Princes' Islands, Moda is an unexpectedly swish residential neighborhood with some trendy restaurants and bars. Although there may have been a settlement here since Phoenician times, Moda only really became fashionable (which is what its name means in Turkish) in the dying days of the Ottoman Empire when many Greeks and Armenians made it their home. Buried in the back streets are several churches that serve as a reminder of those lost Christian populations. One of the most imposing is the 19th-century Catholic **Church of the Assumption**, which was built by the French. Considerably smaller is the Anglican **Church of All Saints**, built in 1878 to a design by **G. E. Street** who was also responsible for the Crimean Church in Pera. Just across the road from Barış Manço's house (see below), it holds services every Sunday morning.

Many of Istanbul's ferry landing stages are an architectural cut above their mundane function, and Moda's, built in 1917 by architect **Vedat Tek** as the first stop for ferries en route for the Princes' Islands, is certainly one of the finest. Destroyed by a high wind in 1937, it was restored in 2000 with a little help from pop star Barış Manço.

Old Moda ferry terminal

Mahmut Muhtar Paşa Mansion

Settlement in Moda dates back to the 1850s. The few mansions which have survived will pop up as if they are reminding you of the old aristocratic days of Moda as you are strolling among its streets. These mansions, some in good condition and still trying to survive among modern buildings and some others about to fall down, are the last witnesses of Moda's bygone days.

Mahmut Muhtar Paşa Mansion

The building which is also called the Marble Mansion because it is covered with marble was built for an Englishman named James Baker in 1886. The mansion is located within the walls of the school close to the pier as you walk along Moda Street. It was later bought by Princess Nimetullah Hanım and her husband Mahmut Muhtar Pasha. Princess

Nimetullah Hanım, daughter of the Egyptian Khedive İsmail Pasha, lived there until her death. After their demise, the mansion was inherited by their children. However, because of the disagreements among them, they sold the mansion to the Ministry of National Education. The valuable pieces of furniture and objects in the mansion were put to sale on auction. The two statues in the garden of the mansion were among these objects. The horse statue was bought by the Sabancı Family after a heated competition at the auction and it is currently located in front of the restaurant building of Sakıp Sabancı Museum (see p. 146). The gazelle statue, which can be seen in front of the Divan Hotel in Elmadağ, was bought by the Koç Family. The building has been used as the Kadıköy High School for Girls since 1957; it was later named Kadıköy High School. The high school is still open, but the mansion stands in a derelict condition in its garden.

Dr. Arif Sarıca Paşa Mansion

The mansion is on the left side once you leave behind the Mahmut Muhtar Pasha Mansion. It used to belong to Arif Sarıca, the physician of Sultan Abdülhamit II. Arif Sarıca Pasha's brother was one of the eminent bureaucrats of the period and he also had a mansion on the Caddebostan coast. The mansion was built by the Greek Pape Kalfa in 1903 as a 5-storey building made of cut stone. The building, which still belongs to the Sarıca Family, is inhabited by the pianist Ayşegül Sarıca who was honoured as a State Artist in 1971.

Antipa Mansion

This grey building which will strike your eyes immediately as you stroll on the Cape of Moda was built for a Greek physician named Dr. Andreas Antipa. The last owner of the mansion was Ferit Tek who was the Tokyo Ambassador. The street was later named after him.

St. Katerina Holy Spring 14

An important feature of the Meyhane Koço, serving since 1928 and located on the slope going down to the Moda Pier, is its underground ayazma (holy spring). Later an entrance was built next to the restaurant for the ayazma which is dedicated to Sainte Katerina, an important religious figure for the Greeks.

St. Catherine's Holy Spring

A tea garden in Moda

Moda streets

All Saints Anglican Church

Catholic Church of the Assumption

Barış Manço House

Memorial gate

Barış Manço House

The much-loved Turkish pop singer Barış Manço (1943-1999), whose music spanned the spectrum from supermarket favorite "Domates, Biber, Patlıcan (Tomatoes, Pepper, Aubergine)" to the sublime "Gülpembe (Pink Rose)", had a house on Yusuf Kamil Paşa Sokak in Moda, and regularly signed off his TV show with an airy "Barış Manço 81300 Moda", the postcode to which fans could write in the days before email. When he died the outpouring of grief was compared to that bestowed on Princess Diana of England. Now his personalized car number plates hang off one gate while another shows the Messiah-like singer greeting his youthful followers. The house is now a **museum** containing reminders of the Istanbul of the 1970s.

Tel:0216 337 94 13
www.barismanco.kadikoy.bel.tr
Closed Mondays

23

Gateway to Anatolia

Haydarpaşa and Selimiye

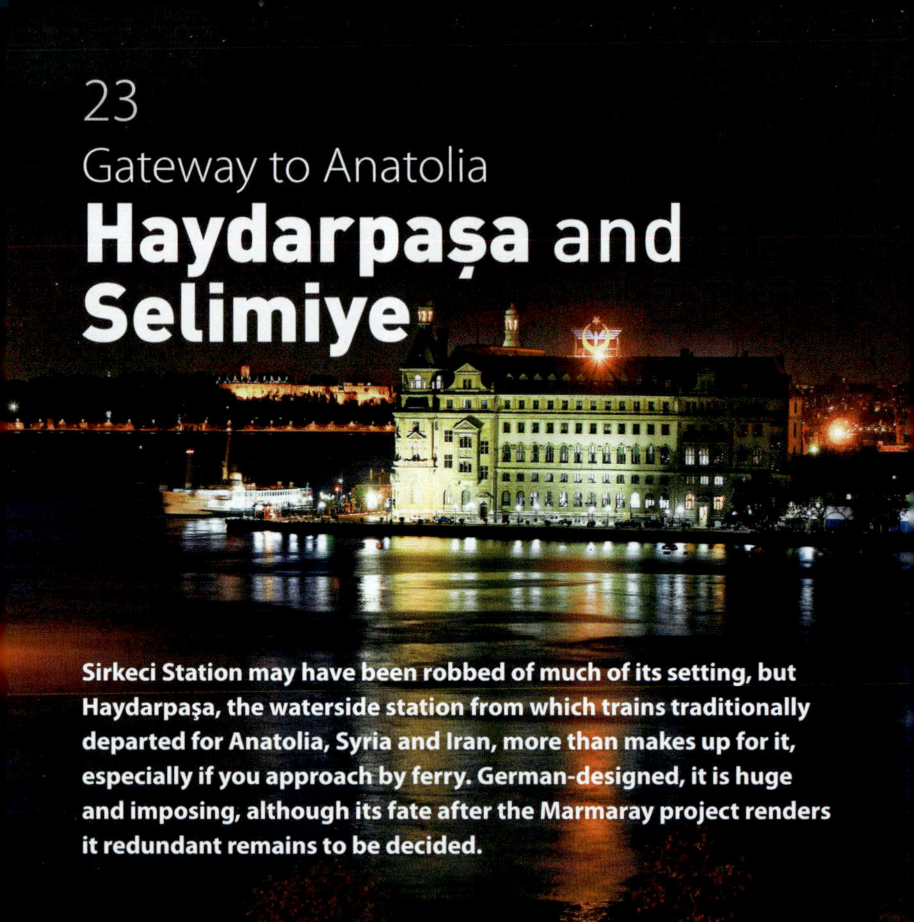

Sirkeci Station may have been robbed of much of its setting, but Haydarpaşa, the waterside station from which trains traditionally departed for Anatolia, Syria and Iran, more than makes up for it, especially if you approach by ferry. German-designed, it is huge and imposing, although its fate after the Marmaray project renders it redundant remains to be decided.

The piece of land immediately to the north of Kadıköy was named after one of two Ottoman grand viziers: either **Hadım Haydar Paşa**, who served **Sultan Süleyman the Magnificent** (1520-1566), and owned a local vineyard, or the **Haydar Paşa** who served **Sultan Selim III** (1789-1807) and had barracks built here. It seems to have remained mainly agricultural land right through until the 19th century when it became the assembly point for armies heading east. The original station was built in 1833 and the port beside it in 1899, after which time the entire area took on an industrial hue.

The Station

In 1898 **Kaiser Wilhelm II** visited Istanbul, a visit most famously commemorated by the fountain that still stands in the Hippodrome. This state visit was instrumental in improving relations between the Ottoman and German courts as a result of which the business of building a railway network for Turkey was transferred from the British to the Germans. In 1906 when a new station was required for Istanbul the work was funded by the German government as part of their plans for a **Berlin to Baghdad railway**. Responsibility for its design was given to two German architects, **Otto Ritter** and **Helmut Cuno**, who created the present monumental building. Ironically it is Sirkeci on the European side of town which favors the oriental look; in contrast, Haydarpaşa on the Asian side of the town looks as if it has somehow strayed from its natural home on the Rhine.

Despite damage caused by accidents in 1917, 1979 and 2010 the station still appears much as it did when it first opened to public in 1908.

The fate of this splendid building which has become the symbol of the migration from Anatolia to Istanbul stayed obscure for a long time after the closing of the suburban line. The building is one of the most beautiful examples of the German style. After some heated arguments over the possibility of its being turned into a hotel, it was decided to be used as part of a High-Speed Railway project planned to operate between Ankara and Istanbul. The urban line is united with Marmaray and it operate between Halkalı and Gebze. There were occasional small-scale events during the time it stayed vacant. The book days organized on the platforms in 2017 piqued the interest of both book-lovers and fans of trains.

If you arrive at the station by ferry you will disembark at the pretty little landing stage provided for it by architect Vedat Tek in 1917. It is decorated with fine Kütahya tiles by Hacı Hafız Mehmed Emin Efendi. What looks like a chimney jutting out of the roof turns out to be a bird house.

Haydar Baba Shrine

The number of shrines in Istanbul is quite high. Although their real stories are not known much, all of them has a special meaning for people. Here is a shrine for you, with an obscure story and an interesting location. Although the shrine, located among the railways in the platform, is called Haydar Baba, the inscription of the tomb belongs to Lahuti Abdullah. All the machinists used to visit the shrine before embarking on their journey and they used to salute him as they pass in front of the shrine so that they would have a safe trip. Throughout the years, this person who rests here has become a protector of railways like the saints who were believed to protect sailors.

The birds of Haydarpaşa

For keen ornithologists one of the pleasures of the boat ride to Haydarpaşa will be the long sea wall that juts out from the shore and provides a preening post for hundreds of cormorants and gray herons.

Haydarpaşa ferry terminal is decorated with Kütahya tiles.

Haydarpaşa Campus

Created in 1894 to house the **Imperial School of Military Medicine**, this imposing building, which is visible from the ferry as you approach Haydarpaşa and from Topkapı Palace, was designed by **Alexandre Vallaury** and **Raimondo d'Aronco** in a style known as Neo-Ottoman. The striking clock towers on either side of its entrance are actually the minarets of a mosque. The building went on to serve as a **high school** for boys before becoming the medical faculty of Marmara University in 1983. It was later acquired from Marmara University and allocated to another foundation university. Behind the building lies the **Crimean War Cemetery** where many British and Commonwealth soldiers who succumbed to their wounds in the Selimiye Barracks or at Gallipoli were buried. Alongside them lie prominent members of the 19th-century expat community. Also here is the tomb of **Edward Barton** which was relocated here from **Heybeliada** in the Princess' Islands.

Crimean War Memorial

Garden of Hardarpaşa Campus

Selimiye Mosque

Across the road from the barracks is the baroque-style mosque that **Sultan Selim III** had built for the soldiers in 1803-1804. Its twin minarets proved too weak to support themselves and had to be completely rebuilt. Selimiye itself was the city's first officially planned neighbourhood.

The famous Lady with the Lamp was named after her birthplace of Florence.

Who were the Janissaries

The Janissaries were one of the world's first uniformed standing armies and provided the household guard of the Ottoman sultans right through from the 14th century, when the corps was probably established by **Sultan Murad I**, to 1826 when **Sultan Mahmud II** abolished them. The original Janissaries were **Christians** seized as **slaves**, converted to Islam, and turned into soldiers loyal to the sultan. However, by the early 18th century they had become so powerful that they could often dictate policy to the sultans; even as their once formidable power as a fighting force declined, they were still able to remove any sultan foolhardy enough to try and improve matters. Eventually, Sultan Mahmud II inspired them to rebel by threatening to set up a modern army. During the ensuing riot, a fire broke out in the barracks and thousands of Janissaries were killed. This so called "**Auspicious Incident**" marked the end of their power. To find out more about the Janissaries visit the **Military Museum** in Harbiye.

Low-ranking Janissary officer flanked by orderlies

Selimiye Barracks

Centuries in the planning, the Selimiye Barracks were first built to the north of Haydarpaşa in 1799, and took their name from **Sultan Selim III** who intended them to act as a base for the new army with which he was hoping to replace the troublesome Janissaries. In 1808 the barracks were burnt down, only to be rebuilt in much stronger materials in 1825 by **Sultan Mahmud II**, just two years after he finally saw off the Janissaries. Mahmud II's barracks only had one wing; the other three were added by architect **Krikor Balyan** during the reign of **Sultan Abdülmecid** to create an enclosed parade ground. During the early years of the Republic, the barracks were turned into a **school**, only to revert to their original function in 1963. Today the vast four-towered structure still houses the headquarters of the **Turkish First Army**, the largest division in the country. Even for those not generally gripped by military history the Selimiye Barracks are interesting as the site of the **British military hospital** where **Florence Nightingale** worked during the Crimean War (1853-1856). The famous "Lady with the Lamp" is credited with having reduced mortality from war wounds enormously by introducing simple rules of hygiene. One tower of the barracks now houses the small **Florence Nightingale Museum**, with mementoes of the nurse preserved rather soullessly in her living room and surgery; there's also some information about the Crimean and other wars in which Turkey has been involved.

24

The Snake in the Basket

The Maiden's Tower

Just off the Bosphorus coast at Üsküdar, the cute little Maiden's Tower (Kız Kulesi in Turkish) crops up in many old pictures of Istanbul and has attracted many romantic stories over the years. After the most recent restoration, it houses a restaurant and small café, and offers 360-degree city views from its balcony.

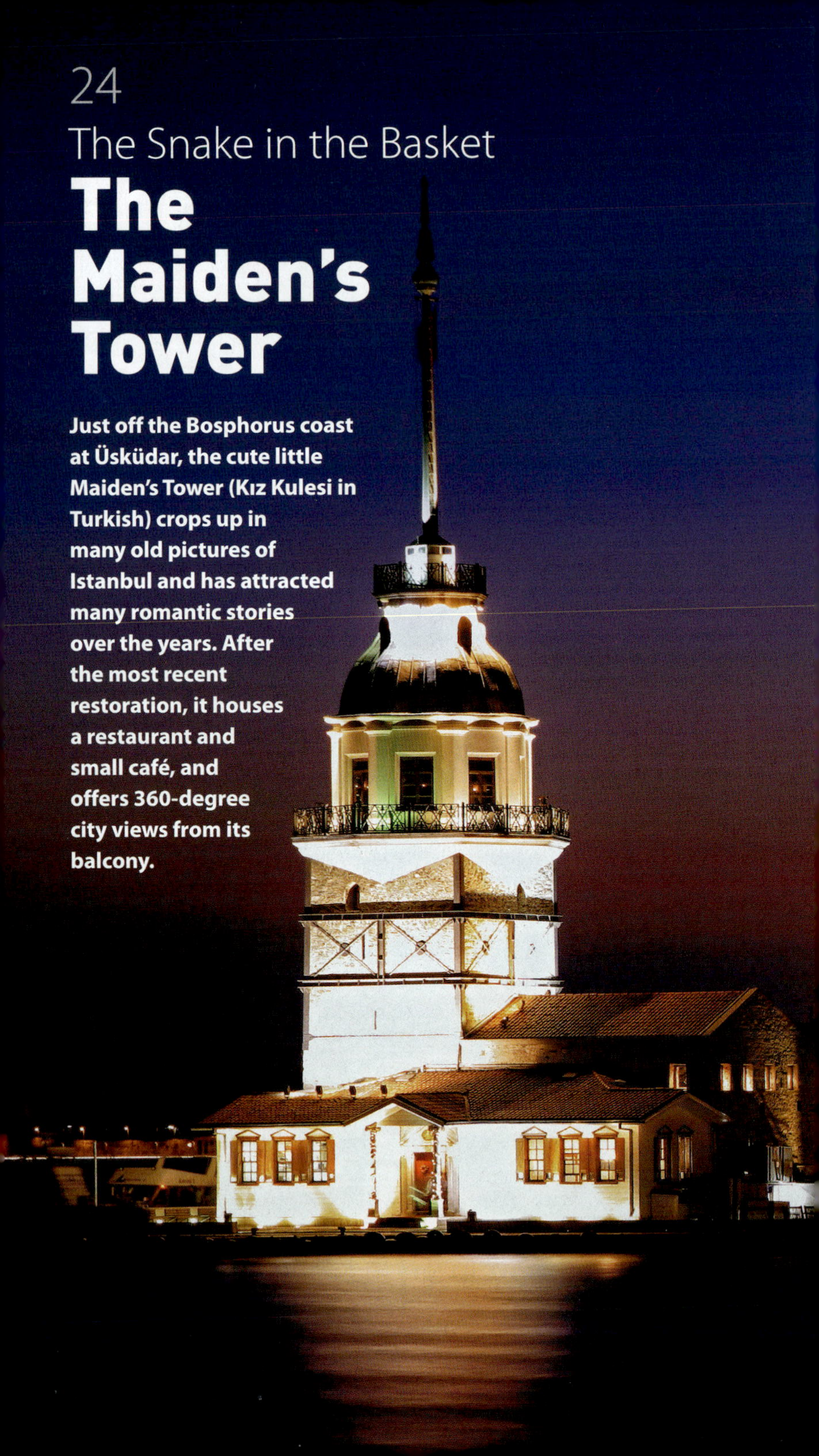

Although the tower currently standing on the rock off Üsküdar dates back only to the 19th century, the earliest building there seems to have been a small fort built by the Athenian general **Alcibiades** in 408 BC to keep the Persians at bay. Later the Byzantine Emperor **Manuel I Comnenos** (1143-1180) had a miniature castle created to discourage invaders. **Sultan Mehmed the Conqueror** replaced this mini-castle with one of his own which was restored by **Sultan Selim I**. Like Istanbul's larger islands, this islet also served time as a **prison**, with Sultan Mahmud I locking up the **Chief White Eunuch Beşir Ağa** here before beheading him, and then Sultan Osman III locking up his **Grand Vizier Hekimoğlu Ali Paşa** here before exiling him to Cyprus.

The Athenian General Alcibiades

Like so many Istanbul buildings, the Maiden's Tower has also fallen foul of a fire, this time one started by torches at a party that got out of control in 1719. It was replaced almost immediately by Sultan Ahmed III's Grand Vizier **Damat İbrahim Paşa**, at which point it appears to have been turned into a **lighthouse**. The final version was created by **Sultan Mahmud II** in the early 19th century.

Since then the rock has served a predictable collection of functions as a **semaphore station**, a **quarantine outpost** during a cholera outbreak, and a **tollbooth**. It was completely restored in 2000, and now houses a café, restaurant and lookout balcony.

Fabulous stories

There's something about off-shore islands which brings out the fantasist in everyone, so it's hardly surprising that a story rather like that of Rapunzel crossed with Cleopatra quickly developed around the Maiden's Tower. According to the tale, a king had a beautiful daughter whom he loved greatly although a prophecy had predicted that she would be killed by a snake bite. Anxious to circumvent cruel fate, the king had his daughter confined on the rock until eventually someone delivered a basket of fruit to her that turned out to contain the predicted snake. The rest, as they say, is history. That story is fanciful enough, but a second version stirs the Turkish hero **Battal Gazi** into the mix. Battal Gazi was an eighth-century Umayyad soldier who used to farm land immediately across from the tower and fell in love with the Byzantine emperor's daughter. While he was away fighting in Damascus, the emperor imprisoned his daughter on the rock. On his return Battal Gazi was able to free her, but only with the help of a highly unlikely-sounding 700 soldiers. A third version of the story has a fairy-tale ending with the princess rescued from the tower by a **Persian prince** but only after she had been poisoned by a snake hidden in a basket of flowers that he sent to her. Finally the story of the Maiden's Tower, sometimes called Leander's Tower, became hopelessly entangled with that of **Hero and Leander**, lovers who lived on opposite sides of the Dardanelles near Çanakkale. Every evening Leander would swim across to meet Hero, guided by a light that she hung in a tower. One night the wind blew the lamp out, and Leander was swept away by the tide and drowned. Cast into despair, Hero committed suicide by jumping from the tower. How the two disparate venues became so mixed up is, however, unclear.

James Bond in town

In 1999 the Maiden's Tower featured as a hideaway for the fiendish Elektra, played by Sophie Marceau, in the James Bond movie "The World is Not Enough". It also featured in the smash-hit Turkish television series "Kurtlar Vadisi (The Valley of the Wolves)".

Maiden Tower's restaurant

TRANSPORT

Regular ferries to the tower run from Salacak on Üsküdar's waterfront promenade immediately facing the rock. There are also a few ferries from Ortaköy, as well as a couple from Kabataş to suit night-time diners.

Salacak and Çürüksulu (Muharrem Nuri Birgi) Yalı

Overlooking the Maiden's Tower, the Üsküdar shore road is perfect for promenading. Perched as though hanging from a cliff above it, the ruddy-colored Çürüksulu (Muharrem Nuri Birgi) Yalı is one of the finest examples of 18th-century Ottoman architecture and was restored by the architect **Turgut Cansever** in 1971. Later, Ambassador Birgi bequeathed the building to Selahattin Beyazıt, owner of a magnificent yalı in Kandilli (see p. 281). The world-renowned violinist **Yehudi Menuhin** (1906-1999) was a guest in this yalı whose interior decoration is truly impressive. I visited it to listen to a concert and was struck dumb by the incredible view of Istanbul to be had from the balcony.

Salacak in an old engraving

With the shore road passing in front of it, this yalı looks as though it is hanging from the cliff.

Muharrem Nuri Birgi (1907 - 1986)

The first known owner of the 18th-century Çürüksulu Yalı was a merchant named Tırnakçızade. Later on, it was transferred to the Çürüksulu Family. Its previous owner was the famous diplomat, Muharrem Nuri Birgi (1907-1986). A graduate of Galatasaray Lyceé, Birgi was assigned to the Turkish Delegation of the United Nations General Assembly in 1946 after several postings abroad. From 1957 to 1960 he was ambassador to London, and was known as the only diplomat who managed to make **Queen Elizabeth II** laugh. After spending an uninterrupted 12 years representing Turkey at the highest level in NATO, he was not only accepted into the secretive **Bilderberg Group**, which brings together the richest and most influential individuals on both sides of the Atlantic, but also became a member of its administrative committee.

Entrance

Living room

Main hall

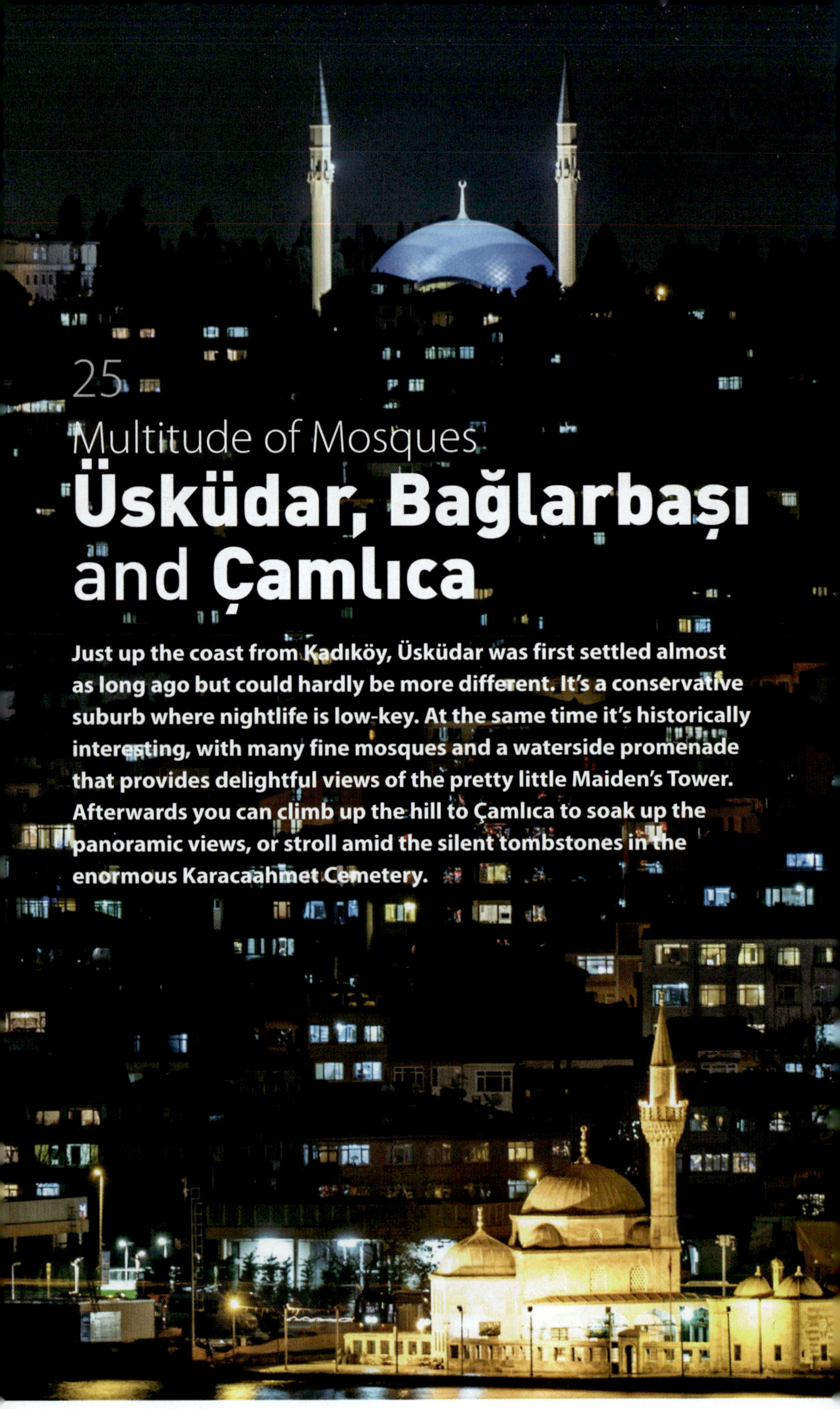

25

Multitude of Mosques

Üsküdar, Bağlarbaşı and Çamlıca

Just up the coast from Kadıköy, Üsküdar was first settled almost as long ago but could hardly be more different. It's a conservative suburb where nightlife is low-key. At the same time it's historically interesting, with many fine mosques and a waterside promenade that provides delightful views of the pretty little Maiden's Tower. Afterwards you can climb up the hill to Çamlıca to soak up the panoramic views, or stroll amid the silent tombstones in the enormous Karacaahmet Cemetery.

The area that is now Üsküdar appears to have been settled at about the same time as Kadıköy. It was originally called **Chrysopolis** (the City of Gold), although whether because the Persian invaders stored their plunder from Anatolia here, or because of the way the setting sun lit up the Bosphorus in front of it is unclear. Although **Chalcedon** (Kadıköy) was originally the more important of the two settlements, Chrysopolis grew very quickly and soon became the main departure point for military expeditions into Anatolia. Over time its name changed to **Scutari**, which could have been derived from the Greek word "skitos", which described the leather used to coat the shields of the imperial guards stationed here; or from Scutarion, the name of a long-lost Byzantine palace situated on land immediately across from the Maiden's Tower. This in turn evolved into the modern Üsküdar. Legend has it has it that the neighbourhood was named after in reference to its geographical characteristics. Since it has a wide coastline which gets narrower towards the slope, it was defined as "narrow at the top".

Although Chrysopolis pre-dated Byzantium, it lacked the other city's naturally defensible site and was occupied several times before the Turks finally seized it in the 14th century. Today visitors who arrive by ferry find themselves in a fairly chaotic transport interchange which stands where the great caravan trains bearing pilgrims to Mecca for **the Haj** used to start out. Once upon a time many of Istanbul's rich and powerful came here to make their homes in what Italian writer Edmondo de Amicis could still describe in the second half of the 19th century as "like a rural city." Today only the great mosques they endowed survive.

Recent excavations associated with the **Marmaray project** have uncovered traces of a medieval bazaar, tannery, monastery, and wooden pier near the ferry terminal.

Harbor (Mihrimah Sultan) Mosque

Harbor (Mihrimah Sultan) Mosque

Facing the ferry landing stage across the busy main road is the magnificent mosque built by Mimar **Sinan** for **Mihrimah Sultan**, daughter of Sultan Süleyman the Magnificent and wife of his grand vizier **Rüstem Paşa**, in 1548. It was the first building in which he made use of the semi-domes that were to become one of his trademarks. When it was first built the mosque stood right on the **waterfront** and the sultan was able to disembark straight from his caique onto its steps; the view from the şadırvan (fountain) was regarded as one of the best in Istanbul. The medrese to the side that was once part of the complex now houses a local **clinic**, while the school on the other side now houses a **children's library**. Note the fine **sundial** attached to the wall as you exit at the back towards the library. In front of the mosque amid the swirling traffic is the free-standing baroque **fountain of Sultan Ahmed III** dating back to 1728. All four sides are decorated with **poetry**, including a couplet composed by Ahmed III himself. It's a less elaborate version of the one in front of Topkapı Palace.

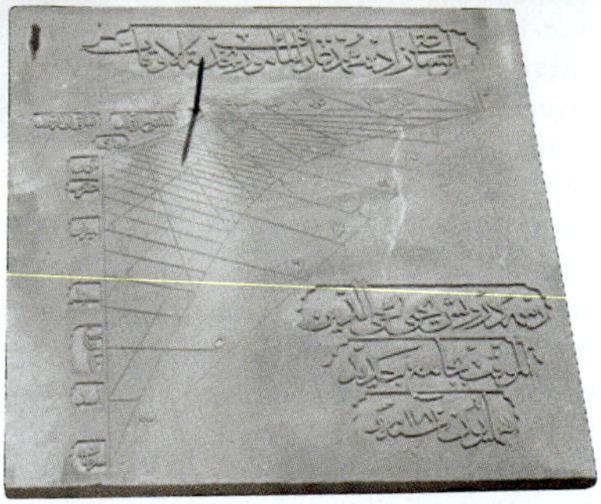

Sundial

Sultan Ahmed III Fountain

Shrine of Aziz Mahmud Hüdayi Efendi

In Aziz Mahmud Efendi Sokak, this shrine (1541-1628) commemorates a holy man born in Koçhisar, near **Tuz Gölü** (Salt Lake), who lived through the reigns of eight different sultans and founded the **Celveti sect**. Asked a question by Sultan Ahmed I in a letter, he sent back his reply without even needing to open it. An inscription inside the **Bulgurlu Hamam** records that he was the imam who read the first sermon in the **Blue Mosque** in 1616.

Yeni Valide Mosque

Very close to the ferry terminal is the imposing Yeni Valide (Queen Mother) Mosque built by **Sultan Ahmed III** for his mother **Valide Rabia Gülnüş Ümmetullah** in 1710. Despite its huge size it has a pleasingly rustic appearance brought about by the combination of the queen mother's tomb, which has been described as resembling a giant aviary, the house-like wooden façade of the sultan's pew, and an especially beautiful fountain. Of relatively late date, it was still designed with a large courtyard surrounded on three sides by domed porticoes and with an elaborately carved şadırvan (ablutions fountain) as its centerpiece. Not much else of the complex survives apart from a small **school** building and much larger **imaret** (soup kitchen).

Across the road an **old hamam** has been converted into a small shopping center. Its attribution to Sinan is unlikely to be true although it may well date back to the 16th century.

On the left the Valide Sultan's tomb

Marmaray

The project, which was launched in 2013 as a solution for the traffic issue in Istanbul and especially to ease the Bosphorus transits, started to operate with 5 stations between Ayrılıkçeşme and Kazlıçeçme (Ayrılıkçeşme-Üsküdar-Sirkeci-Yenikapı-Kazlıçeşme). The project consists of an immersed tunnel, approximately 1.4 km in length, and bored tunnels on both sides, each almost 11 km in length. The project, integrated with the suburban line between Gebze and Halkalı, significantly eases public transportation in Istanbul. The first project to build a tunnel under the Bosphorus from Üsküdar to Sarayburnu was designed in the 1860s. The project which had been planned for years came to realization with Marmaray for the first time. During the construction work of the Yenikapı station, the Byzantine Port was unearthed. The excavations, which ignited great excitement all around the world, the world's largest port from from antiquity and 37 shipwrecks dating back to periods between the 5th and 11th centuries, bones of humans and animals and more than 35,000 artefacts dating back to as far as the Neolithic Period were discovered. Even the loads of the ships survived. The findings of the shipwrecks which survived to this day in the mud carried over by the Lykos Stream and the photographs of the excavation work were exhibited at Istanbul Archeology Museum in recent years. According to Istanbul University Research Center for Yenikapı Wrecks (www.yenikapibatiklari.com), the findings from Yenikapı might again highlight the role of Byzantine shipbuilding and maritime commerce in Constantinople and Late Roman period. The conservation and reconstruction work of the wrecks is ongoing as part of the project. 'Yenikapı 12', whose reconstruction is completed had her first sailing course in the Sea of Marmara and it was put on exhibition at Istanbul Archaeology Museum. The project to exhibit the artefacts kept in the stores of the Archeology Museum is still waiting.

Ayazma Mosque rises above the Şemsi Paşa Mosque

Şemsi Paşa Mosque

As you follow the road round towards the Maiden's Tower you will pass the twin-domed **Cedid Valide Soup Kitchen** (İmaret) and the wooden **Balaban Lodge (dervish tekke)** which has been completely rebuilt. Finally you will reach the small Şemsi Paşa mosque complex that was designed by Mimar Sinan in 1580 for the Vizier **Şemsi Paşa** whose tomb opens, unusually, straight into the mosque. It overlooks the point where the Bosphorus meets the Sea of Marmara.

Another name given to the mosque is "Kuşkonmaz" (birds don't land). Since the mosque is located at the intersection of the air streams from Marmara and the Black Sea, the reverse effect of the wind and the boom penetrating into the minarets prevent birds from perching in the mosque. Legend has it that the reason for choosing such a location was because Şemsi Ahmet Pasha wanted a mosque which could not be dirtied by birds. The mosque, enjoying the nice view of this location, was restored in 2012.

As you walk along the coast road towards Salacak and the ferry to the Maiden's Tower you will pass two **sculptures** - 1453 and 1923 - by Faruk Akın (the artist also responsible for the giant alarm clock facing the ferry terminal). Also on the coast road you will see an imposing building originally erected in 1842 to house a **police station** but since given new life as the Air Force Club.

Interior of Şemsi Paşa Mosque

Ayazma Mosque

Close to the Rum Mehmed Paşa Mosque is the huge baroque **Ayazma Mosque** complex built by Sultan Mustafa III for his mother Mihrişah Emine Sultan in 1760, and designed by Mehmed Tahir Ağa.

Interior of Ayazma Mosque

Note the small birdhouses on the façade and on the gateway. Look out, too, for what are probably the last remaining Janissary tombstones in the city, identifiable from the flamboyant headgear carved onto the top of them. This is the mosque that dominates the eastern skyline of Üsküdar as you approach by ferry.

Rum Mehmed Paşa Mosque

A short walk away from the Şemsi Paşa Mosque is this small mosque built in 1471 for one of Fatih Sultan Mehmed's grand viziers. Mehmed Paşa was a "Rum", the Turkish word for a Greek, which is sometimes offered as an explanation for why this building, with its taller than average central dome, is so Byzantine in appearance.

Nevmekan-Sahil, which was transformed from the former Üsküdar Registry Office to a library, offers you a different experience with its architecture and unique sea view.

Cannonball dating back to 1453

Nurbanu Sultan

Atik Valide Mosque

High up on a hill and with particularly tall minarets, Üsküdar's most important mosque is another work of **Sinan**, this time designed in 1583 for **Nurbanu Sultan**, the wife of **Sultan Selim II**. To find it you need to walk up Eski Toptaşı Caddesi (Old Cannonball Street), readily identifiable by a small monument in the middle of the road incorporating a cannonball said to have been used during the siege of Istanbul in 1453.

Described by **John Freely** as one of the half-dozen most impressive Ottoman monuments in the country, the Atik Valide Mosque has a delightful **courtyard** filled with plane trees and rosebushes, a place where old men while away the day over glasses of tea and their newspapers. A narthex of twelve arches filled with fine metalwork opens onto an interior that seems unexpectedly small after the grand exterior. The mihrab is surrounded with İznik tiles but of a late period when the colors tended to run.

Unfortunately, the surrounding complex is not being well maintained. Not only are the walls of the mosque and medrese plastered with graffiti, but the lovely old **caravanserai** with its fine wooden portal leading into a domed antechamber is falling into rack and ruin despite being the property of Marmara University's School of Fine Arts. **The sıbyan mekteb** (school) at the back is also in ruins, as is the **imaret** (soup kitchen) with its graceful brick chimneys. Külliye (social complex) went through a bad restoration which looks good from the outside in 2014.

Ablutions Fountain

Ahmediye Mosque

Inland on Gündoğumu Caddesi the Ahmediye Mosque complex was built in 1722 by **Eminzade Hacı Ahmed Paşa** who was in charge of the arsenal during the reign of **Sultan Ahmed III**. It still retains many of its subsidiary buildings including a **sebil** (water dispensary), **medrese** (seminary) and **kütüphane** (library) grouped round a small courtyard.

The Çinili Mosque is remote from the center.

Mehmet Naci Aköz Kite Museum

The small, special museum which you will see in Üsküdar will surprise you. This is Turkey's first and only, and one of the world's eighteen kite museums. Exhibiting about 750 colourful kites collected from all over the world, the museum has a collection of more than 2,500 pieces collected from six different continents and thirty-three countries (kites, publications, materials and various objects). It is located just across the Municipality of Üsküdar, at the end of Uncular Main Street on Bakıcı Street. Open on weekdays, the museum can be visited by appointment on Saturdays. There are kite-making courses as well.

@ucurtmamuzesi, Tel: 0216 553 23 37
www.ucurtmamuzesi.net

Tiled (Çinili) Mosque

Kösem Sultan

It's even further uphill to this mosque but you won't regret it once you persuade the caretaker to unlock the door so that you can inspect the fine **İznik tiles** on its walls. The mosque dates back to 1640 when it was built by **Mahpeyker Kösem Sultan**, the mother of **Murad IV** and **İbrahim the Mad**. Facing it across a square is the **Çinili Hamam** which, despite its name, is not tiled at all.

Karacaahmet Cemetery

Heading south towards Kadıköy the hillside is covered with a vast cemetery, the largest in Turkey and second only to Eyüp for the quality of its Ottoman tombstones. Named after a warrior companion of Orhan I whose tomb is still greatly revered, the cemetery was seen as being on the side of the city closest to the holy cities of Mecca and Medina, hence its great popularity as a burial place. The artist **Fikret Mualla** was buried here in 1967 as was the rock musician **Cem Karaca** in 2004.

Abdülaziz Hunting Lodge (Abdülaziz Av Köşkü)

The Abdülaziz Hunting Lodge stands in the **Validebağ Wood** off Tophanelioğlu Caddesi in **Altunizade**. Built in 1856 in neo-Turkish style, it features a delightful wooden portico. There was a scout museum which I thought was never open when I visited. There is a "Writing Workshop" signboard placed on the lodge which was restored for a second time later on. Its present use is still not in harmony with its texture and history. The Validebağ Grove, a First Degree Protected Area, offers you some fresh air in the middle of the city.

The Adile Sultan Mansion

Altunizade İsmail Zühtü Paşa originally commissioned a splendid villa in the district that was named after himself. Later he presented it to **Sultan Abdülaziz**, who was particularly fond of the site. Abdülaziz tore down the existing villa and commissioned **Nigoğos Amira Balyan** to design the present one for his younger sister, Adile Sultan. Beside the Abdülaziz Hunting Lodge, the Adile Sultan Mansion currently serves as the Validebağ Teacher's House. Early episodes of the Turkish comedy series **Hababam Sınıfı** (Outrageous Class) were shot here and one room was turned into a Hababam Sınıfı Museum.

Zeynep Fadıllıoğlu

Şakirin Mosque

On the north-eastern side of the cemetery, facing the Zeynep Kamil Hospital, is the brand-new **Şakirin (Gratitude) Mosque**, a futuristic building commission by the **Şakir Family**, which mixes minarets of reinforced concrete with a sweeping dome that looks like an off-cut from the Guggenheim in Bilbao and a courtyard centered on a giant silver ball symbolizing the world that reflects the mosque back to itself. It was designed by **Hüsrev Tayla** and decorated by **Zeynep Fadıllıoğlu**, already well known for her work on the **Ulus 29** restaurant, who thereby became the first woman in modern times to adorn a mosque in Turkey. With its utterly original **arched mihrab** of turquoise and gold, a **minbar** decorated with stylized leaves, and a **chandelier** of dripping plastic adorned with the **99 names of Allah** and the **Nur** (Light) verse of the **Koran**, the mosque is a first in every way and a godsend to those whose hearts sink whenever they see yet another debased version of Sinan's great masterpieces. Conservatives have criticized the Şakirin as resembling a casino. I prefer to congratulate the architects for their originality.

The Balyan tombs

The prolific family of architects, the Balyans, are buried in the Armenian Cemetery in Nuh Kuyusu Caddesi in Bağlarbaşı.

Çamlıca' Girls High School

Above Üsküdar is Çamlıca (Pine Wood), which is best known for its large public parks. Here, too, is **Acıbadem** where **Vice-Admiral Ahmed Ratip Paşa** commissioned a fine mansion from **Kemaleddin Bey**; unfortunately for him, he was exiled for taking bribes over the building of the Hejaz railway before he got to live in it. The work was completed in 1908 and in 1938 the 54-room mansion was turned into **Çamlıca Girls' High School**, albeit a high school decorated with **Murano glass** stair rails and Villeroy and Boch bathroom tiles. Now that a new modern school has been built right next door for the girls, this masterpiece is standing sadly empty.

Marmara Faculty of Theology Mosque

The mosque was rebuilt with modern architecture in 2012 when it had been demolished because it was against the earthquake regulation. The mosque was opened for service again in 2015. As part of the Marmara University Faculty of Theology has a capacity of 4,500 people and covers an area of 30,000 square meters with its square and cultural center. Its helix-shaped dome with glass tunnels and minarets with different styles are striking.

Hamam

Üsküdar retains several historic Turkish baths that receive relatively few foreign visitors and all of which have separate sections for men and women. The oldest of them is the **Şifa (Healthy) Hamam** which appears to have been built in the late 15th century. The Valide Atik Hamam is a work of Sinan dating back to 1583. The **Çinili (Tiled) Hamam** dates back to 1648 and was carefully restored in 1964; unusually, the women's section is larger than the men's. The **Bulgurlu Hamam** proudly preserves the basin used by Aziz Mahmud Hüdayi Efendi (see p.218). Finally there is the **Ağa Hamam** that dates back to 1610.

Çamlıca Mosque

The Büyük Çamlıca Mosque that was recently added to the silhouette of Istanbul has increased interest in the area. The construction of the mosque began in 2013 and was opened for worship in 2019. It's the largest mosque in Turkey with a capacity of 65,000 people. As we are familiar from historical mosques, most typically those in Süleymaniye, there are several symbols contained within its architecture. Four of the minarets are 107.1 meters high, referring to the Victory of Malazgirt, which was the turning point that brought Turks into Anatolia. And the diameter of the dome is 34 meters, the number that represents Istanbul.

Küçük Çamlıca

Less well known but perhaps even prettier is Küçük Çamlıca, a hillier park covered with trees and recently adorned with a complex of kiosks loosely based on **Topkapı Palace**. Between them stands a copy of the İftariye Canopy from which you can gaze out on the city, a **magnificent panorama** stretching from the Princes' Islands on the left, through Fenerbahçe and Haydarpaşa in the middle, to Topkapı Palace on the right.

Less well known but perhaps even prettier is Küçük Çamlıca, a hillier park covered with trees and recently adorned with a complex of kiosks loosely based on **Topkapı Palace**. Between them stands a copy of the İftariye Canopy from which you can gaze out on the city, a **magnificent panorama** stretching from the Princes' Islands on the left, through Fenerbahçe and Haydarpaşa in the middle, to Topkapı Palace on the right. A television tower with a height of 388.5 meters is being built to prevent the visual pollution caused by the radio and television towers in Büyük Çamlıca. The tower, which will be visible from many parts of Istanbul, will also have two restaurants on 39th and 40th floors and viewing platforms on 33rd and 34th floors.

Büyük Çamlıca

The 262-meter-high Büyük Çamlıca on **Mt Bulgurlu** is Istanbul's highest point, and used to be a famous beauty spot, much hymned by writers as various as **Procopius, Evliya Çelebi, Lady Mary Wortley Montagu,** and **Lord Byron**. Now, however, its beauty is marred by serried ranks of radio and phone masts although the views are still magnificent, and there's an inviting Ottoman-style coffee house as well as a restaurant and private picnic kiosks to make up for them. There are also shady walks to be had beneath the pine trees (çam) that gave their name to the site.

Marmara Faculty of Teology Mosque with European Shore behind it.

26

Television's Favorite Suburb

Kuzguncuk

On the Asian side of the Bosphorus, just north of Üsküdar, Kuzguncuk is a pleasant, leafy suburb with many old wooden houses and a mosque, church and synagogue virtually side by side. Its traditional appearance has made it a favorite with Turkish television companies who have used it in several recent soap operas, including "Ekmek Teknesi (Bread Boat)" and "Perihan Abla (Big Sister Perihan)".

Church cross on top of what looks like a mosque dome.

Kuzguncuk harbor in the 1890s

Simotas Building with date according to three calendars

The Byzantine **Kosinitsa**, Kuzguncuk lacks any major attractions although it is a great place to wander around and admire the frilly wooden houses that dot the main drag or perhaps come for a bite to eat in one of several unexpectedly sophisticated restaurants. Unusually, it has a **church, mosque and synagogue** all grouped together near the waterfront, a reminder of how cosmopolitan a city Istanbul was in the 19th century. It's thought that the first settlers were **Jews** expelled from Spain at the end of the 15th century who were followed here by **Greeks and Armenians**, before Turks finally moved in too. At one time there may have been as many as 10,000 Jews living here and the area was sometimes called "**Little Jerusalem**". Today there are hardly any Jews, Greeks or Armenians left, although their place is slowly being taken by expats from the USA and the UK.

According to **Evliya Çelebi** the area was named after a wise man called Kuzgun Baba who lived here in the 15th century. However, others think it took its name, more prosaically, from the Turkish word for "little raven". In reality, it's probably a corruption of the original Kosinitsa.

Can Yücel

Kuzguncuk was sometime home to the translator and poet **Can Yücel** (1926-1999), known for his prolific use of slang. It also features as the setting for **Buket Uzuner**'s best-selling novel "Mediterranean Waltz".

"I Anatolia"

Güngör Dilmen

One of Kuzguncuk's most famous residents was the playwright **Güngör Dilmen** (1930 - 2012) whose most famous play, "I Anatolia", relates the history of Anatolia through the mouths of 16 famous women.

Fine example of a wooden house in Kuzguncuk

Mosques

Built in 1860, the waterside **Üryanizade Mosque** was intended for Sultan Abülhamid's religious leader Üryanizade Ömer Efendi. It boasts a distinctive **wooden minaret** and a design that recalls the neighboring yalıs.

The much newer **Kuzguncuk Mosque** dates back only to 1952 hence its nickname, the "Yeni Cami" (New Mosque) and stands right beside the Armenian church of **Surp Krikor Lusavoriç**. The domes of the mosque and the church have the same shape and reach the same height.

Üryanizade Mosque

Synagogues

The **Beth Ya'akov synagogue**, in İcadiye Caddesi, was built in 1878 and used to provide services in summer; in winter the congregation would move to Yakup Sokak to another synagogue, **Kal de Ariva**, that dated back to 1840; its name meant "lower synagogue" to distinguish it from Bath Ya'akov which was also called **Kal de Abaşo** (Upper Synagogue). The hamam next door to Bath Ya'akov used to function as a **mikvah** (ritual bath) for the Jewish community.

Beth Ya'akov Synagogue

Hagios Panteleimon Greek Orthodox Church

Churches

Beside the main road, the huge Armenian church of **Surp Krikor Lusavoriç** was built in 1831 and rebuilt in 1861. On İcadiye Caddesi, the Greek Orthodox **Church of Hagios Panteleimon** was built in 1821 on the site of an earlier church dating back to 550. Its magnificent detached bell tower (1911) doubles as an entrance gate. The church also has a holy spring. A third, smaller church, dedicated to **Hagios Georgios**, stands beside the Beth Ya'akov synagogue.

Surp Krikor Lusavoriç Armenian Church

Nakkaştepe

On the lower slopes of **Nakkaştepe** (Embroiderers' Hill), just to the east of Kuzguncuk, there's a walled Jewish cemetery full of gravestones with inscriptions in Hebrew, Ladino, Ottoman and Turkish. Views from the top of the hill are superb. Tourists are sometimes brought to cafes here in the mistaken impression that it is Çamlıca Hill.

Abdülmecid Efendi Mansion

A very beautiful and colourful mansion strikes one's eye just across the Jewish Cemetery on the Gümüşyolu Street. The mansion located in Bağlarbağı Grove was built at the end of the 19th century as a hunting lodge by the Egyptian Khedive İsmail Pasha. Its original size was bigger but only its Selamlık (the portion of a house reserved for men) part has survived. A Cufic inscription at its entrance writes "God is the only victor".

Its architect is Alexandre Vallaury who designed many beautiful buildings including Istanbul Erkek Lisesi (High School for Boys), Archeology Museum, SALT Galeri and the former Haydarpaşa High School. Following the death of İsmail Pasha, Sultan Abdülhamid II bought the mansion for the last caliph Abdülmecid Efendi, who was the son of his uncle. Abdülmecit Efendi lived in this mansion located in its land of 200 decares for 28 years. Sultan Abdülhamid II, his cousin who granted him the mansion, did not allow him to come to the city. Hence, Abdülmecid Efendi told Pierre Loti that he saw the place as his grave.

Known his love for the arts, Abdülmecid Efendi used the mansion for meetings on art and literature. Abdülmecid Efendi, son of Sultan Abdülaziz, is a well-educated personality of parts. He is especially known for his paintings; his work has been exhibited even in Europe. Moreover, he worked on nudes on a couple of his paintings and produced ground-breaking work for his time.

Abdülmecid Efendi was the honorary president of the Ottoman Artists Association founded in 1909 and he offered financial support for the publication of the newspaper of the Ottoman Artists Association. The 1918 Vienna Exhibition, the first exhibition to be opened by Turkish artists in Europe, included 4 works of him. During the time of Kâzım Taşkent, founder of the first private Turkish bank Yapı ve Kredi Bankası, the mansion was bought for protection. All its originality was preserved during the renovation work and it survived to this day. Its entrance hall, the tiles decorating the walls, the fireplace, the fountain and all its details are the reflections of fine taste. Thanks to the occasional exhibitions held in the mansion, you may catch a chance to admire both the works of art and this beautiful structure.

Abdülmecid Efendi the painter born to be sultan

His name may not ring many bells with foreign visitors but Abdülmecid Efendi was an extraordinary man who would, had he been born just a few years earlier, have become sultan. The son of **Sultan Abdülaziz**, he was born in 1868 either in the old Beşiktaş or new Dolmabahçe Palace. In 1922 the sultanate was abolished but he was appointed **caliph**, or head of the Islamic congregation worldwide. Exiled in 1924, he died in **Paris** in 1944 and was later re-buried in **Medina**. In the meantime, he had made a name for himself as an **artist** of considerable ability. His paintings are on display in the **Dolmabahçe Palace** (see p.79), Aşiyan (see p.133), and the **Istanbul Modern** (see p.65), and the **Sakıp Sabancı Museum** (see p.146).

This old photo shows Caliph Abdülmecid Efendi with his daughter Dürrüşehvar and son-in-low Azam Cah grandson of Hyderabad Nizam. The other bride is Nilüfer Sultan, the granddaughter of Sultan Murad V who is married to Muazzam Cah, the other grandson of Hyderabad Nizam.

Cemil Molla Mansion

Cemil Molla Mansion

Heading north from Kuzguncuk you are soon forced to divert inland by a waterfront naval base. Just as the road turns you will see on the right a wonderful wooden house with a turret that was built by the Italian architect **Albeti** in 1885 for **Mahmud Cemil Efendi**, a Minister for Justice under Sultan Abdülhamid II. Its decor was so impressive that it was sometimes nicknamed "**the eighth wonder of the world**", and it was regularly used for poetry readings and musical recitals.

At the time that it was built the only building allowed to be illuminated using electricity was the Yıldız Palace. Regardless of this, Cemil Molla had an **electricity generator** installed in the grounds of his house and on the anniversary of the sultan's accession to the throne risked his wrath by turning it on to light the building. His argument that the only way to commemorate such an important occasion properly was with electricity eventually won the day, and so he paved the way for the rest of the city to be electrified. The mansion also housed one of the Empire's first telephones, as well as a private **cinema** and **photographic studio**. Today, sadly, all this remarkable history has been forgotten.

Modern versions of the old sultans' caiques are used for Bosphorus tours

Hüseyin Avni Paşa Fountain

Paşalimanı

Just before Kuzguncuk on the way from Üsküdar is Paşalimanı (the Paşa's Harbor) which acquired its name when **Admiral Piyale Paşa** built himself a palace here (since lost). Facing the waterfront a large, newly restored **warehouse** used to store tobacco; it has now been restored to provide administrative offices for the Istanbul opera, ballet and orchestra. Immediately opposite it is what used to be the monumental **Nemlizade Tobacco Warehouse**, built by **Vedat Tek** in 1923.

Old warehouses

The Nemlizade Tobacco Warehouse now houses the headquarters of Ciner Holdings.

Kuzguncuk *Yalıs*

The Arapzadeler Yalı on the right of this photo and the Baştımar Yalı on the left stand in front of the Fethi Ahmed Paşa Woods.

Baştımar Yalı

The Baştımar family, descendants of **Gazi Edhem Paşa**, who was a military commander during the reign of Abdülhamid II, had a very beautiful yalı in Rumeli Hisarı (see p.135). The Secretary General of the Turkish Communist Party, **Nihat Sargın** (1929-2010), who married the sister of **Dündar Baştımar**, lived in this yalı for many years.

Arapzadeler Yalı

Born in the year 1719, **Arapzade Ataullah Efendi** was promoted from the post of a military judge to that of the chief religious official of the Ottoman Empire at the age of 66, serving only two months in this position before he died in 1785. The yalı was first (before Arapzade Ataullah Efendi) the property of **Arapzade Mehmed Arif Efendi**, who passed it onto his son **Sadullah Efendi**. It became the property of the Governor of Erzurum, **Halil Kemal Paşa**, during the reign of **Sultan Abdülaziz**.

Sculptor İhsan Bey Yalı

İhsan Özsoy (1867-1944) was Turkey's first sculptor and lectured at the **Istanbul Fine Arts Academy**. When he died this yalı was bequeathed to his sister, **Nimet Hanım**, and then to her son and daughter. It was sold to **Mehmet Doğan** in 1971. Normally the haremlik of a yalı was the bigger part of it. Here, though, the men's section, which consists of two buildings, is larger.

Fethi Ahmed Paşa Yalı

Kuzguncuk's finest building is the **Fethi Ahmed Paşa Yalı**, otherwise known as the **Pink Yalı**, which was built in the 18th century. Fethi Ahmed Paşa was married to Sultan Abdülmecid's sister **Atiye Sultan** and was responsible for the yalı's interior decoration. The building was apparently a favorite of the Swiss-French architect **Le Corbusier** who made two visits to Istanbul in 1911 and 1948. The composer **Franz Liszt** also stayed here when he visited the city. Only the men's part of the mansion survives; the women's quarters were used as a tobacco depot and burned down in 1927.

Le Corbusier

Franz Lizst

In 1846 **Fethi Ahmed Paşa** became responsible for the creation of Istanbul's first military museum, then housed in **Hagia Eirene** church in the old city.

Who was Şevket Mocan?

Fethi Ahmed Paşa's grandson was a playboy who became MP for Tekirdağ during the period when the **Democratic Party** led by **Adnan Menderes** was in power. A habitué of the Tokatlıyan Hotel in Beyoğlu, he fell in love with **Gönül Yazar** who was nicknamed "Taş Bebek" (The China Doll). His daughter **Ayşe** married the nephew of the leader of the Communist Party **Zeki Baştımar** which so enraged her father that he called for membership of the CP to attract the death penalty. Baştımar's family owned the **Zeki Paşa Yalı** in Rumeli Hisarı (see p.135). The Fethi Ahmed Paşa Yalı is sometimes called the **Mocan Yalı** after this man.

Kamil Paşa Yalı

The ambassador to St. Petersburg, Kamil Paşa, acquired this yalı, which had been used as a courthouse, and bequeathed it to his brother, **Yusuf Ziya Bey**. After his death, his son-in-law acquired the other shares in the property and, after tearing down the northern portion towards the Bosphorus Bridge, had the **Halil Haşim Bey Yalı** constructed. Only a section of the Kamil Paşa Yalı is still standing.

Madam Agavni Muratyan Yalı

Dating from the second half of the 19th century, this Art Nouveau yalı belonged to an Armenian family of Iranian descent. It passed to **Şerif Gazioğlu** until 1988, when it was sold to **Vildan Gürani** and **Canan Subaşı**. Its latest owners are the Kibar family, who also own yalıs in Bebek and Rumeli Hisarı. The yalı was completely renovated in 2004.

Halil Haşim Bey Yalı

The northern portion of the Kamil Paşa Yalı was constructed by **Raimondo d'Aronco**, who was responsible for many fine works in Istanbul. After the death of Halil Haşim Bey, the yalı was bequeathed to his son, **Mukbil Moralıoğlu**. The spectacular **Cemil Molla Mansion** rises up behind it.

Kuzguncuk Garden

The story of the "Ilia's Vegetable Garden", as mentioned by the locals, dates back to the 1990s. The locals of the neighbourhood united under the name "Garden Solidarity Volunteers". The garden is a refreshing area both for the locals in Kuzguncuk and visitors coming from other places with its cultivable areas, a small park, openair cinema open during summer months and as a gathering place for the locals on religious holidays.

27 The Empress' Love-Nest

Beylerbeyi

The 1st Bridge separates Kuzguncuk from Beylerbeyi, best known for its palace but also home to a fine baroque mosque, a yalı-hotel and a collection of inviting restaurants grouped together around the ferry terminal. It was used as a setting in the famous 1964 heist movie "Topkapi" starring the late Peter Ustinov.

Beylerbeyi is sneakily two-faced. From the water its charms are immediately obvious as you drift past the palace and its alluring landing stage. From the road, however, it appears at first sight to be just another congested suburb, the only hint of something more interesting being the imposing gateway leading through to the mosque.

The area was originally called "**Stavros (The Cross)**", apparently because of a large cross erected here by **Constantine the Great**. Later it was renamed "Lord of the Lords", possibly in memory of **Mehmed Paşa** who served as Governor of Rumelia (the Balkans) during the reign of **Sultan Murad III** and built himself a fine house here (although the name could be much later in origin). In the dying days of the Ottoman Empire this was a place where religious leaders made their homes. Today it's a suburb that has moved steadily upmarket, and there's a very chi-chi corner full of restaurants, art galleries and upscale shops tucked away out of sight of the busy main road near the ferry terminal and the exclusive Villa Bosphorus. Think of 2the **Ortaköy** (p.104) of the Asian shore and you'll get the general picture.

A lion decorating the palace entrance

Beylerbeyi Palace

Sultan Abdülaziz

The first Beylerbeyi Palace was built here between 1829 and 1832, but, as so often, fell victim to a fire in 1851. Although enough of the palace survived for him to continue to use it, **Sultan Abdülmecid** never returned there, and in 1865 **Sultan Abdülaziz** had it replaced with the present relatively restrained baroque building that was designed by **Sarkis Balyan**. It was here that Sultan **Abdülhamid II** lived after he returned from exile in Salonica in 1912, and here that he died in 1918.

Originally the palace would have been approached from the Bosphorus, and it has a delightful **private landing stage** of marble flanked by exquisite **boathouses** that look like tents rendered in stone. Today of course most visitors have to be content with creeping up on it from the rear before joining a guided party in the hall.

Intended for summer use and to house official guests, the palace has a very manageable 26 rooms divided into the public male and private female's quarters. The single most impressive room is focused on a large **marble pool** with a fountain carved with dolphins; the sound of the cascading water must have been marvelously cooling in summer. Also very impressive are two rooms facing

If you click on www.3dmekanlar.com you will be able to see images of Beylerbeyi Palace and other important buildings in 3D.

each other across a hallway whose walls, ceilings and furniture are all carved with **Moorish-style woodwork**. Like the larger and older Dolmabahçe Palace (see p.74), Beylerbeyi is decorated throughout with Hereke carpets, Baccarat glass and Yıldız porcelain. However, one of its more conspicuous features is the omnipresence of **maritime scenes** painted by **Stanislas Chlebowski** (1835-1884), a Polish artist much admired by Sultan Abdülaziz, on the walls and ceilings. There is also a series of decorative panels inscribed with poetry and with quotations from the Koran.

Empress Eugenie

Famous visitors to the palace included the **Shah of Iran**, and those other well-known British socialites, the **Duke and Duchess of Windsor**. But the most famous visitor was **Empress Eugenie** of France who dropped by on her way to the **opening of the Suez Canal** in 1869 and was supposedly so impressed by what she saw that she had copies of the windows made for the Tuileries Palace in Paris. She is believed to have embarked on an affair with **Sultan Abdülaziz**, as described in **Pablo Martin Asuero's book "El Palacio de las Columnas Azules (The Palace of the Blue Columns)".**

A particularly delightful feature of the palace is the **terraced garden** that rises up the hillside behind it. Here can be found the **Ahır Köşk (Stables),** one of the few imperial stable blocks to survive, as well as the decorative **Sarı Köşk (Yellow Pavilion)** and **Mermer Köşk (Marble Pavilion)**, the latter overlooking a small **lake** on which swans used to swim. A unique **tunnel** was built beneath the terraced part of the garden during the reign of Sultan Mahmud II; this enabled road traffic to pass without it being cut off from the waterside part. Some might wish that a similar solution could have been found so that the 1st Bosphorus Bridge did not soar so noisily above it today.

Tel: 0216 321 93 20
www.millisaraylar.gov.tr
Closed Mondays and Thursdays.

Stairways of Selamlık

Blue Hall

Kürsü – preacher's chair

Mosque interior

Beylerbeyi Hamam

Inconspicuously located behind what looks like the façade of a wooden house **Beylerbeyi Hamam** was built in 1789 as part of the Beylerbeyi Mosque complex. It still serves men and women, with women mainly welcomed during the middle part of the day and men in the early morning or evening.

Tel: 0216 321 46 83

Beylerbeyi Mosque

Right on the waterfront, this large mosque with a small garden was built by **Sultan Abdülhamid I** for his mother **Rabia Sultan** in 1778; the architect was **Mehmed Tahir Ağa** who was also responsible for Laleli Mosque. A second minaret was added in the early 19th century by Sultan Mahmud II. Beside it stands an attractive two-storey oval building that used to house a **library** and **time-keeper's lodge**. The mosque boasts a particularly fine minbar and a priest's chair made from wood inlaid with ivory.

Beylerbeyi *Yalıs*

Özdemir Sabancı Yalı

The youngest son of **Sadıka** and **Hacı Ömer Sabancı**, Özdemir Sabancı persuaded **Toyota** to set up a 50% joint-venture factory in Turkey, the first such enterprise outside Japan. In 1996 he was assassinated in his office in Levent in somewhat mysterious circumstances that were being reexamined. Since his death, Özdemir Sabancı's family has been living in the yalı, which features contemporary architectural elements. His son, **Demir**, moved into the adjacent **Hasib Paşa Yalı** after it was restored.

The villa behind the Özdemir Sabancı Yalı belonged to Faruk Süren. Ali Sabancı, the owner of Pegasus Airlines, later acquired it.

Hasib Paşa Yalı

The yalı of Hasib Paşa, who served as vizier (minister) during the reigns of Sultans **Abdülmecid** and **Abdülaziz**, burned to the ground in 1972. The reincarnated Hasib Paşa Yalı belongs to **Demir** and **Aslıhan Sabancı**. The first member of the Sabancı family to break away from Sabancı Holdings, Demir Sabancı is the **CEO of Sedes Holdings**, which deals with everything from insurance to grocery shops.

Mabeyinci Faik Bey Yalı

Once the property of the Kalkavan family, this fine yalı was once home to **Esra Bereket**, the wife of **Hyderabad Nizam Bereket Jah**, who sold it to **Hacı Sabancı**. It featured in Topkapı, the cult 1964 film starring **Melina Mercouri** and **Peter Ustinov** in which thieves attempted to steal the **Topkapı Dagger**. The yalı to its left belongs to Jak Kamhi (see p.158).

The pink-hued **Hüseyin Kazım Kadri Yalı** is currently serving as a restaurant. The yalı on its right belonged to **Hamid Paşa** who served in **Yıldız Palace** during the reign of **Abdülhamid II**.

28

Anchor Village

Çengelköy, Kuleli and Vaniköy

North of Üsküdar, beyond Kuzguncuk and Beylerbeyi, lies the waterside suburb of Çengelköy, known for its pretty main square which is shaded by ancient plane trees. This is not a place to come in search of major sights so much as somewhere where you can while away a few hours beside the water and shop the way the locals do. The most prominent landmark between Çengelköy and Vaniköy is the lemon-walled, twin-towered, oddly asymmetrical Kuleli Military School, clearly visible as you cruise along the Bosphorus.

In Turkish, Çengelköy means "Anchor Village", and two possible explanations have been given for how it acquired this strange name. The usual story is taken from the Ottoman travel writer **Evliya Çelebi** who suggested that a stash of Byzantine hooks and anchors had been found here after the Conquest of Istanbul in 1453. However, it is also possible that the village was named after **Admiral Çengeloğlu Tahir Paşa** who built a waterside mosque here.

As long ago as the 6th century the Emperor Justin II had a palace built for his empress **Sophia** after whom the area that is now Çengelköy was called **Sophianae**. In the 19th century a summer palace, the **Hümayun Kasrı**, stood here, its grounds watered by streams that flowed down from the forests on the hillside above. Today no trace of either structure survives.

Vahdeddin Mansion

High on the hillside above Çengelköy stands a huge 19th-century mansion distinguished by a tower topped with an onion dome. Originally built for the **Armenian Köçeoğlu family**, it became home to Sultan Abdülaziz's nephew **Prince Burhaneddin** and then to **Vahdeddin Mehmed VI**, the last of the sultans who reigned from 1918 to 1922 before being sent into exile. It is used by Presidency of Turkey.

Hagios Georgios Church at Easter

Church of St George

At the Kuleli end of Çengelköy, in Tanrıverdi Sokağı, the large 19th-century Greek Orthodox church of **Hagios Georgios** (St George) stands on sloping land with a bell tower at the top of a flight of steps. From the outside (which is all that you are likely to be able to see) it looks almost like a warehouse. Inside, however, it contains a particularly fine iconostasis.

On 6 January (**Epiphany**) swimmers retrieve crosses thrown into the sea during an ancient ceremony known as **tossing the cross** at Çengelköy, Kuzguncuk, Fener, Ortaköy, Arnavutköy and Yeşilköy.

Macar (Hungarian) Feyzullah Paşa Villa

One of the finest examples of mid-19th-century Ottoman architecture in Istanbul, the villa was constructed as a hunting lodge in a lush green valley by the Hungarian **Josef Kohlmann**, AKA Feyzullah Paşa, in the 1860s.

Originally close to the sultan's Beylerbeyi summer palace, it was sold after remaining in the family for several generations. Once considered a masterpiece for its intricate interior décor, the building was allowed to fall into disrepair until it was acquired by the famous art historian, **Serdar Gülgün**, who now lives in it, having restored it to its former glory. It holds his vast art collection, which includes fine examples of calligraphy, embroidery, **Uşak** carpets, furniture inlaid with mother-of-pearl, and blue and white **Chinese** porcelain from various periods. It is one of the three finest private homes that I have visited in Istanbul.

Garden pavilion

THE GARDEN AND FAÇADE

The villa was built in a secluded valley, which boasts a more temperate climate than the rest of Istanbul, allowing different types of plant to be raised in its garden. The palms, laurels, lemon, pistachio and linden trees succeed perfectly in keeping the city's concrete tentacles at bay, while the mulberry trees are old enough to have witnessed most of the villa's history. Today some fine roses still grow here and a pretty pavilion lets visitors appreciate the garden's peaceful beauty.

View of the hall from the staircase

THE GROUND FLOOR

Giant guillotine (double sash) windows let light and air flood into the villa; they're so large that they were crafted in three sections instead of the normal two.

A classic Ottoman house plan was applied to the villa's architecture, with nine rooms opening off central lounge areas. A lath plaster technique was also applied in an attempt to minimise potential damage during an earthquake.

The villa is entered through a marble hall. The three rooms situated on the right-hand side are used as the owner's bedroom and workrooms while those to the left serve as the dining room and kitchen. The engraved penwork on the ceiling was crafted over canvas in order to prevent cracks appearing after an earthquake. The 4,000 thumbtacks that fasten the canvas were positioned so meticulously that it is almost impossible to see them. The incredible chandelier hanging from the ceiling is a **Venetian Murano** work from the 18th century. The walls are decorated with twin Ottoman mirrors inlaid with mother-of-pearl and roundels inscribed with thuluth calligraphy.

Guests ascend to the first floor via a magnificent staircase with wooden banisters.

The dining room is to the left on the ground floor

The Oval Hall resembles that of the Sadullah Paşa Yalı (p. 258).

THE FIRST FLOOR

The divanhane is situated on this floor and is covered with a dramatic oval dome that mimics one of the sultan's tents. Its hub is carved in a style associated with **Edirne** craftsmanship and is a work of art in its own right. Always regarded as the most important section of an Ottoman home, this grand reception hall takes up 150sqm of space and is shaped like a cross. One of the rooms off it was used as a Turkish bath. Its marble was renewed during the restoration but the portion bearing **Sultan Mehmed Reşad**'s tuğra (seal) is original. Its dome is decorated with **kündekari** (carved wood) work.

The ceilings of some of the other rooms are also decorated with kündekari woodwork, which gives them the feel of exquisite jewellery boxes.

The villa is full of wonderful antiques.

Private Turkish bath bearing the sultan's seal

The Cihannüma feels like a completely separate building.

CİHANNÜMA

At the top of the villa is an attic called a 'Cihannüma', which means 'showing the world' in Turkish. It was where the paşa would come to admire the view and is embellished with elegantly crafted penmanship inspired by the **Fruit Room** (Yemiş Odası) of Topkapı Palace.

WHO WAS MACAR FEYZULLAH PAŞA?

Born in **Moravia** in 1808, Josef Kohlmann graduated from the military academy in Vienna and was then assigned important duties in the Austrio-Hungarian Empire. However, in the 1840s he and around 20 colleagues carried out an unsuccessful attempted coup to liberate the Hungarians and were forced to take refuge in the Ottoman Empire. A diplomatic crisis then ensued between the two empires, with the Hungarians demanding the repatriation of Kohlmann and his colleagues. The matter was resolved when he converted to Islam becoming an Ottoman citizen and changing his name to Feyzullah. He was promoted to paşa when he fought for the Ottomans during the Crimean War. When he retired he had this hunting lodge built for himself, and it was here that he died in 1889.

SERDAR GÜLGÜN

Born in Istanbul, Serdar Gülgün studied Ottoman art at London's School of Oriental and African Studies and worked in London for some time at **Sotheby's Auction House's Islamic Arts Section** as an Ottoman art specialist. Having written about Istanbul for the **Louis Vuitton** European city guidebooks, the talented Gülgün turned his hand to fabric and porcelain design, but he also restores Ottoman works and has lectured in the Ottoman art doctorate program at the British Museum. Published his **"The Grand Bazaar"** and **"Ottoman Chic"** which are splendid books.

Çengelköy *Yalıs*

Sadullah Paşa Yalı

Sadullah Paşa

Like most of the Bosphorus suburbs, Çengelköy and Vaniköy still retain plenty of lovely old waterside mansions in varying states of repair. One of the oldest in Çengelköy is the burgundy-colored Sadullah Paşa Yalı which was given to **Mehmed Ağa**, a eunuch at Topkapı Palace, by **Sultan Abdülhamid I** in the late 18th century. Its baroque-style upper floor contained a room designed to imitate an Ottoman tent (otağ).

After the death of **Necibe Hanım** (see The haunted house p.258) the house passed to Ferit Tek, a distant relative. His daughter married an Egyptian prince and set up a foundation to maintain it. One tenant was **Ayşegül**

Tecimer who married **Asil Nadir**, the Polly Peck entrepreneur who fled the UK for Northern Cyprus when his business empire collapsed. She was later accused of selling antiquities illegally and left Turkey to live in **Marrakesh** in Morocco.

The Haunted House

In 1872 the Mehmed Ağa Yalı was bought by **Sadullah Paşa** who fell from favor with the court. Suspected of plotting against the sultan, he was sent as an ambassador to **Berlin**, and forbidden to return. Eventually he fell in love in **Vienna** and committed suicide there in 1892. Unable to believe he was never coming back, his wife, **Necibe Hanım**, continued to keep the house spotless and waited for his return clad in a dress he loved. She was still wearing it when she, too, died in 1917. Some people believe that her **ghost** haunts the house to this day.

Garden

Ayşegül Tecimer Nadir

Cemal Emden's photographs of the oval hall and back entrance to the **Sadullah Paşa Yalı** are reproduced with the permission of the **Tek-Esin Foundation**.

Entrance to the yalı from the garden

Oval Hall

Bostancıbaşı Abdullah Ağa Yalı

The early 19th-century Bostancıbaşı Abdullah Ağa Yalı was built for a man who rose from poverty to become a grand vizier to **Sultan Mahmud II** for a brief four months and who was nicknamed **"Deli Abdullah" (Crazy Abdullah)**. The mansion was expropriated by the Ministry of Culture and Tourism in 1981. All its original pieces were preserved before its demolishment in line with the relief and restoration projects prepared by the Taç Foundation. It was rebuilt with a concrete-brick interior and a timber-covered façade. It was planned to be turned into a Judgeship Building and was transferred to the Ministry of Justice. The mansion was restored under this function and assumed its present shape. It is currently home to a branch of an old pudding shop, which is now a worldwide chain store.

The yellow building behind the ferry terminal is a church

Server Bey Yalı

Right next to the landing stage is the recently restored and elegant four-storey Server Bey Yalı that has changed hands many times.

The staircase of the Muazzez Hanım Yalı is enclosed inside an elegant tower. The Baha Bey Yalı beside it was up for sale for $6 million in 2011.

Muazzez Hanım Yalı

This yalı belonged to one of Turkey's first industrialists, the sugar baron, **Hayri İpar**, who also owned the Cemil Topuzlu Villa in Caddebostan. He was forced to flee the country during the military takeover of 1960. His wife **Emine Tevhide İpar**, his daughters **Şaziye** and **Muazzez**, and his son, Ali, who was married to the Hollywood filmstar, **Virginia Bruce**, were prominent Turkish socialites. Muazzez İpar, after whom the yalı is named, was married to the painter **Rasin Arsebük** and lived here. Once known for her great beauty, she sadly committed suicide in 1972.

Kaymak Mustafa Paşa Mosque

This pretty wooden mosque was built in 1720 for Kaymak Mustafa Paşa whose father, **Boşnak Kara İbrahim Paşa**, had been brother-in-law to the **Tulip Age Grand Vizier Damat İbrahim Paşa.** Like him, Kaymak Mustafa Paşa was killed during the **Patrona Halil** uprising of 1730. The mosque was restored by **Sultan Mahmud II**.

The area in front of the Kuleli Military High School is perfect for fishing.

In this old engraving a ship called The Jason can be seen moored in front of the Kuleli Military High School.

Kuleli Military High School (Kuleli Askeri Lisesi)

When the Janissaries were disbanded in 1826, **Sultan Mahmud II** founded a regular army to take their place, and a wooden barracks was built for them on the shores of the Bosphorus just up from Çengelköy. After it burnt down **Sultan Abdülmecid** commissioned **Garabet Balyan** to build a stone replacement which came to be known as the **Tower Barracks** after its most conspicuous feature. Following another fire **Sultan Abdülaziz** had it rebuilt with a second storey. During the Crimean War of 1855-1856, the barracks were turned into a **military hospital** supervised by **Florence Nightingale**. Over the years the building has served as a school, orphanage, and military high school. One of its most famous students was **İrfan Orga**, the author of the poignant "**A Portrait of a Turkish Family**". After the decision to close down the military schools in the aftermath of the July 15 coup attempt, this building full of memories was also evacuated. It was planned that the front part of the building will be transferred to the Ministry of Culture and Tourism and it will be turned into a museum. It was announced the function of the remaining part will be decided on later. The site on which the Military High School now stands has been identified as the probable location of a convent called **Metanoia (Repentance)** established by the Emperor Justinian's wife **Theodora** to house forcibly reformed prostitutes, a story gleefully related by the Byzantine historian **Procopius** (c. 500-c. 565) who claimed that Theodora herself had started out as one of them.

YAL ARTILLERY DISEMBARKING FROM "THE JASON."

Vaniköy *Yalıs*

Just after you pass the Kuleli Military High School you'll see two unexceptional yalıs sharing a garden. They belong to the Ülker family, Turkey's most famous chocolate-makers. The brown one is the **Neşet and Şirin Yalçın Yalı**, the yellow one the **Yusuf Paşa Yalı** (Formerly Abdülgaffar Karacadağı Yalı).

Mahmud Nedim Paşa Yalı before restoration

Mahmud Nedim Paşa Yalı

Further north in Vaniköy, the **Mahmud Nedim Paşa Yalı** was built for an Ottoman ambassador to Vienna and grand vizier who was so fond of the Russians that he was nicknamed "**Nedimof**". It features a distinctive wooden tower. The yalı came into the hands of Kızılay (the Red Crescent) who sold it to Yalçın Sabancı for just $3 million in 2004. It has since been beautifully restored.

The yalı on the right is the İffet Hanım Yalı. To the left stand the selamlık and harem quarters of Mahmud Nedim Paşa Yalı.

Anadolu Kazaskeri Necmeddin Efendi Yalı

The building has had a troubled history featuring damage caused by fires and boat collisions. It belonged to the **Sapmaz**, a wealthy family of textile manufacturers from Adana. In 1973 Coşkun Sapmaz married the Turkish pop singer and actress **Ajda Pekkan** but his family disapproved so strongly of the match that it lasted only six days. Later the family was hit by a financial crisis and lost everything including this yalı.

The Anadolu Kazasker Necmeddin Efendi Yalı now belongs to the jewellery designer Tansa Mermerci Ekşioğlu.

Serasker Rıza Paşa Yalı

Next door to the Anadolu Kazasker Necmeddin Efendi Yalı, the **Serasker Rıza Paşa** Yalı, which dates back to the late 19th century, retains more of its original appearance. Rıza Paşa was an ambassador and a favorite of **Sultan Abdülhamid II**. During the Second Constitutional Period he was forced to flee to France. His son Süreyya İlmen became an MP and established the **Süreyya Beach** and the **Süreyya Opera House** in Kadıköy (see p.198).

Designed by Sedad Hakkı Eldem, this yalı belongs to the philanthropists Suna and İnan Kıraç who gave the wonderful Pera Museum to Istanbul. Originally it was the harem of the Serasker Rıza Paşa located next door.

Vaniköy Mosque was built in 1665 Vanlı (by Van) **Mehmed Efendi** who gave his name to the suburb. The Sultan's Lodge was added in **Sultan Mahmud** I's reign.

Ahmed Nazif Paşa Yalı

Ahmet Nazif Paşa (1842-1905) was three times Minister of Finance under **Sultan Abdülhamid II** and had a great reputation for being well-adjusted and honest.

The larger building on the left was the harem of his yalı while the separate smaller building on the right was the selamlık.

This yalı belongs to Ender Mermerci of Akfil Holdings

Dining room

Evrenosoğlu Hamid Bey Yalı

This yalı took its name from Hamid Bey, who was descended from the family of **Gazi Evrenos**, a man said to have lived from 1288 to 1417 which would have made him 129 when he died! Tracing their lineage back to the early Ottoman days of the Akıncı warriors, this family played a significant part in the founding of the Ottoman Empire. With a distinctly European flavor, the yalı once belonged to **Esin-Yaşar Yılmaz Başkaya**, but has since changed hands and been thoroughly restored.

Winter garden

Living room

The photographs of the Evrenosoğlu Hamid Bey Yalı were taken by Engin Aydeniz.

Mihrengiz Kadın Efendi (Melek Hanım) Yalı

Due to financial difficulties, Melek Hanım, the daughter of **Esvapçıbaşı Sabit Efendi**, rented out the small yalı seen to the right in the photograph. Amongst its notable tenants were the archeologist **Halet Çambel** and the writer and translator **Mina Urgan**. The large, three-storey yalı on the left was once the Kadınefendi Yalı. It belonged to a fourth wife of **Sultan Reşad** named **Dilfirib**. Following the declaration of the Republic, the dynasty was sent into exile, but she was allowed to stay in Istanbul because of her poor health. She died in her villa in Erenköy in 1952.

Recaizade Yalı

The **Recaizade Yalı** belonged to Recai Mehmed Efendi and was the birthplace of his son, the poet **Mahmud Ekrem Bey** (1847-1914), author of "Araba Sevdası (Carriage Liaisons)", regarded as one of Turkey's first realist novels. Mahmud Ekrem had his own yalı in **Yeniköy**. Accused of secretly signaling to **Khedive Abbas Hilmi Paşa** over in Çubuklu, he was forced to sell it and move to Cihangir. Until the 1980s the Vanıköy yalı was used as a corn-oil factory. It was then seized by the local authorities, but is now back in private ownership. The garden boasts some beautiful bougainvillea plants.

Recaizade Mahmud Ekrem

Vaniköy in 2012. To the left is Ender Mermerci's yalı with the Ahmed Nazif Paşa Yalı beside it. The tower of the Mahmud Nedim Paşa Yalı appears after its restoration.

Postcard of Vaniköy at the end of the 19th century with the Anadolu Kazasker Necmeddin Efendi Yalı in the foreground and the tower of the Mahmud Nedim Paşa Yalı to the right.

29

The Hilltop Observatory

Kandilli and Küçüksu Mansion

The Kont Ostorog and Hadi Bey yalıs are backed by the Cemile Sultan Woods

For Turks the suburb of Kandilli is best known as the location of a famous observatory that issues bulletins after earthquakes. It is home, too, to the Küçüksu Mansion, perhaps the prettiest of the minor 19th-century imperial lodges. Kandilli also boasts many fine yalıs, including the Kıbrıslı Yalı, the longest such waterside mansion on the Bosphorus, and Abud Efendi Yalı, the setting for popular soap operas.

Lost churches

Although it was one of the smaller villages on the shores of the Bosphorus, Kandilli once had **three churches and a mosque**. The Catholic Church was converted into a house, and although the other two churches still exist they are no longer in operation. The **Istanbul Riots** of 6-7 September 1955 left an indelible mark on Kandilli; the minority religious populations disappeared, and the Greek primary school, which had boasted 88 students in 1914, closed in 1972 (I later found one of its old desks, still with the old pupil's names carved into it, on sale in an antique shop). At that time, **the sense of community** was still strong. Everybody knew and greeted each other, so a stranger really stood out. One day I spotted a stranger standing on the quayside. The village headman identified him as his old friend, Marko, who had to leave along with the other Greeks. Now he had returned to visit his elderly aunt and his old homeland before he died. In the 1990s his aunt, the last Greek in the village, passed away and the Greek cemetery opened and closed its doors for a funeral for the last time. It was the end of an era. Neither Kandilli nor Istanbul was ever the same again.

The **mansion of Fatin Gökmen**, founder of the Kandilli observatory, stood beside the old Greek cemetery. A gorgeous structure originally built for a Levantine family, it was converted into a monstrous shape in the process of "restoration". Another stone building in the same street was built for the Glavany family after whom **Kallavi Street** in Beyoğlu was named. Despite the magnificent murals decorating its walls and ceilings the house was turned into a social facility for a school, leaving only the original outside walls still standing. In their heyday, these two houses boasted **breathtaking views** of a small forest and a valley running down to a beach. Then, despite the fact that construction along the shore of the Bosphorus had been prohibited, they were suddenly surrounded by serried ranks of new villas.

The Glavany family mansion and coat of arms

Greek Orthodox Church of Christ

Surp Yergodasan Arakelotz (12 Disciples) Armenian Church

The Greek Orthodox Primary School has been closed for decades

The lost mansions

Like so many areas of Istanbul, Kandilli has suffered from relentless and often unthinking "development". In particular, the number of wooden houses declines day by day; some were supposedly being restored although the end results often look nothing like the originals. A more conspicuous victim of brutalist restoration was the **Demosten Corpi Mansion**. This four-storey building in Sıraevler Street, opposite the Armenian church, was built by members of the same Italian family responsible for the **old American Consulate (Soho House)** in Tepebaşı. Its walls and ceilings were once richly decorated with especially adorable animal paintings. The exceptionally big and beautiful garden embraced a chalet and pool. But then one day the walls were suddenly whitewashed, an act of vandalism almost as crass as whitewashing over the walls of the Sultanahmet Mosque.

Demosten Corpi Mansion

When this photo was taken in the 1980s some of the paintings still survived.

Casanova's Bosphorus bolthole

The façade of another traditionally maroon-colored building known as the Casanova Mansion conceals an interesting footnote to **erotic history**. When describing his varied experiences on a visit to Istanbul in 1745 in his 12-volume "**Story of My Life**", the famous Italian playboy Giacomo Casanova (1725-1798) mentioned in particular the love and kindness shown to him by , Reis-ül Küttap İsmail Efendi. Later an artist named Türkan Hanım lived here. Finally it was bought and restored by the construction company STFA.

Casanova Mansion

The white building on the right is the Dabcovich mansion.

Giacomo Casanova

Kurtbağrı Sokak

Bülent Bulgurlu Mansion

Kandilli Yokuşu (Kandilli Hill)

Kandilli Yokuşu contains the mansion home of the **Trabzon MP Şükrü Bey** whose huge, tree-filled garden contained an ayazma (sacred spring). Eventually this fine building also fell victim to the sort of "restoration" that effectively replaces an old building with a brand-new one. In this case, however, the good news is that the building had provided an inspirational childhood home for **Bünyamin Derman** who went on to become an award-winning architect.

Poetic inspiration

I lived in Kandilli for 25 years. It is and always will be the most special place in the world for me. As I was writing these lines, I remembered a poem of **Constantine Cavafy** entitled "**The City**" which reads:

"You will not find new places; other seas
you will not find. This city will follow you.
You will walk the same familiar streets,
Get older in the same neighborhood,
Grow white hair in the same house.
Always you will return to this same city.
Don't expect anything elsewhere;
There is no ship, no road.
As you have destroyed your life here
In this little corner,
So you have ruined it
Everywhere in the world.

Saffet Emre Tonguç

Amazingly, people still lived in this house a few years ago.

Kandilli Ferry Terminal

Sultan Murad IV

Kandilli

In Turkish Kandilli means **"with oil lamps"**, and there are several suggested reasons as to how the suburb acquired such a romantic name. Two of them relate to **Sultan Murad IV** who is said to have built a palace here and ringed it with oil lamps; alternatively, he is said to have hung a cypress tree with decorative lamps. In another version of the same story a priest in need of a favor is said to have placed candles in the sultan's garden every evening, thus giving rise to the name. More prosaically, lamps are thought to have been placed at **Kandilli Point** as a form of primitive lighthouse. Finally, the name could have come from the proliferation of candle-makers' workshops in the area. Take your pick.Today the **Küçüksu River** is a polluted trickle of water and it's hard to believe that it was once, with the Göksu River at nearby Anadolu Hisarı, one of the two stretches of water to which revelers flocked in the 18th century and which were known collectively as **"the Sweet Waters of Asia"**. Dredging work currently in progress should eventually improve its appearance and smell, a step in its rehabilitation, and already the excursion boats are starting to reappear.

The Observatory (Rasathane)

Takiyuddin

Istanbul's first observatory was built above **Tophane** in the 16th century, roughly where the Maison de France is now in Tom Tom Kaptan Sokak. It was the brainchild of **Takiyuddin** (1526-1585), a talented astronomer and physicist who had worked at the observatory in **Samarkand** and arrived in Istanbul in the 1550s. However, after the religious authorities ruled that it was a sin to study the heavens, **Sultan Murad III** ordered **Admiral Kılıç Ali Paşa** to destroy it. A surviving account of the first observatory describes several different instruments that were in use there. It is thought that it may have had an influence on the work of the famous Danish astronomer, **Tycho Brahe**. Two years later a new observatory, the Rasathane-i Amire, was established in **Beyoğlu**, before being moved again, this time to Maçka. Finally in 1911 the Observatory arrived in its present location on İcadiye Hill where once there had stood a mansion called **Hekimgörmez Sarayı (Never Needs a Doctor Palace)**, a name apparently given to it because the strong sunlight on the hilltop was believed to keep its residents healthy. Until this time the religious authorities had been in control of everything to do with **time-keeping** but from then on this responsibility passed to the observatory. Today as part of the **Bosphorus University** the observatory also serves as an earthquake research institute. One of its managers **Ahmet Mete Işıkara** made a name for himself in the aftermath of the 1999 earthquakes when people hung so desperately on his words that children started to call him **"Deprem Dede" (earthquake grandpa)**.

Observatory

You can find out more about the Observatory at the Museum of Islamic Science and Technology in Gülhane Park (see p.26).

On the hilltop stands the Adile Sultan Palace. On the shore to the left is the Edib Efendi Yalı. The twin green-roofed yalıs belong to Yalçın Sabancı and Hasan Aslanoba.

Adile Sultan Palace

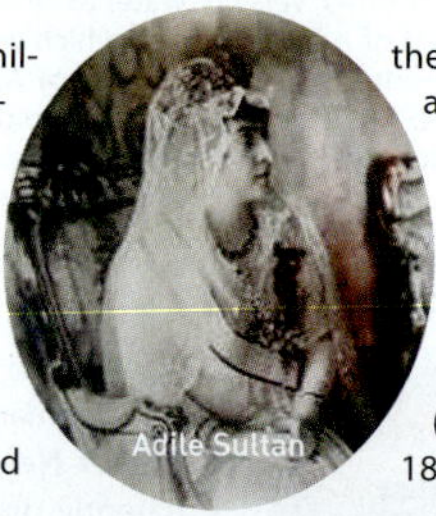

Adile Sultan

One of Sultan Mahmud II's 31 children, Adile (1825-1898), a published poet and philanthropist whose life was blighted by the deaths of her husband, children and younger brother **Sultan Abdülaziz**, employed the **Balyan** family to build a palace for her in Kandilli. In 1916 it became Turkey's second girls' school, and then a girls' high school. Destroyed in a fire in 1986, it has since been restored with grants from an ex-pupil, Prof. **Dr. Turkan Saylan** (see p.116), and the businessperson **Sakıp Sabancı** and reopened in 2006 as an **education and cultural center**, and **restaurant** (see p.290) with a spectacular 180-degree view of the city.

Oval Salon

Kandilli *Yalıs*

Fuat Bayramoğlu Yalı

This is another yalı designed by the famous architect **Sedad Hakkı Eldem** but in our opinion it is less impressive than the **Suna-İnan Kıraç Yalı** in Vaniköy (see p.266). Fuat Bayramoğlu (1912–1996) was a former ambassador, foreign minister and presidential general secretary. Having begun his career in 1945, he was first appointed to ambassadorial duties in Oslo in 1957, continuing as ambassador to Baghdad, Teheran, Rome, Brussels and Moscow. After marrying Nesteren Hanım, the daughter of **Vehbi Koç**'s sister **Zehra Kütükçü**, Fuat Bey traced the Koç family tree back to descendants of **Hacı Bayram Veli**, founder of the **Bayrami Sufi** sect. He became known for writing poetic quatrains and wrote a book on Turkish glass and the Beykoz factory.

One of his quatrains:

The heart is always ready for a new love
The heart is always in love with anyone else
Our spirit has an eternal and inextinguishable fire
The heart is a kind of wine that is distilled with love potion…

Clifton Yalı

From 1881 to 1907 the British woman **Dorina Lady Neave** lived in the **Clifton Yalı** at Kandilli that was eventually burnt down by the Germans. In her *Romance of the Bosphorus* left a lively account of growing up there that includes descriptions of an earthquake, seeing **Sultan Abdülhamid II** visiting the mosque for Friday prayers, and an extraordinary day when many Bosphorus fish literally froze to death.

One of the Bosphorus radar stations can be seen behind this yalı

Edib Efendi Yalı

Visible from a waterside walkway at the Bosphorus' narrowest point and overlooking the city's fastest-flowing current, **Şeytan Akıntısı (Devil's Current)**, the Edib Efendi Yalı has borne the name of many Ottoman officials over the years. Unusually, it features the same ground plan for the male and female sections of the building (the female part is usually larger).

Entrance

Dining room

These photographs of the Edib Efendi Yalı were taken by Engin Aydeniz.

Edib Efendi Yalı Living room

The Selahattin Beyazıt Yalı is a rare example of a single-storey Bosphorus building. The Muharrem Nuri Birgi Yalı (see p.213) at Salacak also belongs to Beyazıt.

Hadi Bey Yalı

Once called the Manford House, this beautiful 19th-century Ottoman-rose-colored yalı was bought by a Greek ship-owner called **Licardopulos** after the British occupation of Istanbul. The lawyer Hadi Bey later acquired it from a Salonican Turk in settlement of a debt. It now belongs to **Hasan Çolakoğlu**, the owner of the TEB bank.

Hadi Bey Yalı

Kont Ostrorog Yalı

Kont Ostrorog Yalı

Of the many other yalıs, one of the most impressive is the **Kont Ostrorog Yalı**, built in the 19th century for the Polish count Leon Ostrorog who was an advisor to the Ottoman court. It was visited in the past by the French novelist **Pierre Loti** (1850-1923), after whom a famous café overlooking the Golden Horn is named. It's now owned by **Rahmi Koç**.

Ancient columns in the garden

Dining room

It's possible to see some of Rahmi Koç's private collection in his study.

The study has a great view of the Bosphorus.

Abud Efendi Yalı
Kont Ostrorog Yalı
Hadi Bey Yalı

Cemile Sultan Woods
Neslişah Sultan (Monheim) Yalı
Çolakoğlu Yalı

Abud Efendi Yalı

Situated between the Ostrorog and Kıbrıslı yalıs, the Abud Efendi Yalı is named after an early 20th-century owner. It was originally designed by **Garabet Amira**, a member of the Armenian Balyan family that was responsible for many of Istanbul's palaces and important buildings, for **Altunizade Recip Bey** who lived in it from 1835 to 1855 before selling it to a French baron. Abud Efendi's daughter, **Belkıs**, was a socialite of the 1920s and an unforgettable wedding reception was held for her in this building. The yalı was purchased in the 1980s by the **Özdoyuran** family, which had made its fortune in the sun flower oil sector. Unfortunately the interior of the yalı turned out to be a great disappointment.

Back garden

Living room

Gümüş

The Abud Efendi Yalı was used as the setting for the popular soap opera "Gümüş (Silver)", starring the dishy **Kıvanç Tatlıtuğ** who has been described as Turkey's answer to Brad Pitt. So popular did this series prove in the Middle East (where it was renamed "Nur") that it has been credited with kickstarting a surge in visitors to the country from the Arab world. It also featured in the TV series **Lale Devri** (Tulip Age).

Cast of Gümüş

This old lithograph depicts a pair of Bosphorus oarsmen above an image of people enjoying themselves at the Sweet Waters of Asia.

1.—BOATMEN OF THE BOSPHORUS. 2.—THE SWEET WATERS.

Kıbrıslı Yalı

Kıbrıslı (Cypriot) Yalı

Of all the Bosphorus yalıs, the 21-room Kıbrıslı (Cypriot) Yalı, which was built in the 18th century for the Grand Vizier **Mehmed İzzet Paşa**, is the longest. Later it passed into the hands of Kıbrıslı Mehmed Emin Paşa whose wife **Melek Hanım** wrote a book called "**Thirty Years in the Harem**" which was published in 1872 and is still in print. Past guests at the yalı included **Pierre Loti**, the **Empress Eugenie** and **King Faisal II**, the last king of Iraq.

Entrance from the back garden

Entrance hall

Library

On the lefthand corner of the hall stands a piano.

Sitting room

Main hall

Who was Melek Hanım?

An Ottoman woman of Greek, Armenian and French lineage, Melek Hanım met **Kıbrıslı Mehmed Emin Paşa** in Paris and married him in Istanbul. As the wife of a grand vizier she traveled extensively with her husband.

However, in his absence she seems to have plotted to replace her sickly son with another child in the event of his death. The child survived, but one of her co-conspirators killed another one, and in the ensuing **scandal** her husband divorced her. Sent into exile, she passed her time plotting to get revenge on him, and writing an account of the life of upper class women in late Ottoman society, which, despite being called "Thirty Years in the Harem", had little to do with what most people think of as the harem at all.

The Kıbrıslı Yalı in an early 20th-century photo.

Kandilli Park

The parapet bears the monogram of Sultan Abdülmecid

Küçüksu Kasrı

Küçüksu Kasrı (Mansion) makes the perfect escape for those who want to see how the 19th-century sultans lived but find the Dolmabahçe Palace overwhelming. Designed by **Nigoğos Balyan** in 1856-1857 as a hunting lodge for **Sultan Abdülmecid I** on the site of an older wooden palace, it has only eight perfectly maintained rooms, enough for you to appreciate the lavish baroque decoration without feeling swamped by it.

Bohemya kristali avizeler.

The mansion stands on the banks of the **Küçüksu River** in a pleasant small garden complete with lily ponds. Of course the sultan would have approached in his **caique** from the Bosphorus where he would have been looking straight at the elaborate ornamentation of the façade. Today's visitors, however, approach from the rear which is a great deal less heavily decorated.

Inside, a delightful double staircase spirals round beneath an internal dome that is painted, like all the ceilings, with goldleaf. The rooms all feature **parquet floors** made from walnut, mahogany and chestnut, on top of which are laid Hereke carpets and one fine Persian carpet that is distinguished for its animal designs. Most of the chandeliers are Bohemian crystal, although one was made in Italy. It's worth taking a peek at the bathroom which features an over-the-top marble sink, and then a super-plain shower unit. Because it was just a **hunting lodge** there was no formal bedroom, although Turkey's fourth president **Cemal Gürsel** (1895-1966) sometimes slept here, hence the daybed in one of the upstairs rooms.

Tel: 0216 323 33 03, www.millisaraylar.gov.tr
Closed Mondays

The fountain in an old photograph

Mihrişah Sultan Fountain with Küçüksu Mansion in the background

Mihrişah Sultan Fountain

As if it wasn't enough that Küçüksu Mansion is the prettiest of the imperial lodges, it also has, right next door in the shape of the **Mihrişah Sultan Fountain**, which was commissioned by Sultan Selim III for his mother in 1807, the most elegant fountain to be found anywhere along the Bosphorus. Much hymned by writers and artists, it stands on a plinth to protect it against flooding roughly midway between the "**Sweet Waters of Asia**".

The view from Sevda Hill behind the Kıbrıslı Yalı.

Kavacık
Otağtepe

30

The Junior Fortress
Anadolu Hisarı

It was here at the narrowest point of the Bosphorus that Sultan Beyazıd I chose to build his castle, and it was here, much later on, that many wealthy individuals chose to build their yalıs, including the magnificent Amcazade Hüseyin Paşa Yalı, the oldest such waterside mansion to survive. This was also the part of Istanbul famed as the "Sweet Waters of Asia".

The white yalı at the far left by the entrance to
Göksu River is named after Riyaziyeci İzzet Bey

Anadolu Hisarı is the suburb that grew up around the "**Anatolian Castle**" started by **Sultan Beyazıd I** and completed by **Sultan Mehmed II**. Today the remaining fortifications are overshadowed by the **2nd Bridge**, the Bosphorus, although this is still a pretty place with a number of impressive **yalıs** clustered around the castle. The banks of the **Göksu River** may be built up now but they once served as one of Istanbul's premier pleasure gardens and even today there's the occasional whiff of the Thames at Maidenhead in England about it.

Anadolu Hisarı in an old engraving

2nd Bridge and yalıs

The castle

Long before Sultan Mehmed II rode up to capture Istanbul in 1453 the early Ottoman sultans had yearned to seize the city, and in 1394 **Sultan Yıldırım (the Thunderbolt) Beyazıd** identified the site of an ancient temple to Jupiter at the narrowest point on the Bosphorus as the best location for a castle. It was from here that he launched the first Ottoman attack on Constantinople which came to an unsuccessful end in 1402 when Tamerlane came thundering across the country and carted the sultan off in chains. Later Sultan Mehmed II decided to expand his great-grandfather's fortress at the same time as he built his own much more magnificent castle on the opposite shore at Rumeli Hisarı (European Castle); Anadolu Hisarı is sometimes called the **Güzelce Hisar** (Rather Pretty Castle) to distinguish it from its more impressive rival.

The new Anatolian Castle consisted of a keep with a surrounding wall enclosing an area of some 7,000 square meters/23,000 square feet together with an outer barbican with three towers. Unfortunately, in the 20th century a road was driven through the walls rendering them considerably less impressive.

From the bridge over the Göksu River a narrow road winds down to the river and in one of the gardens in front of the fortress you can see a rare **namazgah**, an outdoor prayer arena complete with stone mihrab and minbar that was probably built in the early 18th century.

Göksu in the past

Göksu River

While fairly insignificant today, the stream that runs beside the fortress was once extremely important as one of the two waterways (the other was the Küçüksu River), which together made up the playground called "**The Sweet Waters of Asia**". Its banks were once lined with parks and green spaces, and wooden bridges allowed pedestrians to gaze down on boats bringing yet more visitors to frolic on the banks. The area was especially busy on Wednesdays, Fridays and Sundays when people flocked in to participate in what were called the **Göksu Galas**. As recently as the 1960s the area was still undeveloped. Even in 1972 **John Freely** and **Hilary Sumner-Boyd** could write: "If you continue up the valley on foot, you find at the beginning of spring banks and meadows covered with the earliest snowdrops of the year and with wild cyclamen." Now, of course, they are solidly carpeted with concrete, although pleasure boats still moor in picturesque order alongside the banks.

Anadolu Hisarı *Yalıs*

Komodor Remzi Bey Yalı

Built in 1917, the Komodor Remzi Bey Yalı, a grey-painted mansion right on the waterfront, was bought by **Erdal İnönü**, a son of Turkey's second president and a prime minister in his own right, in 1972.

Bahriyeli Sedad Bey Yalı

Constructed in neo-Baroque style in the late 19th century, the Manolyalı (Magnolia) Yalı is divided into two separate properties. The section on the left belongs to the owner of the **Doğuş** schools and universities, **Doğu Gözaçan** while the former president of Boğaziçi (Bosphorus) University, **Üstün Ergüder**, owns the white-colored **Rıza Bey Yalı** on the right of this yalı.

Zarif Mustafa Paşa Yalı

The Zarif Mustafa Paşa Yalı at Anadolu Hisarı is one of the most beautiful and valuable of the Bosphorus mansions. Right beside it is the Amcazade Hüseyin Paşa Yalı, the oldest such mansion on the Bosphorus shore. Below in a nutshell is the story of the 300 years of history that lies behind its lovely façade.

The yalı's second floor extension is supported by five huge wooden brackets.

One of the biggest and most conspicuous of the mansions is the Zarif Mustafa Paşa Yalı, built on the site of a **Byzantine monastery** with an ayazma (sacred spring) in the ground and purchased in the early 19th century by **Kani Bey**, official coffee-maker to Sultan Mahmud II. In 1848 it passed into the possession of the **Zarif Mustafa Paşa** after whom it is named. The paşa's son-in-law Sadık Bey soon tired of all the partying that went on there and bought the selamlık (male quarters) and boathouse for himself before erecting a high wall between the two properties.

The family were related to **Şeyh Talat Efendi** from whom they acquired a piece of the Prophet

The boathouse to the left of the yalı was sold as a separate property for $12 million in 2011.

Mohammed's beard. After Sadık's son **Esat Bey** donated one hair to the **Fatih Mosque** the yalı was sometimes called the Esat Bey Yalı in his honor. The mansion's cihannüma (lantern) was used to display the rest of the beard.

The yalı stayed in the same family until 1992. During the Turkish War of Independence and the British occupation of Istanbul Esat Bey's sons used it to store weapons to be smuggled to the resistance in Anatolia. Because the harem section had been used by English soldiers it was later pulled down. In 1926 the building was painted yellow in celebration of the wedding of Sadiye Hanım, after which it was sometimes called the **Yellow Yalı**.

The elegant Mustafa Paşa Yalı is one of the few historic buildings along the Bosphorus which still retains its beauty.

The Montreux Convention of 1936 had designated the Bosphorus an international waterway which meant that all non-military shipping was free to pass through it, a potentially dangerous situation. Sure enough, in 1974 a ship hit the yalı and severely damaged it. Speedily restored, it fell victim to another **shipping accident** in 1990. After a long legal struggle the owners finally sold the remains for $7 million to the then **Saudi energy minister** whose mother had wanted to live somewhere where she would be able to hear the call to prayer. A stroke meant that she never actually lived in the mansion but it was nevertheless restored by her family.

Since 2000 the house has been back in Turkish hands and the current owner acts as an unofficial ambassador for the country, wel-

The wooden wall panels are decorated with floral designs that evoke the Fruit Room (Yemiş Odası) of Topkapı Palace.

coming such eminent visitors as **Madeleine Albright, Colin Powell, Oprah Winfrey** and the **Grand Duchess Maria Vladimirovna Romanova of Russia** to her home.

It retains many **original features** including a *mehtabiye* (room for looking at the full moon) and a *maltalık* (fruit room) whose walls are decorated with painted fruit and flowers; a built-in **sea hamam** filled with water from the Bosphorus that once allowed the women of the house to bathe in privacy now serves as an indoor fish pond. In the past a **track** used by horse carts passed through the garden but the family eventually donated some land behind it to create a proper road.

Sitting Room

Hamam

Through the glass in the floor of the Coffee Room you can still see the old sea hamam.

Amcazade Hüseyin Paşa (Köprülü) Yalı

It may not look much now but this yalı is very important not only architecturally but because of events that took place inside it. It was built in 1698 for **Grand Vizier Hüseyin Paşa**, nicknamed "The Wise", a member of the powerful Köprülü family who also bequeathed several buildings to **Divan Yolu** and **Çemberlitaş**. As the representative of Sultan Mustafa II, Hüseyin Paşa negotiated with the Europeans at Carlowitz in 1698, and the final articles of the **Peace of Carlowitz**, which resolved the Austro-Ottoman War (1683-1699), were signed in this house in 1699. Its terms forced the Ottomans to cede many of their European holdings to Poland, Russia, Austria and Venice, and marked the beginning of the end of their power.

Today all that survives of the yalı is the central section with its cumba (bay window), both wings having long since collapsed. It's painted the popular rust-red color that was called "**Ottoman rose**". 19th-century drawings show an interior of unmatched sumptuousness, and **Pierre Loti** was one of those who campaigned to save the building for posterity. In 2009 restoration work on the yalı finally began.

Nuri Paşa Yalı

The **Nuri Paşa Yalı**, built in 1895 for an officer of **Sultan Abdülhamid II**, was for some time the home of industralist **Rahmi Koç**. After he moved to the Kont Ostorog Yalı in Kandilli, it became the home of his son **Ali Koç**. According to the gossip Nuri Paşa's son Hami ran away with the daughter of **Marki Necib Bey** who owned the yalı next door.

Marki Necib Bey Yalı

The **Marki Necip Bey Yalı**, believed to date back to the early 19th century, took its name from that of a Frenchman who became a Muslim in order to be able to marry the woman he loved. The building with a tower immediately behind it was used as a winter home. The yalı was restored after a fire in 1983.

Hekimbaşı Salih Efendi Yalı

In much better shape although minus its left wing is the yalı built in the mid-19th century for **Salih Efendi** who was the court physician in attendance when **Sultan Abdülmecid I** died of tuberculosis in 1861. He didn't challenge the verdict that **Sultan Abdülaziz** had committed suicide in 1876 even though he may well have been murdered. However, he drew the line at agreeing when, in the same year, **Abdülhamid II** deposed his brother **Murad V** on the grounds of "emotional instability" and took his place on the throne. Despite the new sultan's efforts to exile him, Salih Efendi was able to retire to the yalı he had bought in the 1840s where he planted a **physic garden** and remarried at the age of 63 a beautiful 16-year-old Circassian girl called Payidar.

Hekimbaşı's diploma

Some of his medical instruments are still preserved in the house. In the mid-20th century British travel writer **Freya Stark** was a guest here. Beautifully restored, the yalı is still in the hands of Salih Efendi's descendants and was restored in 2010.

In 2005 the yalı appeared in Conde Nast Traveler magazine's "Fabulous 50" list of places that are not always open to the public but which give an added insight to a culture. I think it has an air of the "1001 Nights" about it and love its original Turkish bath.

Unfortunately the sea mansion had its share from the traffic in the Bosphorus and a ship struck the mansion in April in 2018 and its façade was severely damaged.

Hekimbaşı's medals

Sitting room facing the Bosphorus before the accident

Bridal room

Hamam

Hekimbaşı's bedroom

Fatih Woods

On **Otağtepe (Tent Hill)** in Kavacık above Anadolu Hisarı, this small and rather overgrown park offers fine views along the Bosphorus in both directions.

Bosphorus view from Otağtepe

Üsküdar Şemsi Paşa Mosque
Maiden's Tower
Savarona
Galatasaray Island
Ciner Holding Building in Paşalimanı
Edib Efendi Yalı
Kandilli Devil's Current

31

Yoghurt and Yalıs
Kanlıca

Dominated today by the 2nd Bridge, Kanlıca's great claim to fame is its yoghurt which has been held in high regard since the 17th century when the Ottoman travel writer Evliya Çelebi spoke of it in mouth-watering terms. Modern passengers on the longer Bosphorus cruises will have a chance to sample it without leaving the boat since yoghurt-sellers always board at Kanlıca to sell their wares. Otherwise, the main reason to visit the suburb is to inspect some of the finest surviving Bosphorus yalıs, none of them open to the public.

Originally Kanlıca seems to have been called **Glaros (Seagull)**, but there is uncertainty over the origin of its modern name, which means "**quite bloody**" in Turkish. Some suggest that it is a corruption of "**kağnis (ox-cart)**" since such carts were once made in this area. Others suggest that local cows used to graze on a **red grass** that turned their milk pink; this grass was supposedly called "kanglı" which might have evolved over time into Kanlıca.

The Kanlıca landing stage opens onto a pretty little main square with a handful of fishing boats still moored alongside an inlet running up to the mosque. It has something of the feel of the old Istanbul, the one jarring feature being the white radar tower, which competes for height supremacy with the minaret. It would have had poor Mimar Sinan turning in his grave.

Gazi İskender Paşa Mosque

This small, much modernized mosque facing the ferry landing stage was originally built by **Mimar Sinan** in 1559-1560 for **İskender Paşa** (1492-1571), a governor of Van, Erzurum, Diyarbakır and Baghdad during the reign of Sultan Süleyman the Magnificent, who is buried in a tomb attached to the time-keeper's lodge beside his son **Ahmed Paşa**. Today there's nothing left of Sinan's handiwork.

Keeping Time

Accurate time-keeping is important in most societies, but in Muslim tradition it's especially critical because of the need to summon the faithful to prayer at the correct times in the day which change according to the phases of the moon. Pinpoint accuracy becomes even more important during Ramadan when the start and end of each day of the month-long fasting period is announced from the mosques. In the past the start of each day of fasting was taken to be the point at which it was light enough for someone to be able to distinguish between a black and white thread. Today telling the time is a mechanized business, but once it was the responsibility of special time-keepers (*müneccim*), and many mosques had special lodgings (*muvakkithane*) where their time-keepers could sleep. You can see many devices to do with time-keeping in the **Museum of the History of Islamic Science and Technology in Gülhane Park** (see p.26).

Astrolabe

Timekeepers in an Ottoman miniature

Mihrabat Woods

On the hillside above Kanlıca a 200-acre wooded park with marked walking trails offers a pleasant place to drink tea, smoke a nargile, and gaze out over the Bosphorus and its two bridges. There has been woodland here since the reign of **Sultan Mahmud I** (1696-1754), and the Grand Vizier **Damat İbrahim Paşa** built a mansion here as a gift for **Sultan Ahmed III** (1703-1730). The mansion may be long gone, but many writers and poets, including **Yahya Kemal Beyatlı** (1884-1958) and **Özdemir Asaf** (1923-1981), used to come here to draw inspiration from the view.

Kanlıca *Yalıs*

Prenses Rukiye Yalı

This late 19th-century yalı, once one of the largest of all the waterside mansions, was a gift from her husband's family to Princess Rukiye, the daughter of **Khedive Abbas Hilmi Paşa**. The yalı in the Mihrabat Woods behind was bought in 1957 by **Özdemir Atman**, a stalwart of the Turkish Jockey Club (TJK).

Yağlıkçı Hacı Raşid Bey Yalı

Built in the 1850s, this yalı was restored in the 1980s by Barlas Turan. The bay here was a popular venue for **moonlit musical soirees** in late Ottoman times.

Süleyman Dırvana Yalı

The burgundy-colored yalı with a boat tied up in front of it belongs to Cem Boyner, who acquired it for $4 million in 1997 from Cerrahpaşa Faculty of Medicine's Professor of Neurology, Dr. Nedim Zembilci, and his wife, Esin Zembilci, one of the first female jockeys of Turkey. Süleyman Dırvana Yalı is next to it behind the pine trees.

Prof. Dr. Süleyman Dırvana (1915 – 2010) was one of the giants of Turkish sailing. He was born in the **Kıbrıslı Yalı** (p.288) in Kandilli and his nanny was Tolstoy's niece who had fled the Bolshevik Revolution of 1917. His father was in the service of **Sultan Abdülhamid II**. In order to construct this yalı in Kanlıca Bay, he sold his share in the Kıbrıslı Yalı. He sailed his 7.5-meter-long, 50-year-old ketch, the **Seddülbahir** up and down the Bosphorus.

At the start of the season, it would cruise from the Bosphorus to Bozburun, before sailing back up to the Bosphorus at its end. He had more than five vessels and would haul them all onto land and conduct their maintenance himself. Besides his maritime activities, Süleyman Dırvana was also an accomplished surgeon. In 1980 he retired and rented out the yalı. He and his wife, **Zeynep Hanım**, settled in Bozburun.

Entrance from the garden

Bosphorus view from the sitting room

Hall

Fireplace in the library with a Bosphorus view.

The photos of the Süleyman Dırvana Yalı were taken by Koray Erkaya.

Sadrazam Kadri Paşa Yalı

Built in the mid-19th century, this yalı belonged to **Kadrı Paşa**, a grand vizier and **governor of Edirne** who married the daughter of İsmail Paşa, Sultan Abdülmecid's personal physician. This is one of those unlucky waterside mansions that was hit by a ship as recently as 1991. It has since been restored and members of the same family still live in it. When you look at it from the water, the tiny yalı to the left belongs to pop superstar **Sezen Aksu** while the one to the right belongs to **Cem Boyner**, owner of the Boyner chain of clothes shops.

An ad of the cream

Edhem Pertev Yalı

Most distinctive of all the Kanlıca yalıs is the graceful Ethem Pertev Yalı which was built for Saraylı Fatma Hanım in the 1860s but is named after an Ottoman pharmacist who created a famous **skin cream** (Krem Pertev) that is still on sale today. Unfortunately one of his sons was killed when a wave hit their boathouse, and in 1932 his other children sold the building to a sea captain. The influence of **Art Nouveau** is apparent in the frilly balcony on the ground floor, hence its nickname the "**Süslü (Decorated) Yalı**". The sea mansion was severely damaged when a cargo ship's steer was locked in 2015.

Hacı Ahmed Bey Yalı

Atatürk is known to have attended a circumcision celebration in this late 19th-century yalı that belonged to the Ramazanoğlu family by then.

Saffet Paşa Yalı

Built in 1907, this yalı has one of the longest mooring places on the Bosphorus. It was completely rebuilt in 2008 after a fire destroyed the original. It takes its name from the grandfather of Sedat Simavi who set up the **Hürriyet** newspaper in 1948.

Yağcı Şefik Bey Yalı

This yalı was built in 1905 on the site of the lost Cemile Sultan Palace and beautifully restored in 1989. A successful businessperson, **Şefik Bey** built the larger structure as the *haremlik*, or family quarters, and the smaller one as the *selamlık* for the men. The current owner is the daughter of multi-millionaire tycoon **Faruk Yalçın** who founded the **zoo in Darıca**.

Yedi-Sekiz Hasan Paşa Yalı

The late 19th-century **Asaf Paşa Yalı** is also known as Yedi-Sekiz Hasan Paşa Yalı because the illiterate paşa used to sign his name as 7/8 – "yedi-sekiz" in Arabic numbers. It was bought by **Barut** family who owns **Abdi İbrahim** one of the leading pharmaceutical companies of Turkey. It was restored to its former glory in 2012. Down below you see its living room.

Otherwise known by its historic name of the Elbiseci (Dressmaker) Ahmed Bey Yalı, the Necmettin Erbakan (former prime minister of Turkey who died in 2011) Yalı was put up for sale for $12 million in 2012.

Kanlıca Yoghurt

The original Kanlıca yoghurt was made with a mixture of cow, buffalo and ewe's milk and, like Maraş ice-cream, was thick enough to slice with a knife. Much of the ready-packaged stuff sold today comes automatically sweetened although the waterside retailers will ladle in as much or as little icing sugar as you want. In and around the main square, shops compete to sell the famous local yoghurt. If you take one of the longer Bosphorus cruises you will be able to buy it to eat on deck.

Ahmet Rasim Paşa Yalı

You've seen the yalıs and admired them. Now comes the chance to stay in one too. The 16-roomed hotel is in the beautifully rebuilt 19th-century Ahmet Rasim Paşa Yalı right on the edge of the Bosphorus, which is decorated on minimalist lines with barely a nod of acknowledgment to the Ottoman era. The yalı was built for an Ottoman governor who became mayor of Istanbul briefly in 1878 but was ejected from office after being suspected of siding with the deposed Sultan Murad V against Sultan Abdülhamid II.

32

The Egyptian Summer-House

Çubuklu and the Khedive's Villa

One of Istanbul's more easily overlooked delights is the Khedive's Villa (Hıdiv asrı) at Çubuklu near Kanlıca on the Asian side of the Bosphorus, which is clearly visible from the ferries and from the grounds of the Sakıp Sabancı Museum but which vanishes from sight once you get closer to it.

In Turkish the word "çubuk" has several meanings, so inevitably there are several stories about how the suburb of Çubuklu got its name. In the more prosaic version the "çubuk" refers to the stems of the clay pipes that were manufactured here in the 19th century; in the more romantic version the "çubuk" was a cornelian cherry tree planted by the later **Sultan Selim I** who visited here when he was just a crown prince. The sapling matured and produced fruit overnight, a phenomenon miraculous enough to justify its name being bestowed on the surrounding area.

A short walk to the right of Çubuklu landing stage is the late 19th-century neoclassical **Halil Edhem Yalı** that was built for Edhem İbrahim Paşa, a grand vizier to Sultan Abdülhamid II and the father of Osman Hamdi Bey. Unlike many other yalıs, it still retains its architectural integrity. It was restored in 1988.

The Villa

The Khedive's Villa (Hıdiv Kasrı) was intended as a summer home for the **Egyptian Khedive Abbas Hilmi Paşa** whose mother commissioned the fabulous building used as the Egyptian Consulate across the water in Bebek. Abbas Hilmi already owned a palace on two waterside plots of land in Çubuklu, but in 1907 he bought the slope behind them and began work on a property that was called the **Çubuklu Summer Palace**. Hard though it is to believe that the architect of such a superb and prominent building could be unknown, there is no certainty about who created it; some list it as a work of **Raimondo d'Aronco**, others as the handiwork of the Italian architect **Delfo Seminati** or the Austrian architect **Antonio Lasciac** (Beltur, current operators of the property, favor Seminati).

The Khedive used the villa in summer right through until the 1930s when **Pierre Loti** visited it and expressed a preference for the original waterside palace. Eventually the Egyptian sold his retreat to the Istanbul authorities and departed for Switzerland where he died in Geneva in 1944. In the way of things, the beautiful building was then left to molder until 1984 when the Turkish Touring and Automobile Association under the far-sighted leadership of **Çelik Gülersoy** took it over and restored it. It now offers a **restaurant** and **garden café**.

The villa was designed in a style, which has been dubbed **neo-Renaissance**, and its most striking feature is the lofty flat-roofed tower, which offers panoramic views across the Bosphorus. In the elaborate metalwork over the main entrance the Khedive's coat of arms can be seen, while inside **Art Nouveau** glass doors open onto a circular lobby ringed with paired marble columns with a fountain playing in the center. In its heyday a steam-powered elevator with padded velvet seats would whisk the favored to the top. A circular restaurant is wrapped around this lobby, but don't miss the **door-frame** that leads into the main dining room which is decorated with gilded bears, leaves thrown over their shoulders like cloaks, happily plucking berries from the trees. Even the rest rooms merit a quick look as they still retain their original Art Nouveau tiles.

Behind the villa is a formal **rose garden** laid out in 1909, and a park shaded with pine trees and full of hydrangeas. It's at its fragrant finest in spring when the lawns are planted with tulips and the sweet scent of hyacinths fills the air.

Garden of Khedive's Villa

Who was the Khedive?

"Khedive" was a term used to describe the virtually autonomous governors of late Ottoman Egypt. From 1892 to 1914 **Abbas Hilmi Paşa** was the last khedive of Egypt and Sudan while they were a British protectorate. In 1914 he was deposed by the British who feared that he would side with the Ottomans in the First World War. Stripped of his property and forbidden to return to Egypt, he finally accepted defeat and abdicated in 1931.

Abbas Hilmi Paşa

The Halil Edhem Yalı belongs to the Konukoğlu family, owners of Sanko Holdings, a company involved in everything from construction to textiles.

33

From Nightingale to Kitchen Glass

Paşabahçe and Beykoz

Towards the northern end of the Asian shore of the Bosphorus are the twin suburbs of Paşabahçe and Beykoz, the former well-known for the glassware that used to be produced here. Both are very built-up today, although large stretches of woodland still survive behind Beykoz. Some of the best views of this end of the Bosphorus can be had from the Hill of Joshua.

Fishermen taking a break in Beykoz

Paşabahçe Bay

It was in Paşabahçe Bay that the British and French fleets assembled in 1854 before setting sail through the Black Sea to take part in the Crimean War.

Paşabahçe

Once known as **İncirliköy** (Fig Village), **Paşabahçe**, "the Pasha's Garden", took its modern name from the gardens of **Hezarpare Ahmed Paşa** that existed here in the 17th century. Today it's best known for the large glass factory that was founded in 1934. Although the factory has been relocated, the Paşabahçe name lives on, and modern Paşabahçe glassware is sold all over the world.

Paşabahçe products

There's a small **ayazma** (sacred spring) in the main square, while the Greek Orthodox **Church of Agios Constantinos and Agia Eleni** dating back to 1894 can be found in the back streets just a little way inland. Both are likely to be locked. The large and undistinguished modern **mosque** in the main square was built in 1971 and replaces a wooden one dating back to the reign of Sultan Mustafa III.

Agios Constantinos and Agia Eleni Greek Orthodox Church

Paşabahçe *Yalıs*

Originally the twin Andronaki yalıs were symmetrical, in the photo they didn't match! In 2011 the yalı on the left was finally completed.

A few wooden yalıs still survive in Paşabahçe.

Beykoz

Beykoz has a somewhat enigmatic name which means "**the Sultan's Walnut**" in Turkish. This seems to have been bestowed upon it by **Osman Gazi**, the first of the Ottoman leaders, in memory of one of his commanders, **Akçakoca Bey**, although conceivably it was derived from the Persian word "koz", meaning village. Before that it had been called Amycus after **King Amycus**, the ruler of a people called the Bebryces, who used to challenge all comers to boxing bouts which he would invariably win until he met his match in Polydeuces, one of the heroes traveling in the Argo with Jason in search of the Golden Fleece.

On (10) Fountain in Beykoz, by Hoca Ali Rıza (1858-1930)

İshak Ağa Fountain

Beykoz's attractive main square is dominated by the **İshak Ağa Fountain**, a magnificent structure with 10 water spouts (hence its alternative name, the On Çeşme (Ten Fountains), and a large water tank which is accessed via steps down into a dip. The original fountain dated back to the reign of **Sultan Süleyman the Magnificent**, but it was completely restored in 1746 by **İshak Ağa** who was customs superintendent during the reign of **Sultan Mahmud I**. Restored again in 2008, it now boasts glittering new paintwork but no taps on the spouts. In spite of this snag there's nothing else quite like it in Istanbul.

Near the fountain the 18th-century **Beykoz Mosque** is architecturally undistinguished but still retains a little time-keeper's lodge.

An inscription dates the Serbostani Mustafa Ağa Mosque, with its intricate wooden craftsmanship, back to 1809.

Nightingale glass

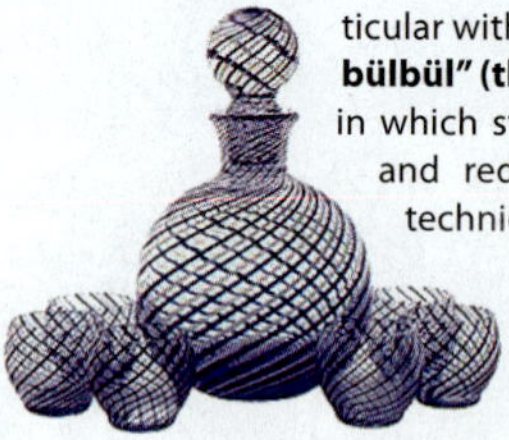

Historically the area around Beykoz was strongly associated with glass-making and in particular with a technique called **"çeşm-i bülbül" (the eye of the nightingale)**, in which stripes of blue, white, green and red glass were created. The technique was apparently introduced from Venice in the 18th century by a dervish and craftsman called **Mehmed Dede**. It took its name from the fact that the first factory set up to produce it in 1843 was right beside the **Çeşm-i Bülbül** fountain, now lost.

Field Marshal Fevzi Çakmak

Beykoz high street is named after Field Marshal Fevzi Çakmak (1876-1950) who was born locally and fought alongside Atatürk at the Battle of Dumlupınar in 1922.

Kavalalı Mehmed Ali Paşa

Hünkar Mansion (Beykoz Mecidiye Kasrı)

On a hilltop a little way west of Beykoz stands an imposing marble mansion designed by **Sarkis and Nigoğos Balyan** for **Kavalalı Mehmed Ali Paşa** who, as Governor of Egypt, led an uprising against the Ottomans. This was only suppressed with Russian assistance, and the **Treaty of Hünkar İskelesi**, signed in Beykoz in 1833, resulted in the Ottomans having to cede to the Russians the right to move their warships through the Bosphorus and Dardanelles. To try and make up for this Mehmed Ali began work on the mansion in 1855 during the reign of Sultan Abdülmecid; his grandson **Said Halim Paşa** saw it through to completion in 1866, by which time Sultan Abdülaziz was in charge of things.

Empress Eugenie

Empress Eugenie of France was one of its more illustrious guests.

After serving as an orphanage and hospital, It was taken over by the Turkish Grand Assembly National Palaces in 1997. After the restoration work completed in 2016, the pavilion was reopened for service as a museum.

The large grounds contain a European-style **grotto** studded with seashells, but the mansion is not currently open to the public.

www.millisaraylar.gov.tr, closed Mondays

Beykoz Wood

Originally called Abraham (Avram) Paşa Wood, this extensive stretch of forest on the hillside between Paşabahçe and Beykoz was laid out in the 19th century during the reign of **Sultan Abdülhamid II**. Today it's a popular recreation area with cafes and children's play areas. **Abraham Paşa** (1830-1918) was a fabulously wealthy Armenian civil servant, hunter and gambler, the owner of the famous **Cercle d'Orient** in Pera (now Emek Pasajı), and vast tracts of the northern Bosphorus. He built himself a house in the woods in which to hold lavish parties. Later debt forced him to sell it and retreat to his yalı in Büyükdere. In 1937 his house burnt down, but in 2007 it was reconstructed and opened to the public as a reasonably priced restaurant.

Tomb of Joshua

Hill of Joshua

For a truly spectacular view of the northern end of the Bosphorus you should make your way up the Hill of Joshua (Yuşa Tepe), at 198m the second highest hill along the Bosphorus, after Çamlıca Hill. On the summit a small 18th-century mosque stands over what are thought to be the remains of the Church of St Panteleimon, dating back to the reign of the **Emperor Justinian**. There's also a beautiful 19th-century fountain. From here you can also gaze down on the **Selviburnu** and **Macarburnu headlands**.

In ancient times a mysterious 12-metre-long trench here was called the **Bed of Hercules**, although it is probably better known as the **Giant's Grave** mentioned in Lord Byron's "Don Juan". Muslims believe it was the grave of **Yuşa**, a local holy man, sometimes thought to be synonymous with the **Prophet Joshua**.

Fountain on Hill of Joshua

Dalyan fishing

Off the coast at Beykoz in spring and early summer you will be able to see an unusual method of fishing that has been in operation at least since the 17th century when it was described in his usual colorful style by **Evliya Çelebi**. Poles are set up in the water with nets attached beneath it. The fish are frightened into swimming towards the nets which are then pulled in around them. Although Çelebi says it was a method used to catch swordfish, today **lüfer** (bluefish) and other common fish are caught in the same way. Dalyan fishing is also carried on near Anadolu Kavağı and Poyrazköy.

Beykoz *Yalıs*

The Hamamcı Hafız and Niyazi Kaptan are among Beykoz's beautiful yalıs.

Some historic yalıs have stood the test of time.

Ahmed Mithad Efendi Yalı

The Istanbul-born writer and publisher Ahmed Midhat (1844-1912) spent some of the reign of **Sultan Abdülaziz** in exile on Rhodes because of his writing. When **Sultan Abdülhamid II** ascended to the throne he wrote in praise of him and was permitted to return. His yalı was built in 1887.

34

Gateway to the Black Sea

Anadolu Kavağı, Poyrazköy and Anadolu Feneri

As its very last stop the Bosphorus excursion boat from Eminönü calls in at Anadolu Kavağı on the Asian shore where the remains of a huge Byzantine-Genoese castle sit astride the hill offering views out towards the Black Sea. Anadolu Kavağı is still a real village separated from Beykoz by dense woodland. However, its main square is full of fish restaurants catering to the boat trippers.

Just as Rumeli Hisarı and Anadolu Hisarı gaze at each other across the Bosphorus, so do Rumeli Kavağı and Anadolu Kavağı, believed to have been the ancient Serapion and Hieron of the Greeks. According to legend, **Jason of the Argonauts** erected altars in both locations to give thanks when he returned from Colchis at the far end of the Black Sea with the fabled Golden Fleece (see p.11). Later, **temples** were erected at both sites, the one on the Asian site being a shrine to the twelve Olympian gods and goddesses of Ancient Greece. Passing mariners would pause here to offer **sacrifices** to Zeus Ourious (of the Favorable Wind) before sailing into the Black Sea.

It's possible that the name Anadolu Kavağı refers to the poplar trees that once grew here, but, as with Rumeli Kavağı, it's more likely that the name commemorates its role as a "border" point where the Black Sea merged with the Bosphorus. Certainly both locations were fortified by the Byzantines who levied **customs dues** on passing mariners.

Anadolu Kavağı's life is firmly focused on the area immediately behind the ferry landing stage which is chock-a-block with fish restaurants ringing the elaborately-carved 18th-century **Cevriye Hatun Çeşmesi** (fountain), sadly reset into a far less impressive modern cistern.

The Clashing Rocks

So important is the passage from the Bosphorus to the Black Sea that it was bound to attract a colorful mythology. In ancient times it was believed that the strait was guarded by two huge rocks, **the Symplegades** or Clashing Rocks, which would move towards each other and clash, making a noise like thunder, thereby deterring ships from passing. On his way to seek the Golden Fleece the famous mariner **Jason** stopped off to help the blind local king **Phineus** who was plagued by monsters that constantly attacked him and ate all his food. Jason and his fellow heroes saw off these monsters, and in return Phineus advised Jason how to trick his way through the Symplegades by sending a pigeon ahead of the ship; if it managed to pass through safely, so would the ship. Jason followed his instructions and the rocks only clipped the pigeon's tail. When the ship followed behind, urged on by the playing of Orpheus' famous lyre, it suffered only minor damage to its stern.

Midillili Ali Reis Mosque

Anadolu Kavağı's small mosque dates back to 1593, but it was thoroughly rebuilt in the 20th century and is of no great architectural significance. There are a few old tombstones in the grounds.

Yoros Castle

It's not clear exactly when the castle on the Asian side of the Bosphorus was built although it's assumed to date from the period when the Palaelogos family ruled Constantinople; it's still possible to make out their motto on an inside wall above the entrance. In 1352 the **Genoese** seized the castle and started to collect the customs dues for themselves. In 1452 **Mehmed the Conqueror** took over the castle, but he doesn't seem to have made use of it, and it was allowed to tall into ruin.

The castle is usually referred to as Yoros Castle, a name thought to derive either from the Greek for "oros (mountain)" or "ourios (fair winds)". Today Rumeli Hisarı may look far more impressive but in its heyday Yoros Castle covered twice as much ground, making it the largest castle on the Bosphorus. In 2010 archeological excavations began at the castle which is currently closed to visitors.

Poyrazköy and Anadolu Feneri

The road north of Anadolu Kavağı leads to Anadolu Feneri (Anatolian Lighthouse) where the eponymous lighthouse sits inside the remains of the **Gözetleme (Watch) Castle** beside a small mosque; it dates back to 1648 but was modernized in 1856. Before Anadolu Feneri, under the shadow of the 3rd bridge, the small beach resort of Poyrazköy is named after the freezing "poyraz" wind which blows down the Bosphorus from the north-east. This is a place to come to sunbathe in high summer although there's also another 18th-century fortress, **Poyraz Castle**, to explore.

Marko Paşa Mansion (Marko Paşa Köşkü)

Inside the grounds of the naval base at Anadolu Kavağı stands the magnificent **Marko Paşa Mansion**, once home to a famously wise Greek doctor **Marco Apostolidis** (1814-1888) who became the chief physician to Sultan **Abdülaziz** and then to the army, and was also the founder of the **Red Crescent** in Turkey. If you catch the ferry to Sarıyer you will get a superb view of it, a white mansion topped with a lantern, as you pull away from the harbor. Marko Paşa died on **Burgaz Island** where he liked to spend his summers. He is buried in **Kuzguncuk** (see p.228) where his winter house has become a primary school. The Turkish expression "**Anlat derdini Marko Paşa'ya** (Tell your problem to Marko Paşa)" parodies the fact that he never actually listened to anyone's problems.

Marko Paşa

Anadolu Feneri

Photo Credits by page number

Saffet Emre Tonguç
(www.saffetemretonguc.com)
VIII, 12, 13, 21, 25, 26, 34, 40, 41, 51, 55, 59, 60, 61, 66, 72, 75, 76, 77, 78, 79, 82, 83, 85, 88, 89, 90, 91, 97, 106, 107, 108, 113, 114, 115, 116, 117, 119, 123, 124, 128, 132, 133, 134, 135, 140, 141, 144, 146, 147, 151, 154, 155, 157, 162, 163, 164, 168, 169, 173, 174, 175, 179, 181, 184, 185, 186, 188, 189, 193, 194, 195, 196, 197, 202, 203, 213, 218, 225, 231, 235, 236, 247, 248, 251, 252, 258, 260, 265, 266, 267, 269, 274, 275, 276, 277, 278, 286, 290, 295, 299, 300, 301, 303, 304, 318, 321, 323, 326, 332, 333, 336

Aydın Sertbaş
(@aydinsert)
VII, IX, X, 4, 5, 10, 11, (16, 17), (22, 23), 27, 30, 35, (36, 37) 39, 40, 44, 48, 49, 64, 66, 68, 73, 76, 77, 83, 86, 87, 88, 90, 91, 94, 95, 98, 101, 103, 107, 108, 110, 111, 112, 115, (116, 117), (128, 129), 136, 137, 144, 151, 156, 158, 159, 160, 162, 166, 167, 168, 169, 176, 189, (190, 191), 194, 195, 197, 199, 200, 203, 204, 206, 207, 208, 209, 210, 211, 216, 218, 220, 221, 223, 224, 225, (226, 227), 232, 233, 234, 235, 237, (238, 239), 241, (242, 243), 244, 247, 249, 251, 262, 271, 278, 290, 292, 294, 295, 308, 313, 316, 317, 319, 320, 321, 323, 327, 336, 337, 346, 348

Halit Bilen
(@bildrone)
4, 7, 10, 11, 38, 58, 74, 76, 104, 109, 124, 130, 136, 187, 217, 296, 312, 323

Sinan Doğan
VIII, 9, 15, 33, 56, 57, 67, 72, 76, 86, 87, 98, 104, 105, 165, 220, 221, 231, 261, 264, 265, 266, 269, 271, 272, 279, 280, 281, 286, 288, 290, 313, 314, 317, 334, 335, 338

Pat Yale
20, 21, 26, 27, 29, 31, 34, 35, 54, 55, 56, 57, 62, 68, 88, 108, 112, 115, 180, 181, 186, 189, 194, 195, 196, 197, 202, 203, 207, 220, 221, 222, 224, 229, 233, 234, 246, 321, 325

Gülgün Asutay
29, 41, 78, 95, 135, 144, 153, 160, 161, 166, 250, 267

Serhan Güngör
14, 25, 26, 54, 75, 91, 229, 285, 311

Şebnem Köken
24, 25, 29, 41, 86, 89, 225, 261

Serkan Eldeleklioğlu
5, 7, 68, 88,152, 198, 262

Rebecca Erol
45, 50, 58, 59, 65, 74, 224

Aydın Kudu
27, 106, 178, 180, 234

Alexandros Massavetas
54, 60, 62, 106, 220, 251

Koray Erkaya
120, 121, 122, 314, 315

Erman Tezgör
54, 138, 144, 206

Fatih Pınar
150, 154

Ali Öksüz
84, 192
Barış Hasan Bedir
(306, 307)

Michael Constantini
5, 45, 118, 120
Kate Russell
19, 42, 43
Engin Aydeniz
268, 280, 281
Ufuk Sarışen
111, 141, 324
Servet Dilber VI, 228
Bahadır Özbayır 177, 225
Alişan Özkan 24, 40
Caner Cangül 143
Mehmet Çabuk 68
Meltem Kızıltan 54
Sibel Şener Çuhacı 161
Didem Alp 113
Katie Albright 63
Bahar Gökten 202
Alp Boneval 21
Ron Lake 28
Kemal Adıbelli 34
Cemal Emden 259
Melih Sular 331
Naren Halitoğlu 348
Serhat Şahin 123

Saffet Emre Tonguç Koleksiyonu
18, 21, 30, 39, 45, 46, 52, 59, 75, 77, 89, 119, 124, 131, 200, 219, 295, 297

Khaftan Koleksiyonu
93, 172, 173, 223, 263, 287

Ali Aral Koleksiyonu
270, 290

İstanbul Modern Arşivi
65, 66

Sakıp Sabancı Müzesi Arşivi
147

İstanbul Büyükşehir Belediyesi Arşivi
138, 139, 322, 323

Index

Ş

T

U-Ü

V

W

Woods

Y

Yalıs

Z

Index

N

O

P

R

S

Ş

T

U-Ü

V

W

Y

Z

Acknowledgements

Ascherson, *Neal Black Sea: The Birthplace of Civilisation and Barbarism*, Virago,1996

Barillari, Diana & Godoli, Ezio *Istanbul 1900*, Rizzoli, 1996

Belge, Murat *Boğazici'nde Yalılar, İnsanlar*, İletişim, 1997

Boppe, *A The Painters of the Bosphorus*, 1911

Byron, Lord *Don Juan*, 1863

Çelebi, Evliya *Seyahatname*

De Busbecq, Ogier *Turkish Letters*, Eland, 2001

Deleon, Jak *İstanbul'un Yaşayan Tadı*, 1989

Deleon, Jak *The Bosphorus: A Historical Guide*, 1999

Di Amicis, Edmondo *Constantinople*, Hesperus Classics, 2005

Diehl, Charles *Byzantine Empress*, 1904

Dorina, Lady *Neave, Romance of the Bosphorus*, 1949

Dünden Bugüne İstanbul Ansiklopedisi, Tarih Vakfı, 1993

Dwight, H.G. *Constantinople: Settings and Traits*, 1927

Erdenen, Orhan *Boğaziçi Sahilhaneleri*, İBB, 1993

Eyüboğlu, Bedri Rahmi *İstanbul Destanı*, 1974

Freely, John *Istanbul: The Imperial City*, Viking, 1996

Freely, John *Stamboul Sketches*, Redhouse, 1974

Freely, Maureen *Enlightenment*, Marion Boyars, 2007

Günay, Reha *A Guide to the Works of Sinan the Architect in Istanbul*, 2006, YEM Yayın

Hinkle, Richard & Vander Sluis Rhonda *Boğaz'dan, Çitlembik*, 2005

Hürel, Haldun *Anlat İstanbul*, 2009, Kapı

Karaca, Zafer *İstanbul'da Tanzimat Öncesi Rum Ortodoks Kiliseleri*, YKY, 2008

Karaların ve Denizlerin Sultanı, YKY, 2009

Karmi, *Ilan Jewish Sites of Istanbul*, Isis Press, 1992

Kayra, Cahit & Üyepazarçı, Erol *Mekânlar ve Zamanlar: Kandilli, Vaniköy, Çengelköy*, İBB, 1993

Kelly, Laurence ed. A Traveller's Companion to Istanbul, Interlink Books, 2005

Kılıçkaya, Ali *Churches of Istanbul*, Uranus, 2008

Loti, Pierre *Constantinople: The Way it Was*, 2006

Mak, Geert *The Bridge*, Harvill Secker, 2008

Mansel, Philip *Constantinople: City of the World's Desire 1453-1924*, John Murray, 1995

Massavetas, Alexandros *Going Back to Constantinople: Istanbul - A City of Absences*, Athens News Publications, 2007

McCullagh, Francis *The Fall of Abdülhamid*, Kessinger Publishing, 2009

Montagu, Lady Mary Wortley *The Turkish Embassy Letters*, Virago 1994

Nicolson, Harold Sweet Waters: *An Istanbul Thriller*, Sickle Moon Books, 1999

Norwich, John Julius *Byzantium: The Decline and Fall*, Penguin, 1996

Pamuk, Orhan *Istanbul: Memories of a City*, Faber & Faber, 2005

Pardoe, Julia *The Beauties of the Bosphorus*, 1840

Petersen, Paulann *Blood Silk*, Quiet Lion Press, 2003

Procopius, *The Secret History*, Penguin Classics, 2007

Seal, Jeremy *A Fez of the Heart*, Picador, 1995

Sepeda, Toni *Life with a View: A Turkish Quest*, Çitlembik, 2007

Shanahan, Brendan *In Turkey I Am Beautiful*, Harper Collins, 2008

Step by Step Istanbul, Intermedia, 1992

Stratton, Arthur *Sinan*, 1972

Sumner-Boyd, Hilary & Freely, *John Strolling Through Istanbul: A Guide to the City*, Redhouse, 2000

Şimşek, Mahmut Sami *İstanbul'un 100 Yalısı*, 2011, İBB

Twain, Mark *Innocents Abroad*, Penguin, 2003

Uşaklıgil, Halit Ziya *Saray ve Ötesi*, 1942

Van den Graven Robert *Byzantine Istanbul: A Self-Guided Tour*, Çitlembik, 2001

Van Millingen, Alexander *Byzantine Churches in Constantinople*, 1912

Villers, James Jr ed, *Turkey, Travelers' Tales*, 2002

White, Charles *Three Years in Constantinople*, 1846